Defensive Environmentalists and the Dynamics of Global Reform

As global environmental changes become increasingly evident and efforts to respond to these changes fall short of expectations, questions about the circumstances that generate environmental reforms become more pressing. *Defensive Environmentalists and the Dynamics of Global Reform* answers these questions through an historical analysis of two processes that have contributed to environmental reforms, one in which people become defensive environmentalists concerned about environmental problems close to home and another in which people become altruistic environmentalists intent on alleviating global problems after experiencing catastrophic events such as hurricanes, droughts, and fires. These focusing events make reform more urgent and convince people to become altruistic environmentalists. Bolstered by defensive environmentalists, the altruists gain strength in environmental politics, and reforms occur.

Thomas K. Rudel is Professor in the departments of Human Ecology and Sociology at Rutgers University. He is the author of *Tropical Forests: Regional Paths of Destruction and Regeneration in the Late Twentieth Century* (2005), which won the 2008 Outstanding Publication Award from the Environment and Technology section of the American Sociological Association. He also authored *Tropical Deforestation: Small Farmers and Land Clearing in the Ecuadorian Amazon* (1993) and *Situations and Strategies in American Land-Use Planning* (Cambridge University Press 1989). Dr. Rudel won the 1995 Distinguished Contribution to Environmental Sociology Award and the 2009 Merit Award from the Natural Resources Research Group of the Rural Sociological Society for his research.

Defensive Environmentalists and the Dynamics of Global Reform

THOMAS K. RUDEL
Rutgers University

CAMBRIDGE
UNIVERSITY PRESS

32 Avenue of the Americas, New York NY 10013-2473, USA

Cambridge University Press is part of the University of Cambridge.

It furthers the University's mission by disseminating knowledge in the pursuit of education, learning and research at the highest international levels of excellence.

www.cambridge.org
Information on this title: www.cambridge.org/9781107448568

© Thomas K. Rudel 2013

This publication is in copyright. Subject to statutory exception and to the provisions of relevant collective licensing agreements, no reproduction of any part may take place without the written permission of Cambridge University Press.

First published 2013
First paperback edition 2014

A catalogue record for this publication is available from the British Library

Library of Congress Cataloguing in Publication data

Rudel, Thomas K.
Defensive environmentalists and the dynamics of global reform / Thomas Rudel, Rutgers University.
pages cm
Includes bibliographical references and index.
ISBN 978-1-107-03052-7
1. Environmental policy – International cooperation. 2. Environmental protection – International cooperation. I. Title.
GE170.R84 2013
363.7′0561–dc23   2012036777

ISBN 978-1-107-03052-7 Hardback
ISBN 978-1-107-44856-8 Paperback

Cambridge University Press has no responsibility for the persistence or accuracy of URLs for external or third-party internet websites referred to in this publication, and does not guarantee that any content on such websites is, or will remain, accurate or appropriate.

In memory of Anne Kiley Rudel, 1915–2000

[They were] country people who did not want to move and therefore got into a revolution. They did not figure on so odd a fate.
>
> John Womack (1969, i) on small farmers
> at the beginning of the Mexican Revolution

Contents

List of Figures		*page* ix
List of Tables		xi
Preface and Acknowledgments		xiii
1	Introduction	1
2	Meta-Narratives of Environmental Reform	10
3	Globalization, Tight Coupling, and Cascading Events	34
4	Partitioning Resources, Preserving Resources?	52
5	Advantaging Offspring, Limiting Offspring	77
6	Choosing Foods, Saving Soils	96
7	Removing Rubbish, Recovering Resources, Creating Inequalities	120
8	Saving Money, Conserving Energy	141
9	Focusing Events, Altruistic Environmentalists, and the Environmental Movement	160
10	A Sustainable Development State?	182
11	Conclusion: Defensive Environmentalists, Sustainable Development States, and Global Environmental Reform	197
References		207
Index		245

List of Figures

2.1	Varieties of Environmental Practice	*page* 11
2.2	Historical Cycles in Human Ecology: Events and Political Pressures across Scales of Human Organization	27
3.1	Global Trends: Population, Economy, and Environment	36
3.2	Chain Reactions from Two Biofuels Initiatives	47
5.1	Declines in Total Fertility Rates, 1960–2008	80
6.1	Trends in Certified Organic Agricultural Lands: Europe and the World	102
6.2	Trends in U.S. Tillage Practices over Time	107
7.1	Trends in Average Tipping Fees at American Landfills, 1985–2010	125
7.2	Doing Without, Reusing, and Recycling across Societies	128
8.1	Global Trends in Energy Consumption and Energy Efficiency, 1970–2005	143
9.1	The Issue Attention Cycle	167
9.2	The Scale of a Focusing Event, Tightness of System's Coupling, and the Length of Chain Reactions: A Hypothesis	168
10.1	Trends in Forest Loss, Brazil, 1988–2010	193
11.1	A Model of Environmental Reform	198

List of Tables

6.1 The Changing Extent of Conservation Tillage in the United States — *page* 108
7.1 Proportions of Households Participating in Recycling in Different Neighborhoods of a New Jersey Community — 126

Preface and Acknowledgments

The quote from John Womack that prefaces this book captures the way in which small, defensive actions, in this instance from *campesinos* south of Mexico City, sometimes scale up to transform the politics of an entire society, as occurred in Mexico between 1910 and 1920. The potentially transformative impacts of small actions have been much on the minds of environmentalists in recent years as larger political structures have remained largely inert in the face of climate change. Of course, as the quotes that preface the first chapter make clear, activities such as eating food grown in a backyard garden or preserving a patch of woods only constitute "drops in the bucket" compared to the magnitude of the environmental reforms necessary to establish sustainable societies. In this context, it becomes important to understand better the ways in which large-scale reforms occur and the role of local environmental activities in these larger-scale efforts. This book uses historical methods to clarify how, periodically over the past half-century, local and global forces have combined to produce moments of environmental reform.

The ideas that organize this book first began to take shape forty years ago when I was a young graduate student taking courses and attending talks on subjects, such as ecology, about which I knew next to nothing. I read an article in *Science* by Eugene Odum (1969) that was ostensibly about changes in plant communities, but it seemed to me to be a good explanation for historical patterns in some human communities. As I learned more about the paths to survival in an academic world, it became clear to me that wild analogies about the similarities between natural communities and human communities did not have a place in any discipline, even one with as expansive a view of its mission as sociology.

Furthermore, the understandable revulsion at the Social Darwinists' self-justifying arguments about the biological sources for high social position had caused many social scientists to look with suspicion at any mixture of social and ecological theory. Even so, the similarities in the meta-narratives of change over time in social and ecological theory seemed too compelling to abandon entirely, so I filed them away. Occasionally, I would mention them in classes to undergraduates, who in most instances were too polite to let me see the full measure of their skepticism.

I could not let go of these ideas in part because I kept running into inexplicable anomalies in the fieldwork that I did on human transformations of landscapes. In particular, the environmentalism that I heard expressed by citizens arguing for restrictions on suburban real estate development did not fit comfortably into prevalent ideas about environmentalism. The anti-growth advocates were too self-interested to be true environmentalists, but they spoke with passion about defending the environment. To see their comments as nothing more than opportunistic rebranding seemed too dismissive. Eventually, I came to regard these people as "defensive environmentalists," people primarily concerned with ensuring the quality of environments close to their homes. They contrasted with "altruistic environmentalists," who pursue goals for the larger society and seem most active during transformative political moments. The defensive environmentalists did things that many other nest-building creatures do, so a mix of ecological and social theory seemed likely to offer persuasive explanations for their behavior. The altruistic–defensive environmentalist binary captured an essential element in the local–global dynamic in movements for environmental reform, so this analytic approach seemed to have promise for explaining the political circumstances in which environmental reforms occur. With this promise in mind, I began to work on this book in 2007.

The work has been made much easier by a great deal of help, much of it unacknowledged until now. The intellectual atmosphere in the Department of Human Ecology, my primary place of employment during all of these years, has proven to be very good for nurturing ideas about relations between society and the natural environment. A small group consisting of Andrew P. Vayda, Bonnie McCay, George Morren, Brad Walters, and Kevin Flesher endorsed intellectual trespassing between the natural and the social sciences and did first-rate field research on environment–society relationships in diverse locales. My second home at Rutgers, the Sociology Department, through its "woodshed workshop," provided a friendly venue for trying out the ideas presented here. On other occasions, audiences in Human Ecology and at the American Sociological Association meetings offered insights that clarified my thinking.

At various points when I was stuck on one or another aspect of the argument, people went out of their way to help me with data or with the substance of an argument. Bonnie McCay and Teresa Johnson helped me understand the dynamics of fisheries. Alan Rudy offered some interesting insights on Andy Szasz's inverted quarantine argument. The late Allan Schnaiberg inadvertently suggested the title for this book in one of his typically trenchant comments about the environmental movement. Samantha MacBride pointed me in the direction of a wealth of data about recycling. Clare Hinrichs shared her knowledge about the food movement in the United States. Norman Uphoff graciously responded to a series of questions about the Gal Oyo irrigation project in Sri Lanka. The members of the Metuchen, New Jersey Environmental Commission helped to gather the recycling data reported in Chapter 7. Bradley Walters, Diana Burbano, Kevin Flesher, and Bonnie McCay read through and commented on the entire manuscript. Diana Burbano graciously allowed me to use a photo from her fieldwork in the Ecuadorian Amazon for the cover of the book. Robert Dreesen and Abigail Zorbaugh from Cambridge University Press and Shana Meyer from Aptara Corporation guided the manuscript and me through the evaluation and production processes at Cambridge University Press. Thank you for your efforts. Three anonymous reviewers read through either the entire manuscript or chapters from it and made comments that improved it substantially. Ellen Dawson remade many of the graphics in the book, improving each one that she touched.

A year-long sabbatical from Rutgers University in 2007 and 2008 gave me the time to organize the argument, gather the empirical materials to evaluate it, and write initial drafts of the chapters. I want to thank Susan Golbeck and Daniel Rudel for putting up with the reclusive lifestyle that I seem to need in order to write a book. Finally, I dedicate this book to my mother. Although she never wrote a book, she loved books and the life of the mind.

I

Introduction

Not only do I think [that] individual efforts are *a drop in the bucket* – but that the cumulative effect of most environmental movement organizations is extraordinarily limited. What I think we need is a far MORE political effort, culminating in enduring political organizations and coalitions, to provide a predictable set of political incentives and penalties for political representatives who preach environmentalism and practice the expansion of production.

Allan Schnaiberg (2007)

Voluntary limits on consumption [produce] little more than "*a drop in the bucket*" compared to the huge flows of resources... [produced] by [changes in] public policy.

Fred Buttel (2003, 330)

Introduction: The Emotional Burdens of Global Environmental Change

These are emotionally difficult times for people who care about global environmental conditions. Report after report provides new evidence of global warming. Greenhouse gas emissions spew forth at accelerated rates from tailpipes all over the world. The prospect of global collective action seems conceivable, but very distant. A sense of frustration, and even despair, at the lack of action creeps into communications by concerned people. "Are words worthless in the climate fight?" asks Andrew Revkin (2007). Myriad reports end with the statement "Technically, it can be done. It is a question of will power" (Kerr 2012). Others talk about the "environmental endgame" (Nadeau 2006). College students characterize their environmental studies courses as "depressing." Plainly, the ominous projections about global environmental change place an emotional burden on people who attend to them.

For very good evolutionary reasons, people tend to focus on the "here and now," and problems of climate in their most acute form have not had immediate effects on most of us. Temporally, "the sting is in the tail," decades from now when average temperatures will have risen two degrees or more (United Kingdom 2006). Spatially, scale mismatches buffer most humans from the consequences of their own actions. Human activities in the densely populated middle latitudes contribute to global warming, which manifests itself most forcefully in the sparsely populated high latitudes, thousands of miles away. Natural scientists refer to these links between physically separated activities as "teleconnections" (Philander 1990). Even when people acknowledge the connections between their daily activities and a changing global climate, the scale of the problem and the magnitude of the necessary transformations discourage people from taking action. As Tom Lowe writes (quoted in Revkin 2007),

A common reaction to this stand-off is for risk communicators to shout louder, to try and shake some sense into people. This is what I see happening with the climate change message. The public are on the receiving end of an increasingly distraught alarm call. The methods used to grab attention are so striking that people are reaching a state of denial. This is partly because the problem is perceived as being so big that people feel unable to do anything about it.

Given the prevalent human focus on the "here and now," we often react to large problems only when they present themselves in our daily lives, and then we react by thinking about what we can do, either personally or locally, to counter the effects of these problems. In one observer's words, "there aren't global pathways of progress, but there is incessant local improvement" (Dennett 1995, 308). David Brower has tried to capitalize on this tendency in human behavior with his call to "think globally, but act locally." Many of these local actions, such as fighting to preserve a patch of woods or strengthen a school recycling program, represent efforts to preserve or clean up personal environments. When someone says, "I care about issues that are close to home; I care if it affects me personally; I care if it affects my children" (Eliasoph 2002, 130), she or he expresses defensive environmentalist sentiments. Defensive environmentalists participate in activities that benefit their immediate environment and sometimes the larger world. Do these activities address global environmental changes in efficacious ways? Brower's slogan would suggest that the answer is yes, but the pessimistic assessments cited above say no. This book says "maybe yes," but only when defensive environmentalists combine with more altruistically oriented activists to produce moments of environmental reform.

Many people already have answers to questions about the global effects of local actions. The many scholarly efforts during the past two decades to understand the workings of local common property institutions testify to the potential that social scientists see in local environmental governance (Ostrom 1990, 2009). Paul Hawken (2007) estimates that worldwide there are now over one million local groups devoted to achieving a more socially just and environmentally sustainable future. Collectively, these groups constitute "global civil society." Federations of local groups exist in some instances, but in other instances group members are not organized beyond the level of the community. They do not profess a single ideology. Rather, they come together around practical ideas that promise to improve the local environment and, more questionably, to provide for social justice. Hawken believes that the members of these groups will in the near future transform our institutional logics in a more sustainable direction.

Lester Brown acknowledges the efforts of local groups but draws a different conclusion. In his words (Brown 2006, 265), "We have won a lot of local battles, but we are losing the war." Vigorous debates about the efficacy of local, voluntary responses fill e-mail inboxes. In an interchange on an environmental sociology listserv during the fall of 2007, several writers, somewhat diffidently, argued for the importance of local, voluntary actions, whereas others asserted, as in the quotations prefacing this chapter, that local actions usually represented a "drop in the bucket" in terms of what needs to be done to stem global environmental change. People of this persuasion argued that, given the existence of a world capitalist system that despoils the environment, only a concerted international effort to rein in global capitalism through reform or revolution could possibly achieve the magnitude of change necessary to address meaningfully the challenges of global warming, fisheries depletion, and biodiversity losses (Roberts 2007; Zavestoski 2007). Taken together, these debates paint a picture of some sustainable localities or practices set in an unsustainable global structure.

The recent history of recycling programs illustrates both the social logic that underlies a localized, defensive environmentalist posture and the overall pattern of environmental conservation. Mandatory municipal recycling programs have spread across a wide range of American communities during the past twenty years. At the same time, cities in China and Japan have begun recycling materials. In most of these instances, governments made recycling mandatory because they had run out of space in the local landfills. The alternative to recycling, long-distance transport of waste to distant landfills, costs more money. People may have begun to recycle during the 1970s out of a generalized concern for the larger environment, an altruistic concern that would not produce personal benefits, but they continue to recycle in part because it removes waste from their houses and saves their communities money. From the twentieth to the twenty-first century recycling changed from an altruistic to a defensive environmentalist practice.

Do defensive environmentalist practices such as recycling move us in a sustainable direction? The answer to this question is not so clear in New Jersey. Many communities in the state ship their recycled cans and bottles to China for sorting. The recyclables go so far because, otherwise, the ships that bring Chinese manufactured goods to the northeastern United States would have nothing to take back to China. Recyclers in New Jersey are defensive environmentalists, but the routes followed by their recycled goods reflect the larger, unsustainable economic structure in which they are embedded.

To some degree, the naysayers in debates about the efficacy of local environmental actions must be right. If local, environmentally friendly actions were quite common and did scale up to address global environmental problems, then we would not be worrying about global environmental changes in the first place. The magnitude of these changes exceeds the remedial capacities of individuals and local groups. This conclusion does not, however, mean that local efforts are insignificant in the global arena. The successful scaling up of some local efforts may suggest effective strategies for environmental stabilization in other times or places. In this sense, a description of the historical circumstances in which local efforts do and do not scale up into significant reform efforts in the global arena has potentially important implications for political action. This book attempts to provide a preliminary accounting of the historical circumstances in which these local-to-global links occur. To do so, it draws upon the two lines of theorizing that run across the divide between natural and social sciences, one concerned with modular changes in the immediate environments of individuals and the other concerned with systemic changes in larger, coupled natural and human contexts.

Theoretical Approach to Understanding Local and Global Changes

Any explanation for environmental reform must navigate the treacherous theoretical waters of the nature–society binary. A long line of Social

Darwinist theorizing, stretching back into the nineteenth century, has ignored the divide between nature and human societies, most notoriously using theories of natural selection to explain stratification in human societies (Hofstadter 1944). More recently, and in part in response to Social Darwinist thinking, social scientists have erected disciplinary divides between nature and humans, insisting implicitly, if not explicitly, that humans are so exceptional that ecological processes do not apply to them. Environmental social scientists have countered that it would be more accurate to regard human societies as a special case of nature (Catton and Dunlap 1978). Viewed in these terms, environmental reforms could conceivably be understood as both social changes and ecological changes. The theoretical tools for explaining environmental reforms might, by extension, come from both social and ecological theories.

Despite the frequent assertions about the gulf that separates natural scientists from social scientists, many of them share a common intellectual point of departure in their research. They think, as Darwin did, in terms of variations across populations and through time (Mayr 1959; Sober 1980; McLaughlin 2012). To explain these differences in populations, scientists typically refer to genetic changes across generations or cultural shifts over shorter periods of time (Richerson and Boyd 2005). These similarities between social and ecological thinking about populations can be exploited heuristically for theoretical gains. A case in point involves waste. Social theorists have next to nothing to say about it, whereas ecological theorists have much to say about it. This discrepancy could mean that there are some important but overlooked social issues in this domain.

The following arguments about defensive environmentalists, altruistic environmentalists, and environmental reforms have two theoretical sources: the much-maligned grand narratives of the twentieth century and coupled natural and human systems theory. The grand narratives have teleological tendencies. They attribute purposive behavior to higher-level aggregates, so societies "progress" and ecosystems "mature." Despite these dubious assertions, the classical theorists deserve credit for asking important questions about the origins of readily observable historical changes such as fertility decline. How, then, do we explain the cluster of historical changes in humans and other organisms as their communities have become more populous and larger in scale over time? One explanation for many of these "close-to-home" changes could lie, broadly, in the growth in the volume of human activities. Put differently, reformulated versions of the grand narratives could draw upon density-dependent processes to explain the emergence of defensive environmental practices. As the scale of human activities increased over the past two centuries, human households and communities tried to exert progressively more control over their close-to-home environments through the adoption of defensive environmental behaviors.

Two venerable theoretical traditions, one in sociology and the other in ecology, provide ways to understand the modular changes that occur in small clusters of human activity in households and communities when the scale and volume of human activities grow (Richerson 1977). Modernization theory, derived in part from the work of a nineteenth-century social theorist, Emile Durkheim, explains how, during the course of economic development, people became occupationally specialized and began living in greater numbers in densely populated places. City residents tried to control the use of neighboring spaces, the size of their households, the quality of their food, the amount of energy that they consumed, and the position of their neighbors in the emerging class system (Durkheim 1893). Waste disposal activities received no attention in modernization theory, but in other respects the theory would seem to explain numerous local-level efforts to improve the environment.

Early in the twentieth century, succession theorists in ecology began to outline an equally venerable line of thought about the ways in which vegetative communities change over time as they age. Like the modernization theorists, the ecologists argued that over time land uses diverge from place to place, reproductive strategies shift, and energy sources change. Unlike the social scientists, the ecologists expected waste disposal activities to become more salient in communities as they age (Clements 1916; Odum 1969). In theory, these changes reflect the outcomes of competitive processes that occur as these communities grow in size over the course of decades. Although the ecologists discussed changes in plants and the sociologists discussed changes in people, they described similar processes. In both instances, individuals responded to increases over time in the numbers and volume of neighbors by trying to control their immediate environments. These efforts gave rise to the defensive environmentalist practices described in this book.

Although theories of modernization and succession contribute to an understanding of localized, modular changes, a relatively new theoretical approach, coupled natural and human systems (CNH), clarifies the dynamics of environmental reforms in larger arenas. For more than a decade, groups of human and natural scientists have written manifestos arguing for a coupled natural and human approach to the study of environmental problems (Liu et al. 2007a, 2007b), and interdisciplinary teams of researchers, funded through governments or large foundations, have initiated field studies using the CNH approach. The most distinctive feature of the CNH approach involves the objects for investigation. CNH studies focus on coupled changes in natural and human systems, on the interactions between changes in natural systems and changes in societies that over time transform both the natural environment and human societies.

The value of a CNH approach has become more apparent in recent years as the scale of human activities has increased and their effects on the natural world have become more visible. When human populations were small, poor, and itinerant, they had a few highly localized effects and little apparent aggregate effect on the larger natural world. In these instances, a CNH approach made little sense because, except in the very-small-scale settings investigated by ecological anthropologists (Vayda 1969), it usually was impossible to trace the effects of human activities on the natural world, and from there back to human societies. Large-scale natural systems had so much slack that the effects of human activities were absorbed into the natural system without apparent changes in its overall structure. Pumping fossil fuel up from subterranean cavities and burning it simply did not create severe enough environmental problems until the volume of burning became very large. Under these circumstances, it made no sense to try to follow the couplings between the natural and the human. The feedback effects from the one to the other were not visible frequently enough to follow.

As the scale of human enterprises grew with the world's population and with globalization, the coupled patterns of change became easier to follow. With the increase in the scale of human enterprises, the natural world had less slack to absorb the large-scale disturbances caused by humans, so humans induced visible changes in the natural world, which in turn had feedback effects on humans and on nature (Liu et al. 2007a). In this sense, one could talk about natural and human communities becoming more tightly coupled, with a reaction in one producing a response in the other. The resulting cascade of effects can best be explained through a CNH approach.

Large-scale events such as a drought in the southern plains of the United States or a hurricane in the Gulf of Mexico often set in motion the cascades of events that culminate in the environmental reform of large organizations. At the same time, more prosaic, local-level defensive environmentalist sentiments, generated, for example, by federal legislators' exposure in Washington, DC, to the remnants of a Plains dust storm in 1934 (Brink 1951), can contribute to an unfolding reform dynamic. This combination of circumstances suggests that the political bases for large-scale environmental reforms emerge when widespread defensive environmental activities in localities coincide with tumultuous events in the larger system that trigger the expression of altruistic environmental sentiments and presage, at least theoretically, fundamental environmental reforms in the larger system.

The Plan for the Book

The following chapter outlines the theoretical argument. It begins by describing how human ecological succession should over time produce the defensive environmentalist postures that seem so prevalent in contemporary human communities. Then, it describes how coupled natural and human dynamics produce focusing events that, in their aftermath, make social movements and people with altruistic environmental sentiments more effective in larger political arenas. In at least some instances, these bursts of political activity, if supported by defensive environmentalists in localities, could lead to fundamental environmental reforms.

Seven empirical chapters follow. After an initial chapter on the globalization of human activity, five of these chapters use historical data on humans and natural resources, combined with a now-extensive case study literature, to outline how humans have become defensive environmentalists in their personal lives while living in a context shaped by an increasingly connected and large-scale system of world capitalism. The methods are largely historical, with a focus on trends over time, substantiated by aggregate data and case studies that exemplify those trends. The cases come from a wide range of people and places in the Global North and South.

The third chapter in the book focuses on global trends. It describes the global expansion of capitalism over the past forty years, with a focus on the trajectory of changes in production processes and personal consumption practices. It pays particular attention to the degree to which changes in these human practices touched off other social and ecological changes. The increasing frequency and length of these chain reactions signal a more tightly coupled natural and human system.

Chapters 4 through 8 represent the empirical core of the book. They examine different varieties of defensive environmentalist activities that reward practitioners and that in some circumstances could produce global environmental gains. Chapter 4 looks at issues of resource partitioning, the carving up of natural resources into private, community, or state-owned areas or preserves. Chapter 5 looks at human population dynamics with particular attention to fertility decline. Chapter 6 focuses on changing food preferences and alternative agricultural practices. Chapter 7 examines the waste stream and efforts to minimize it through recycling. Chapter 8 focuses on efforts by companies to create or adopt cleaner technologies, including alternative sources of energy.

Chapter 9 examines focusing events such as natural disasters that, by disrupting the political system, galvanize social movements and promote an altruistic environmentalism in which environmentally friendly actions bring no personal gains. Chapter 10, a theoretical chapter, traces how focusing events, coupled with social movements, an upsurge in altruistic environmentalism, and continuing defensive environmentalist practices could create the political conditions necessary for the emergence of sustainable development states that pursue hegemonic projects of sustainability and environmental reform. Chapter 11 reviews the argument and suggests areas for further research.

This theoretical and empirical account of defensive environmentalists, focusing events, altruistic environmentalism, and sustainable development states addresses pressing questions about the circumstances that give rise to large-scale environmental reforms. I hope that, at a minimum, this analysis will be "usefully wrong," stimulating others to embark on an effort to explain how defensive environmentalists interact with movement activists in efforts to build more sustainable social orders.

2

Meta-Narratives of Environmental Reform

> Communities reconcile partial with general perspectives. A community must recognize the legitimacy of egoism as a basic aspect of humanity and therefore as a necessary starting point for group life.... [T]he mission of community... is to regulate, discipline, and especially channel self-regarding conduct, thereby binding it, so far as possible, to comprehensive interests and ideals.
>
> Philip Selznick (1992, 369)

Introduction

The circumstances in which local, environmentally friendly actions scale up into global environmental compacts need to be understood in terms of the larger-scale historical processes of which they are a part. The increases in environmentally protective behaviors during the past half-century have had their origins in previous human successes. The enormous increases in the human population and the very uneven but still substantial growth in human prosperity over the past two centuries have generated environmental abuses that humans have tried to counter in a variety of ways. This dynamic implies that explanations for environmental reforms have to be couched in terms of theories that explain how communities change over time as they grow. During the nineteenth and twentieth centuries, meta-narratives emerged in both the social and the biological sciences about how inhabitants change as their communities grow, pollution increases, resources deplete, and governments take countermeasures. These meta-narratives span the divide between the social and the biological sciences, work at different geographic scales (Levin 1999), and make a common set of distinctions about processes of change. These distinctions provide

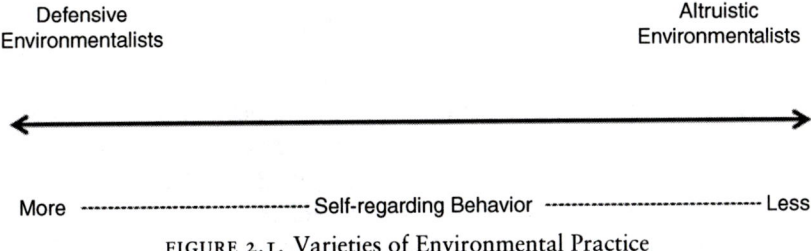

FIGURE 2.1. Varieties of Environmental Practice

an intellectual point of departure for understanding the social dynamics that yield environmental reforms.

One set of converging theoretical expectations derives from succession theory, as developed in both the social and biological sciences. It applies primarily to localized, modular relationships. A second set of converging theoretical expectations focuses on momentous events and their potential for producing crises that transform large-scale, complex socio-ecological systems. These transdisciplinary theoretical strands associate loosely with different types of environmentalists. In localized, modular contexts, defensive environmentalists predominate. They benefit personally from environmentally friendly behaviors. In large-scale arenas, altruistic environmentalists are more common. They do not experience obvious personal rewards from their environmentally friendly actions. Rather than being binary categories, defensive and altruistic environmental activities should be thought of as a continuum, from selfish to selfless activities, as outlined in Figure 2.1. Adaptation and mitigation efforts in response to climate change can be understood in these terms. Adaptation typically involves efforts to prevent damage or enhance a community's resilience in the face of climate change, so it would have a defensive environmental quality. Mitigation, with its focus on reducing greenhouse gas emissions, has a global effect, so it has to be undertaken with an altruistic mindset. It contributes to an aggregate good, but expectations of personal benefits are unrealistic.

For more detailed definitions of defensive and altruistic environmentalist practices, see Box 2.1. The next few pages outline these transdisciplinary theoretical strands, describe the practices of defensive and altruistic environmentalists, and trace out the implications of environmentalists' behavior for the dynamics of environmental reform.[1]

---

[1] The text refers more frequently to "defensive environmentalists" than to "defensive environmentalism" primarily because defensive environmentalists frequently do not frame

> **Box 2.1: Definitions of Defensive and Altruistic Environmentalism**
>
> A person practices *defensive environmentalism* when he or she engages in environmental protection that benefits him or her personally. Oftentimes these efforts occur close to a person's home. If significant numbers of other people adopt these practices, then the collective effects of the individual actions might confer a global environmental benefit. For example, suburban residents benefit personally from limiting real-estate development in their communities at the same time that the global environment benefits from the restrictions on sprawling settlement patterns. People frequently do not frame these activities as "environmental protection."
>
> A person practices *altruistic environmentalism* when she or he works to restore or preserve an environmental resource or service that benefits all of us without deriving any personal benefit from the recovering environment. NGOs could be either defensive or altruistic in their orientation, but almost all large-scale environmental NGOs assume an altruistic environmental posture on the Web sites that describe their activities to the public. Altruistic environmentalists have individual interests, like the rest of us, but they usually realize these interests through salaried employment in an unrelated activity or in organizations that work to safeguard or restore important environmental goods such as tropical rain forests. Defensive and altruistic environmental persuasions can coexist in a single person and can vary over time in their intensity. Under "business as usual" conditions, people may take more defensive environmental actions. During times of crisis, people may see themselves primarily as altruistic environmentalists.

Theoretical Points of Departure

1. Modular Succession and Defensive Environmentalists

The increases over time in population and in economic prosperity have altered human biophysical and social environments, giving rise to pro-environment activities and activism in a dynamic that many observers would recognize as a form of succession. What is succession? Social

---

their practices, such as having only one child, as an environmentally motivated choice. For this reason, someone can be a defensive environmentalist without espousing defensive environmentalism. The same situation could characterize altruistic environmentalists and altruistic environmentalism, although it is less likely.

scientists have used the term to indicate the replacement of one human group by another, usually through a process of invasion (Lee 2007). Ecologists have seen succession differently. They regard it as an endogenous process in which one group gives way over time to another group with different characteristics, in part because the first group has gradually altered the environment in a way that creates disadvantages for themselves and advantages for their successors.

In the words of one ecologist (Smith 1974, 258), succession

> involves a gradual and continuous replacement of one kind of plant and animal by another until the community itself is replaced by another that is more complex. It is brought about by a modification of the physical environment by the organisms themselves. As the environment is modified by their own life activities, the organisms make the habitat unfavorable for themselves. They are gradually replaced by a different group of organisms more able to exploit the new environment.[2]

More simply, "succession includes a series of compositional and structural changes [in vegetation], often in a directional manner" (Meiners and Pickett 2011, 651). The effect of a species on its own environment produces the directional changes over time. These changes, as noted by Smith, gradually transform the environment in ways that prove unfavorable to the original dominant species, thereby opening the door to changes in the composition of species in a place.

Oddly enough, the ecological definition, not the sociological definition, seems most apt for contemporary human societies because the ecological definition, unlike the sociological definition, contains a reflexive dimension in which a species changes its own environment and then has to adapt to the changes. Reflexivity is particularly important in understanding dominant species such as *Homo sapiens* because these species so frequently shape the conditions in which they and their progeny live. Succeeding generations of the dominant species have to revisit and accommodate themselves to decisions made by previous generations of the same species.

In its stress on endogenous forces, ecological succession resembles developmental idealism, the much criticized, but enormously influential,

---

[2] This conceptualization of succession is sometimes referred to as "relay floristics" (Pickett et al. 1987). The notion in theories of succession, that the success of an earlier order lays the seeds for its eventual destruction, is similar to what James O'Connor (1998) has called the second contradiction of capitalism, in which capitalists destroy the natural resource base on which the earlier success of capitalist enterprises depended.

notion that human societies progress as they industrialize and urbanize (Thornton 2005). Modernization theory, derived from the work of nineteenth-century social theorists (Durkheim 1893), argues that as human populations grow, competition between individuals for resources intensifies, and under competitive pressures people begin to specialize in particular occupations. With increased specialization, people become both more productive and more interdependent. Specialization lays the foundation for gains from trade, and the comparative advantages from trade become more compelling. Newly interdependent people cluster, creating cities at the same time that trading networks expand geographically.

Specialization changes landscapes, causing distinct zones of land use to emerge in which the people in each area specialize in a particular activity. The specialists acquire skills through education, and they use the new skills to achieve efficiencies in production, thereby increasing their productivity and disadvantaging people, such as the members of older generations, with less education. The newfound efficiencies extend to fuels. Technological advances make it possible to produce the same volume of commodities with less fuel (Mol, Spaargaren, and Sonnenfeld 2009). When aggregated, the growth in productivity increases the material bases of societies, and issues related to the disposal of these materials become more pressing. At the same time, the costs of acquiring additional skills during childhood drive the overall costs of having children higher, leading to declines in human fertility (Coale and Watkins 1986). Given these patterns, modernization should produce a partitioning of resources into distinct zones, increased efficiencies in energy use, increased attention to waste disposal, and declines in human fertility.

The accumulation of waste and contaminants in the newly affluent societies leads to a "reflexive modernization" (Beck, Giddens, and Lash 1994) in which new problems generated by industrialization preoccupy people. For example, the use of a wide variety of toxic materials in industrial processes spurs people to try to avoid exposure to the toxins (Szasz 2007). Similarly, the increased affluence, generated by modernization, has swelled the streams of waste produced by humans and prompted efforts by governments to deal with waste in new ways (MacBride 2011). Global warming is perhaps the largest-scale example of reflexive modernization, a change in the earth's climate brought on by emissions from the expanded scale of human activities (IPCC 2011).

A venerable theoretical tradition in community ecology comes to some conclusions that are substantively similar to those of modernization theory with regard to changes that occur in populations, in this case plant communities as they age and increase in biomass. This line of theorizing begins with Frederic Clements's (1916) theory of succession, is synthesized in Eugene Odum's (1969) work, and in much revised form persists in the study of "patch dynamics" (Wu and Loucks 1995; Meiners and Pickett 2011). In the early twentieth century, Frederic Clements (1916) outlined with special clarity a pattern of changes that plant communities experience after a large-scale disturbance occurs. Clements argued that recovering plant communities went through a recognizable sequence of changes and eventually reached a stabilized state that in some senses resembled an organism. Beginning in the 1930s, ecologists began to take issue with Clements's arguments (Hagen 1992; Worster 1994; Kingsland 2005). Rather than talking about supra-individual organisms, they introduced the idea of "ecosystems," defined as clusters of interacting organisms in a place, and began to follow energy flows between biotic and abiotic components in small ecosystems such as ponds (Tansley 1935; Lindeman 1942).

In subsequent years, ecologists, most notably Eugene Odum, began theorizing, much like Clement, about patterns of change over time in ecosystems. Odum summarized these patterns in a widely read 1969 article in *Science*, entitled "The Strategy of Ecosystem Development" (Odum 1969). This essay outlines a series of changes in the structure of ecosystems as they undergo "development," in other words, as they progress from aggregations of pioneering species established on a site after a disturbance to older, well-established communities of organisms. Among other things, Odum pointed out how, in the absence of major outside disturbances, ecosystems become over time more spatially heterogeneous with larger amounts of biomass, contain more specialist, long-lived species with low fertility rates, exhibit nutrient flows that support larger amounts of biomass, and develop more extensive detritus cycles for processing waste. For Odum, these trends, taken together, indicated that ecosystems frequently progressed in orderly fashion from "developmental" to "mature" stages of growth. He went so far as to endow ecosystems, at least metaphorically, with "strategies." In so doing, Odum's argument about plant communities became teleological.

Applied to humans, with appropriate acknowledgment of historical contingencies, Odum's model seems more conceivable. Human ecological succession would imply that over time, as the world becomes more crowded and prosperous, new social conditions would reward people less for self-reliant, but sometimes wasteful, activities and more for efficient, specialized activities in places with barriers to entry. As industrializing places fill up over time with people and goods, individuals and small groups would try to exert more control over their personal spaces. To do so, they would adopt defensive environmental practices, drawing boundaries around their home communities, having fewer children, exercising care in the choice of foods, recycling used goods, and pursuing energy efficiencies. These changes resemble those predicted by modernization theory.

Subsequent empirical work both confirmed and cast doubt on different aspects of Odum's generalized account of ecosystem change. Studies of forest recovery in New Hampshire's White Mountains described how the volume of biomass increased and a shifting mosaic of land use emerged over time (Bormann and Likens 1979). At the same time, critics took issue with Odum's emphasis on orderly patterns of change, his teleological imputation of "strategies" to clusters of organisms, and the idea of a climax, a stabilized end state (Botkin 1990; Kingsland 2005). For critics, disturbances, rather than orderly patterns of change, characterized most ecological communities. By extension, random fluctuations, sometimes described as "the accidents of history," characterized most ecosystems.

In response to these criticisms, community ecologists have focused more recently on processes of succession rather than on end states (Pickett et al. 1987). They developed a "hierarchical patch dynamics" paradigm that views communities as "dynamic mosaics of patches differing in successional stages" (Pickett, Steward, and White 1985; Wu and Loucks 1995, 447). The dynamics of change in vegetation became the primary focus for research. Focusing on historical changes in vegetation, ecologists have discussed place-specific trajectories of change and tried to model these changes (Pickett et al. 2009). In its updated form, this body of theory makes no assumptions about equilibria, adopting an almost "Heraclitean" view of patches and connections between patches as places that experience directional changes amid a large expanse of other places that experience almost random disturbances (Kingsland 2005, 254; Meiners and Pickett 2011). Within these islands of order, ecologists might expect over time to see more long-lived species, more prominent detritus cycles, more visible mosaics of patches, and flows of nutrients that sustain larger biomasses. In type these historical trends are close to the ones derived for humans from reflexive modernization theory. They should vary in form from locale to locale in accord with local histories and path dependencies (McLaughlin 2012).

Succession should over time produce defensive environmental practices more frequently in local than in global arenas, because the negative feedbacks from human activities, in the form of pollution and resource depletion, are more obvious close to the source of the activity (Levin 1999; Levin et al. 2001). For this reason, defensive reactions will be evident among people near the source point. Small aggregations of individuals using territorially defined resources harvest or catch less if they fail to organize to halt the depletion of the resource. Similarly, if local residents do not develop ways for disposing of their waste, they will see, feel, and smell the consequences of their failure. When families from one generation bear more children than they can successfully rear, some of these children may die. Finally, corporations that do not limit their use of hazardous materials at production sites run the risk of injuring workers and facing costly lawsuits by people who have been exposed to the contaminants.

In response to these adverse events, actors undertake environmentally friendly actions that benefit themselves and, if widely adopted, the larger ecosystem. Because these actions have a defensive quality, intended to defend an individual's immediate environment, these actors can be characterized as "defensive environmentalists" (A. Owen et al., personal communication). Of course there are defensive actions that do not benefit the environment, like drinking potable water bottled in a portable, throwaway plastic container or driving an automobile that is larger than other automobiles to avoid injury in traffic accidents. Defensive environmentalist practices differ in their consequences from this larger set of defensive practices. For example, a group of fishers who draw boundaries around their fishing grounds and limit their take from the newly bounded fishery gain personally by putting the fishery on a more sustainable basis. Widespread adoption of this sort of regulation would most likely produce global-scale benefits for fisheries. Others might describe these actions as "defensive localism" (Winter 2003), where "local" refers variously to communities, households, or enterprises. "Backyard environmentalists" (Fung and Sabel 2000) and participants in NIMBY (not in my backyard) movements would be defensive environmentalists, but a much wider range of people – for example, people who consume organic foods or people who limit their fertility – could also be described as defensive environmentalists.

Defensive environmental actions may preserve resources, but they also have a stratifying effect. In the fisheries example, members of the in-group who created the regulations benefit from the rules because typically they have preferred access to the fishery, whereas fishers outside of the in-group no longer have access to the fishery. Presumably, the more stratified the society, the more frequently will people pursue defensive strategies because "others" of a different class will seem more alien.[3] Defensive environmentalists adopt a strategy of "inverted quarantine," limiting their exposure to environmental contaminants and disturbances of all kinds (Szasz 2007). At the most general level, this analysis argues that succession in a more populous and materially affluent human context produces over time a human population of defensive environmentalists. Although the scale of defensive environmentalist endeavors may be largest among the upper classes, defensive environmentalist practices can be found among all classes of people.

Practitioners do not always profess defensive environmentalism. Although local activists may express defensive sentiments while embroiled in a struggle against an outside corporation bent on exploiting local natural resources, people do not, with rare exceptions, limit their fertility for ostensibly environmental reasons. In other words, defensive environmentalists frequently do not frame their practices as environmental. For this reason, defensive environmental practices are more pervasive than expressions of defensive environmentalism.

To document the connections between succession in human societies and the emergence of defensive environmental practices, Chapters 4 through 8 outline how, as the scale of human economic activities increased during the twentieth century, people came to adopt defensive environmentalist practices in five domains where human activities have had large local ecological impacts and potentially great global ecological impacts. These domains are natural resource partitioning, reproduction, agriculture, recycling, and energy consumption.

Do these local environmental protection activities scale up into a significant global environmental effect? Szasz (2007) would argue that they do not. Individually oriented strategies adopted by more affluent or advantaged actors offer them alternatives to large-scale collective action to restore environmental resources. By providing an alternative way for advantaged individuals to protect themselves, defensive environmentalist strategies demobilize the larger collectivity and may in this way contribute to further environmental degradation.

This argument, while plausible, discounts the effects of social movements. As defensive environmentalists have become more numerous and the environmental benefits of their actions have become clearer, they have spawned social movements dedicated to the diffusion of their

---

[3] I am indebted to Judith Pajo for this insight.

environmental strategies. The (organic) food movement and the family-planning movement exemplify these types of social movements. Under "business as usual" conditions these social movements may accomplish little, but in politically tumultuous times, oftentimes after momentous events, they may be able to foment large-scale change. I outline this pathway to environmental reforms in the following sections.

2. Focusing Events, Altruistic Environmentalists, and Environmental Reforms in Tightly Coupled Natural and Human Systems

In the late nineteenth century, Herbert Spencer (1876) initiated a line of thinking about large-scale dynamics that has promise as a way to understand when people begin in large numbers to practice altruistic environmentalism. Spencer worried about the consequences of population growth for human societies. Population increase would intensify competition for food and natural resources, which in turn would put strain on the social fabric. Spencer acknowledged, like Durkheim (1893), that competition would lead to increased differentiation among people, but he also argued that increased conflict over goods could lead to the dissolution of societies. Some societies avert conflict and dissolution by creating new organizations that bring the conflicting parties together and resolve the conflicts. With the additional layer of governance, individuals promote the survival of their societies, and perhaps indirectly, themselves.

To be politically effective, the new organizations must incorporate all of the interested parties into their proceedings. For this reason, Mancur Olson (1982) referred to them as "encompassing organizations."[4] Special circumstances that arouse a spirit of altruism accompany the creation of encompassing organizations. The shock of a focusing event or events suspends old social identities and reinforces a sense among the affected people of having a "common fate" (Sell and Love 2009). This sentiment, in turn, persuades some people to become more altruistic and push for the creation of an encompassing organization that brings all parties together to promote their common interest, often by asking their members to make sacrifices for the good of the larger group (Olson 1982, 48).

An historical example may clarify how events contribute to the creation of encompassing organizations. In the early twentieth century, the

---

[4] The narrower the range of members (and the scope of the organization's mission), the more likely it is that the organization will be a distributional coalition. The larger the range of members, the scale of affected populations, and the scope of the organization's mission, the more likely it is that the organization will be encompassing rather than distributional in form.

states of Oregon and Washington in the Pacific Northwest tried to regulate salmon fishing in their boundary water, the lower Columbia River. The initial absence of any regulations, coupled with conflicts between the states' first regulations, created a "chaos" of competition between groups of fishermen. In this unsettled situation the governor of Oregon proposed the creation of a commission to regulate the river's fisheries. Because the proposed commission would have included representatives of all of the river's fishers, it would have been an encompassing organization. For the next seventy-five years, state legislators in the Columbia watershed periodically discussed the idea of a commission, but the legislatures never approved it. In the meantime, the runs of salmon in the Columbia dwindled, falling to very low levels in the mid-1990s.

The decrease in runs in the 1990s finally spurred the legislators to action. The legislatures authorized the creation of a Columbia River Commission in 1999.[5] In the course of setting annual catch limits for commercial fishermen, the commissioners who administer the compact have to consider allowable catches for Amerindians, commercial fishermen, and sport fishermen as well as the population dynamics of the fishery. Born at a particularly acute moment in a continuing crisis, the commission encompasses all of the economic and environmental interests related to the salmon fishery in the Columbia River basin.

Politically tenable proposals for new regulatory organizations, such as an agency to regulate global greenhouse gas emissions, would have to stipulate that the new organization take an encompassing form. Otherwise, some stakeholders, fearing exclusion, would reject the proposal for the new organization. Societies or populations that fail to create encompassing organizations risk dissolution from the turmoil that accompanies worsening environmental conditions.

Although Spencer's ideas about additional layers of governance offer a useful point of departure for understanding how change occurs in a world system, the circumstances surrounding the creation of the new level of organization remain unclear. Game theorists have argued that "new levels of organization evolve when the competing units on the lower level begin to cooperate" (Nowak 2006, 1,563). When do they begin to cooperate? Perhaps it would be easier to answer this question by defining conditions that discourage cooperation.

The absence of negative feedbacks from environmentally damaging acts weakens popular support for global-scale organizations that would curb environmental abuses (Millennium Ecosystem Assessment 2005).

[5] Available at: www.nwcouncil.org/history/ColumbiaRiverCompact.asp.

When consumers purchase commodities sold in global markets, the environmental effects of the purchases often occur thousands of miles from the place of the transaction. For example, when a North American consumer decides that she or he wants furniture made from mahogany (*Swietenia macrophylla*) for the living room, the consumer does not feel the full feedback effects of this choice. The consumer may appreciate indirectly, through high prices, the ongoing depletion of mahogany in tropical forests, but timber market prices do not incorporate the costs of the biodiversity losses that occur when contractors extract 200-year-old mahogany trees from relatively undisturbed tropical forests. Similarly, greenhouse gas emissions from a round of daily activities in a suburban community in North America contribute to changes in the global climate that are felt most keenly in far removed, Arctic places. In this instance, the mismatch in scale and distance between the action (driving a car in a suburb) and its effect (a warmer climate in the Arctic) is so extreme that the feedback effects are imperceptible, and rationales for new levels of governance lose their force (Satake, Rudel, and Onuma 2008).

"Altruistic environmentalists" acknowledge the absence of positive feedbacks from engaging in many environmental practices, but they do them anyway out of a concern for the larger collectivity. For this reason they can be considered altruists (Dietz, Fitzgerald, and Shwom 2005). For example, someone may choose not to fly in airplanes to conferences in order to reduce his or her carbon footprint.[6] This action reduces an individual's contribution to greenhouse gas emissions, but it confers no obvious benefit on the individual, given that the solution requires similar individual actions from many other people that may not occur. Expressions of altruistic environmentalism are ubiquitous. The Web sites of almost all major environmental organizations express lofty, altruistic sentiments about the organizations' commitments to global environmental improvement.

The findings from research by social psychologists confirm the link between altruism and environmentalism (Dietz et al. 2005). A large number of other studies have investigated the attributes of environmentalists (Dunlap and Van Liere 1984; Brechin and Kempton 1994; Dunlap and York 2008). Most of these studies, with some exceptions (Jones and Dunlap 1992), have investigated the attributes of altruistic environmentalists at a single point in time. Game theorists have investigated fluctuations

---

[6] The actual change in a person's carbon footprint would, of course, depend on whether the individual actions, like the cancellation of an airplane flight, make a meaningful difference in greenhouse gas emissions.

in altruistic environmentalism over time (Sell and Love 2009), but only within the confines of experimental situations.

In sum, the accumulated social psychological research offers only suggestions about the historical conditions that induce people to express altruistic environmental sentiments and cooperate with one another to create a new level of governance. A model of the dynamics of change in expanding systems constructed by Per Bak and his colleagues outlines one possible set of conditions that might give rise to the cooperative behaviors that enable encompassing organizations. Bak's model, referred to as "self-organized criticality" (SOC), begins with a system undergoing expansion through the steady addition of new elements. Human population increases would certainly qualify as an enabling condition in Bak's model (Bak 1996). His favorite example involves a sandpile onto which a thin stream of sand falls. As the sandpile grows taller and larger, the elements (grains of sand) become more tightly packed and more transitive. If they experience a disturbance, they will pass the effects of the disturbance on to others, initiating a chain reaction or cascade of events among the elements in the system. In network terms, the connectivity of the system increases; the elements become more tightly coupled, and the system reaches a "critical" or "vulnerable" state (Scheffer 2009, 59) in which small changes within the system radiate throughout it, eventually causing (in the sandpile metaphor) "avalanches." In other words, the progressively tighter coupling that occurs when systems grow in size eventually causes major structural events such as catastrophes or revolutions. All of these events occur without perturbations from outside the system.

Charles Perrow (1999) describes a similar progression over time in technological systems. For example, to heat their homes, the French shifted during the second half of the twentieth century from the loosely coupled technology of coal-fired home furnaces to the tightly coupled technology of nuclear power plants. Loosely coupled systems have "slack," unused or underutilized capacity, built into them. In these settings, a breakdown or increased pressure in one part of the system does not immediately cause adjustments in other parts of the system. The component in question just repairs the breakdown or absorbs the increased pressure with the available slack, so the other components in the system do not have to change. When component failures occur in tightly coupled technological systems such as nuclear power plants, a different course of events ensues.

Tightly coupled technological systems have little slack and many feedback loops, so, on those rare occasions when multiple components fail at the same time, the effects radiate through the system in unpredictable ways, causing in some instances a complete breakdown. Because the structure of these systems contributes to the cascading effects, the accidents that occur, although rare, are in some senses a "normal" part of the system's operation. *The Black Swan* (Taleb 2010) makes a similar argument about both the inevitability and the influence of improbable events in tightly coupled social systems such as large-scale, interconnected financial markets. The growing complexity of these networks, institutions, and organizations generates normal accidents that in turn reduce the economic returns to increased scale and complexity. Archeologists have argued that these diminishing returns to increases in scale and complexity explain the collapse of complex ancient societies (Tainter 1988, 2011).

With some allowances for imprecision, assertions about changes in the relative tightness of coupling can be applied to entire societies. When human activity increases in volume and scale, as it did during the twentieth century, the coupling between the natural and the social worlds should have grown tighter as more and more resources were exploited to meet the demands of a more prosperous and expanding human community. With increased tightness in the system, more feedbacks should occur from the natural to the social world, even in large-scale socio-ecological arenas, as unused resources decline in extent (Liu et al. 2007a). These feedbacks could come in the form of disruptive events.

In writing about global warming, Clark (1985, quoted in Homer-Dixon, 1999, 38) captures well the dynamic leading up to the pivotal moments when disruptive events occur:

> Slow variation in one property can continue for long periods without noticeable impact on the rest of the system. Eventually, however, the system reaches a state in which its buffering capacity or resilience has been so reduced that additional small changes in the same property, or otherwise insignificant external shocks, push the system across the threshold and precipitate a rapid transition to a new system state or equilibrium.

Extreme weather events, particularly in the form of heat waves and torrential downpours, increased in number after 2000 (Coumou and Rahmstorf 2012). At the same time that the number of global warming-induced meteorological shocks appears to be increasing (IPCC 2011), popular appreciation for the political significance of shocks appears to be growing (Klein 2007). These climatic changes represent crucial emergent behaviors in SOC-like systems. They are the avalanches. They cannot be understood in reductionist terms as an aggregate of individual actions.

Whereas SOC could in theory apply to systems at any level of aggregation, Bak and Chen (1991) see it applying primarily to large-scale systems. Their model does appear to have straightforward applications to a globalizing world that seems to grow more interconnected each year. As Lynn writes (2005, quoted in Perrow 2007, 302),

> Our corporations have built a global production system that is so complex, and geared so tightly and leveraged so finely, that a breakdown anywhere increasingly means a breakdown everywhere, much in the way that a small perturbation in the electricity grid in Ohio tripped the great North American blackout of August 2003.

As implied by these comments, the steady increases in connectivity, what some theorists call "lash-ups" (Molotch 2003, 1–2), create over time a pattern of "interdependent security" in which, for example, a homeowner in a densely populated, fire-prone landscape may take all possible precautions against fire, only to see his house go up in flames because the neighboring homeowners did not take similar precautions (Tierney 2011). These tightly coupled systems eventually give rise to threshold-crossing events that initiate a cascade of fundamental changes in the system. As Jervis (1997, 39), a political scientist, puts it,

> Jumps rather than smooth progressions often characterize the operation of systems.... [W]hen variables interact in a non-linear manner, changes may not be gradual.... [F]or a prolonged period there may be no deterioration, followed by sudden collapse or transformation.

This picture of collapse recurs in the literature on an increasingly crowded, connected world (Catton 1980; Diamond 2005; Brown 2006). The pace of change in this model approximates the "punctuated equilibrium" idea outlined by Gould and Eldredge (1977) to explain the pace of evolutionary change. Long periods of relative stasis alternate with shorter periods of rapid, thoroughgoing, sometimes revolutionary change. Similar patterns of alternating stasis and change have characterized recent American politics (Jones, Sulkin, and Larsen 2003) and environmental politics in particular (Gunderson and Holling 2002; Repetto 2006). Focusing events and the "common fate" reactions of those affected produce "sudden qualitative shifts in environment-society dynamics" (Levin et al. 2001, 224) that would create political opportunities for the creation of the new levels of governance that Spencer sees as vital to maintaining social bonds in a growing population (Meyer 2004).

The new organizations are most likely to take an "encompassing" as opposed to a "special interest" form. Prototypical encompassing organizations would include the United Nations, the European Community, and the Intergovernmental Panel on Climate Change (IPCC). Scale matters in the designations of organizations as encompassing. An organization, a federation of labor unions, for example, would be an encompassing organization among labor unions, bringing them together to pursue a common agenda, but in the larger political arena a federation of labor unions could be considered just another special interest. As noted above, the role played by encompassing organizations in achieving sustainability appears to increase in importance with the scale of the threat to the environment.

The circumstances that give birth to encompassing organizations almost always involve some measure of political struggle. Both the United Nations and the European Community emerged in the aftermath of World War II. Elite groups often stand to lose from the restraints on their behavior imposed by encompassing organizations. For example, elite groups composed of executives from coal-burning utilities and oil companies have vigorously opposed the Framework Convention on Climate Change (McCright and Dunlap 2003). This political dynamic explains why encompassing organizations typically appear in the aftermath of threshold-crossing events. The political impetus to create encompassing organizations only has enough force in the aftermath of extraordinary events that have created common-fate sentiments, strengthened the appeal of altruistic environmentalism, and made it apparent to large segments of the elite that they cannot respond to the problem through "business as usual" processes (Olson 1982).

While defensive environmentalist practices emerge gradually over time as successive generations of people contend with a more populous and materially affluent world, the focusing events that transform structures often appear suddenly in unexpected ways. These transformative events become more probable, as argued above, when the system becomes larger and more tightly packed. However, beyond these very general determinants, focusing events occur in ways that are contingent on the particular historical conjuncture in which a society finds itself (Sewell 2005). By extension, any theory of environmental reform that features focusing events must have an open-ended quality to it that reflects the unpredictable historical contingencies associated with the events that precipitate political upheavals.

Meta-Narratives of Reform: Structures and Processes

To summarize the argument to this point about the conditions of environmental reform, it begins with small communities of pioneering individuals that grow in time into larger, interconnected populations of specialized individuals who adopt defensive environmentalist practices in societies that increasingly exhibit the characteristics of "self-organized criticality" (Carpenter and Brock 2002, 425). In other words, small modules of activity characterized by tight feedback loops give way to larger, interconnected aggregations of individuals with more randomized, intermittent feedbacks and periodic shocks that threaten to destroy the entire system. The larger social system exhibits rigidities in the face of reform efforts as elites defend established interests and political entities with diverse interests struggle to find common ground. The absence of a concerted response by large-scale organizations to smaller-scale disturbances increases the likelihood that the disturbances will grow in magnitude over time and eventually cause the larger system to collapse. After the shocks, people express an altruistic environmentalism and mount efforts to reform the system that often involve creating new encompassing organizations.

As implied by this dynamic, local and global aggregates of people innovate at different speeds. Local clusters of people are "fast," quick to experiment and adopt new practices in the face of disturbances, whereas global institutions are "slow," even rigid, in their response to change (Holling, Gunderson, and Ludwig 2002).[7] Local organizations may be

---

[7] The cited authors are all members of the Resilience Alliance, a group of scholars dedicated to studying coupled natural and human systems. Although this book addresses issues similar to those considered by Resilience Alliance investigators, it makes little use of their framework, because it has teleological tendencies. Their "adaptive cycle" model, metaphor, and terminology seem ill-suited to humans, although much of the cycle's underlying logic has a clear heuristic value. The stagelike progression from reorganization to growth, then to maintenance, and finally to disintegration has an internal logic that seems to make the progression through this sequence of stages inevitable, as in most teleologies.

Resilience Alliance authors, usually but not invariably ecologists, regard the current coupled natural and human system as primarily characterized by disintegration or reorganization, the backloop in the adaptive cycle described earlier (Berkes, Colding, and Folke 2004). Although this characterization certainly seems accurate regarding the ecological dimension of the CNH, it does not seem like an accurate description of the human dimension of the CNH, in that it ignores the massive increases in human prosperity and population over the past two centuries. Clearly, the human dimension of the CNH would be most accurately characterized as caught up in the resilience-enhancing activities that would typify the maintenance stage in the cycle.

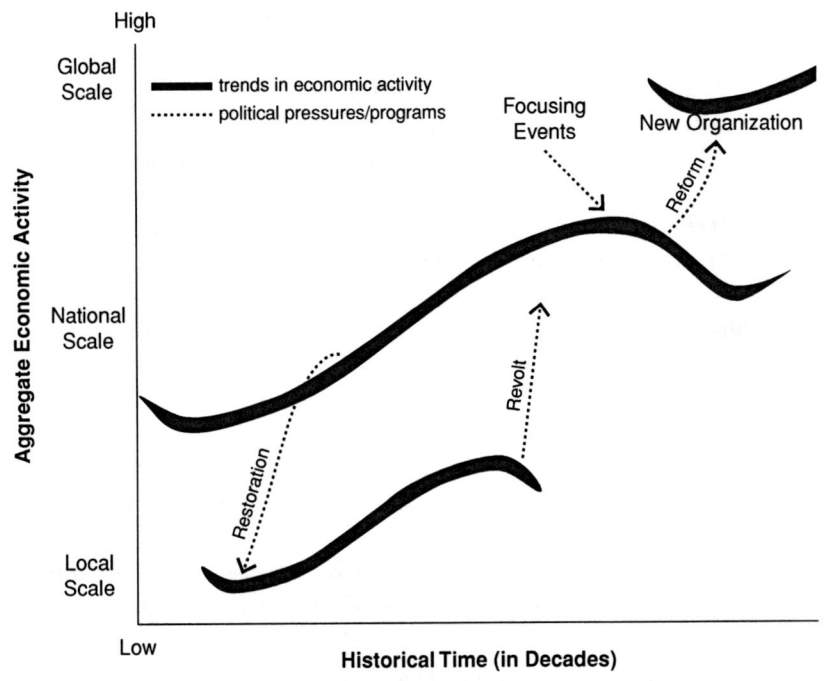

FIGURE 2.2. Historical Cycles in Human Ecology: Events and Political Pressures across Scales of Human Organization

able to take action more easily because they have less diverse interests or non-elite interests that are not wedded to the status quo. The larger organizations with more diverse constituencies and more fully represented elite interests move more slowly. Under these circumstances, local organizations may "revolt," taking concerted action to force change on the larger-scale institutions. The politics of global warming offers numerous examples of this dynamic. California and the northeastern states in the United States take unilateral action to regulate greenhouse gases, while the national government dithers. Figure 2.2 situates the revolt, the restorations, and the creation of new levels of governance in a larger historical framework.

The internal structure of a CNH can affect the historical path it charts in trying to recover from a shock. Optimizing arrangements, frequently promoted by economists in an effort to achieve increased efficiencies, reduce resilience because they eliminate the organizational slack in a system that, in the aftermath of a disaster, might allow an organization to resume operations quickly.[8] Diversity across the different elements in a system increases resilience because it increases the range of strategies that localities adopt in the face of a disturbance. Decentralized societies with local governance have a similar effect because some individual modules continue to work after a disaster and eventually the larger system reorganizes around the more effective of the local survival strategies. Similarly, a decentralization of human activities into smaller communities (in other words, modularization) would reduce our vulnerability because the risks of place-specific disasters such as nuclear meltdowns or devastating hurricanes striking large concentrations of humans would decline (Clarke 2006; Perrow 2007). The strength of feedback effects also contributes to resilience by ensuring that individuals react to incipient trends in the larger environment (Walker and Salt 2006). If individuals do not feel the feedbacks, they will continue to undertake destructive behaviors until the larger system crosses a threshold and undergoes a fundamental transformation.

The variable historical paths followed by CNHs may reflect differences in the forces driving the change. These forces typically take the form of "press" processes such as population growth that gradually apply pressure on a socio-ecological system and discontinuous, sudden, "pulse" processes such as floods that suddenly ramp up the pressure on a system (Collins et al. 2011). The press processes would drive defensive environmentalist practices, whereas pulses would presumably trigger points of punctuation in the political process when altruistic environmentalism surges and governments undertake significant reforms (Repetto 2006).

Cultural changes shape both the pace and scale of human responses to both press processes and pulse events. Cultures provide "toolkits" or "repertoires" of understandings (Swidler 1986) that people can draw upon to justify courses of action. The understandings come in the form of schemata, simplified representations of knowledge, that organize information for people. Individuals recall, use, and assimilate information related to prevalent schemata more easily than they do information that is not consistent with these schemata. In effect, schemata help people frame messages about the environment. When corporate enterprises with an interest in the continued expenditure of funds on fossil fuels pay

---

[8] Resilience Alliance authors regard resilience as the capacity of a system to withstand "shocks," self-organize, and learn from the experience (Berkes et al. 2004).

to have messages about the environment framed, they insist that their message give special salience to climate change dynamics that appear to relieve the corporations of their responsibility for the problem (Boykoff 2011). The combined effect of these messages may be to normalize the problem, framing it as a problem endemic to all growing human populations and, implicitly, discouraging collective action to reduce fossil fuel use. Under these circumstances, a culture of climate change denial and an accompanying social organization of denial may emerge (Norgaard 2011).

Schemata can change rapidly when people think about new courses of action during periods of societal turmoil (DiMaggio 1997). In these circumstances, as for example after a focusing event, stories, ideologies, and world views suggest new strategies of action or assemblages of action in response to unsettling events (Swidler 1986). People override existing schemata when high-profile events take place that do not readily assimilate into the prevalent schemata. Movement activists can expedite these cultural changes by reframing focusing events around new schemata and related ideologies. During periods of cultural flux, ideologies prove especially compelling because they both organize information through cultural scripts and provide strategies for action. Under these circumstances cultural processes accentuate the punctuated nature of political change. Initially, they retard change as people continue to use their old schemata, but after additional events people may convert to new schemata. In this sense, cultural dynamics would contribute to a discontinuous pattern of change (Westley et al. 2002). In the aftermath of a large-scale focusing event that destabilizes a CNH, this kind of cultural shift could reinforce altruistic environmentalist sentiments and stimulate growth in social movements dedicated to achieving large-scale environmental reforms.

Issue attention cycles and the politics of attention in environmental affairs fit this understanding of cultural change (Downs 1972; Jones and Baumgartner 2005). Anthony Downs argued that popular attention to particular environmental issues follows a regular pattern over time, beginning with the pre-problem stage, followed by a stage of alarmed discovery, and ending with a long period of declining public interest in the issue. Following shocking new information from the environment, people develop new schemata, reframe old activities in terms of the new schemata, create a social movement, and elaborate new institutional logics, including new proposals for legislation. Eventually, other problems capture the public's attention, and people lose interest in the original problem. The loss of interest does not, however, signal a return to the "pre-problem" stage, because social movements and new laws enacted during the period of alarmed discovery persist and shape individual behaviors in environmentally friendly ways.

Although Downs's formulation of the fluctuations in media attention seems overly linear and ahistorical (Boykoff 2011), subsequent research has shown the applicability of the issue attention cycle to environmental problems that afflict the larger public periodically, but not constantly (Peters and Hogswood 1985; Howlett 1997). Researchers have connected issue attention cycles to patterns of punctuation in politics, with periods of accelerated policy change following surges in public attention to an issue. The cycles of public attention often begin with focusing events. The surge in public attention to an issue following a focusing event resets political agendas and spurs a period of accelerated policy change, followed by a period of slow decline in legislative activity on an issue (Jones and Baumgartner 2005).

Issue attention cycles point to the crucial role played by social movements in environmental reforms. Focusing events threaten the existing order of things and, in so doing, create political opportunities for reform (MacAdam 1988). To realize reforms in these moments of opportunity, movement activists have to be well organized prior to the event and ready to "strike while the iron is hot" (Boudet 2011). In this sense, the reforms typically build on initiatives that began before the focusing event added a sense of urgency to the reforms. Finally, the ways in which movement activists and associated media frame a focusing event can affect the urgency with which politicians seek reforms (Snow et al. 1986; Boykoff 2011). These findings from research on social movements underline the ways in which the magnitude of a focusing event's effects depends crucially on the strength of the activist organizations that seek change after the event.

Stratification and unequal exposure to environmental abuses figure centrally in modular succession and the defensive environmentalist strategies that drive it, but these inequalities have received little or no attention in discussions. Advantaged groups adopt defensive environmentalist practices in part because they confer advantages. Elites, who, as happens in many cities in Latin America, privatize a public good such as potable water, prevent wide-ranging environmental reforms under "business as usual" conditions (Szasz 2007). Of course, focusing events such as the

BP oil rig blowout in 2010 destabilize "business as usual" politics. The subsequent turmoil sometimes shakes the power elite (Mills 1956), calling into question their legitimacy, destroying some of their wealth, and giving reformers momentum in efforts to wrest political advantages from the elite.

Theorizing Macro-Environmental Reform: A Polycentric, Multiphasic Approach

Demographers have long tried to theorize about large-scale social change over short periods of time, and their work offers useful lessons for efforts to theorize about environmental reforms. Kingsley Davis (1963) outlined a version of demographic transition theory that, in its generality, has considerable utility for understanding how humans respond to the challenges of global environmental change. Davis singled out the fertility declines in Japan and Ireland for special attention. He argued that Japan and Ireland did not differ from other countries in the complex of social changes that drove fertility declines. They differed because the fertility-limiting behaviors were either relatively extreme (Ireland) or rapidly adopted (Japan). The Irish delayed marriage to a greater extent than did other northern Europeans. The Japanese reduced their fertility rates at record rates during the 1950s.

Surprisingly, Davis did not point to the influence of cataclysmic events as possible causes for the extraordinary nature of the fertility declines in the two countries. Between 1845 and 1849 the Irish endured a famine, caused by pest-driven crop failures and England's refusal to provide food relief, in which one million Irish, 10 to 15 percent of the population, perished (Donnelly 2001). Emigration followed almost immediately. Thirty years later, the Irish began to limit fertility through delayed marriage to a degree that was unprecedented anywhere else in Western Europe (Davis 1963; Caldwell 1980). Japan experienced massive destruction and mortality during World War II, so the fertility declines during the 1950s occurred in a context of severe deprivation. The patterns here suggest the historical importance of catastrophic events in propelling change. They make understandable the sense of urgency in Ireland and Japan that would explain both the rapid rates of change and the resort to multiple means of change, what Davis calls a "multiphasic response." Perhaps multiphasic responses tend to occur in contexts marked by the punctuated equilibria described by Bak and others.

So, what did people do in Japan and Ireland? Davis's description (1963, 349) of the changes in Japan during the 1950s captures the general pattern:

What then is the picture that Japan presents? It is the picture of a people responding in almost every demographic manner then known to some powerful stimulus. Within a brief period they postponed marriage, embraced contraception, began sterilization, utilized abortions, and migrated outward.

In other words, Japanese families responded in polycentric and multiphasic ways. Some responses occurred before others. In northern European societies some families delayed the marriage of the younger siblings, so as to prevent the subdivision of the farm. Only later, when the numbers of jobs in cities increased, did the younger generation choose to move away from the farm. The use of contraception came still later. "Grim poverty" did not compel the decline in fertility. Rather, people saw competitive advantages in limited fertility and took measures to limit the size of their families. In a sense, families could see the changing pattern of incentives in front of them. They chose to limit fertility through a means, emigration, that on the one hand took advantage of changing opportunities (jobs in cities) and on the other hand resembled earlier practices of delayed marriage, because emigration, like delayed marriage, did not place additional burdens on the homestead. In Davis's words (1963, 355),

Migration out of agriculture was... an adjustment that was congruent with the response pattern already built into the rural social structure.

Consistent with modular patterns, smallholders experienced the negative feedbacks from high fertility rates almost immediately, and they modified their behavior in a wide variety of ways. A kind of defensive environmentalist posture drove their changes in fertility.

The multiple ways in which people limited their fertility suggests widespread popular understanding of a point made forcefully by Elinor Ostrom and her colleagues (Ostrom, Janssen, and Anderies 2007) that "there are no panaceas" for resolving environmental problems. By extension, human responses to a global environmental problem such as climate change should take a polycentric form, occurring on a local as well as a global scale (Ostrom 2010). Reform at one scale would facilitate reform at other scales. Politicians in the upper levels of government would look for evidence of popular support for environmental reforms at the local level before proposing reforms at their level of governance. Social movements would provide sometimes crucial links between local and centralized levels of governance. In theory, this type of political dynamic could lead to the creation of a sustainable development state. It would be "federal" in its fundamental dynamic. It would strengthen the bonds of community between local initiatives and global transformations (Selznick 1992) at the same time that local variations in history would prevent the uniformity and local repression often attributed to states (Scott 1998).

Next Steps

It is impossible to verify fully this theoretical account about the ways in which defensive and altruistic environmentalists interact in accomplishing environmental reforms because global reforms have not, with several exceptions, occurred. Segments of the argument can, however, be subjected to empirical analysis, and from these assessments we can draw some conclusions about the utility of this theoretical framework for understanding the difficulties surrounding environmental reforms and the conditions in which people overcome these obstacles. The rest of the book undertakes this empirical task.

The next chapter outlines the degree to which processes of globalization and associated environmental stressors have created a highly connected world system that is vulnerable to the accidents and catastrophes foreseen by the focusing event theorists. The following five chapters describe, against the backdrop of a precarious world economic system, the different ways in which small clusters of people, in response to feedbacks from their local environments, have moved, sometimes consciously, sometimes unconsciously, toward defensive environmentalist patterns of behavior during the second half of the twentieth century. The question hanging over these analyses is the degree to which these varied, small-scale efforts aggregate into trends that affect the larger world system. A subsequent empirical chapter looks at the historical record of transformative environmental events and assesses their impact on efforts by altruistic environmental activists to reform the larger political structures in environmentally friendly ways. A final substantive chapter describes the contours of a sustainable development state with a hegemonic project of sustainability that could emerge after a harrowing set of focusing events.

3

Globalization, Tight Coupling, and Cascading Events

> When I stood in the swirling mists of waterfalls deep in the cloud forest along Orellana's route, watching brilliant orange Andean Cocks of the Rock cavorting in the dense canopy, or when I walked these dense forests at night, plucking new species of frogs and lizards from the moss-cloaked vegetation that lines the streams, I found it easy to imagine that I was in the middle of uncharted wilderness. Such illusions were shattered when I realized that the deep throb reverberating through the night... was the whine of pumps that push Amazonian oil up the trans-Andean pipeline.
> Ken Miyata (Forsyth and Miyata 1984, 208)

Introduction: Globalization and the Human Prospect

The authors of the most somber assessments of the human prospect almost always begin with discussions of globalization and global trends in population, economic inequality, and environmental conditions (Catton 1980; Homer-Dixon 1999; Brown 2006; Speth 2008). Understanding the ways in which globalization and related trends have changed the fabric of society–nature links is important for assessing the likelihood of disruptive changes in the global human and natural system. The following pages describe these globalization-induced changes.

Globalization occurs when people from physically separated societies come into regular contact with one another. Tomlinson (1999, 2) describes globalization as "complex connectivity,... the rapidly developing and ever more dense network of interconnections and interdependencies that characterize modern social life." For Scholte (2005, 49) globalization occurs when "transplanetary social connections" spread. A globalized world exhibits "supraterritorial connectivity."

Economically, the growth of transnational corporations, outsourcing by these organizations to worldwide networks of subcontractors, and dramatic increases in direct foreign investment all increase economic connections between societies (Robinson 2004, 51). Culturally, the spread of languages of commerce, the growing volume of foreign travel, and the availability of the same media around the world create cultural connections between societies. Biologically, fire-resistant invasive species, typically shrubs such as *Chromolaena odorata* (Jack in the bush) or *Pteridium aquilinum* (bracken fern), spread across regional landscapes and homogenize them (Schneider 2006). The prevalence of signature invasive species such as bracken fern on every continent provides botanical evidence for the pervasive influence of human-induced globalization. The simultaneous spread of corporations, languages of commerce, and invasive species across the globe reflects the incorporation of human and plant communities into a single, human-driven process of coevolution (Norgaard 1994). Over time, these globalizing trends should create the larger, more tightly coupled natural and human systems envisaged in theories of event-driven, encompassing change in the global system.

Tightly coupled natural and human systems always exhibit cascades of effects. In other words, they tend to be transitive configurations. Whenever an external change has an impact on them, they pass the impact's effects on to other segments of the system. Because tightly coupled systems have little slack built into them, they cannot just absorb the impact of an external change by bringing heretofore unused resources into use. They have to reallocate already committed resources to cope with the new demands. These reallocations, in turn, generate other impacts within the system. In this manner, every significant change in an external condition initiates a chain of events, a cascade of sometimes unexpected effects. The most tightly coupled systems would exhibit the longest cascades of effects following a disturbance.

Aggregate trends in population, world economic product, and greenhouse gas emissions drive the overall process that sets off the long cascades of sometimes disastrous events. Figure 3.1 outlines these major trends: a slowing rate of population increase, a fluctuating but still increasing world economic product, and an accelerated growth in greenhouse gas emissions, especially after 2000.[1] The following pages describe the demographic and political economic drivers of the increased volume of human

---

[1] To make Figure 3.1 legible, I eliminated the scales for each of these variables. In effect, the graphic depicts the changing slopes for the three variables.

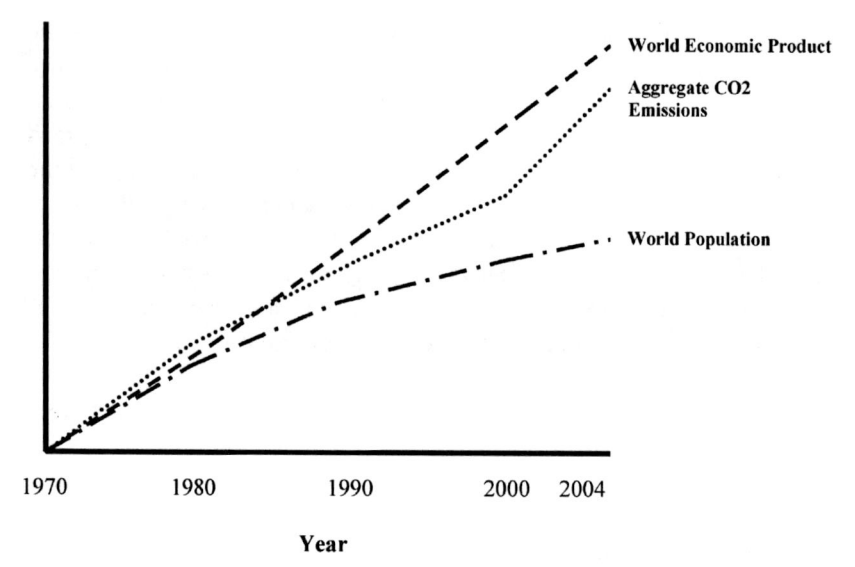

FIGURE 3.1. Global Trends: Population, Economy, and Environment

activities. A comparative analysis of the event cascades unleashed by biofuels directives in the United States and Europe illustrates how disturbances reverberate through tightly coupled natural and human systems. Several examples of event cascades induced by local climate change follow. Finally, the parallel increases in greenhouse gas emissions and extreme weather events suggest links, if not event cascades, between the volume of human activities and climate change.

The Drivers[2]

Population Changes

Although the annual rate of increase in the human population has been declining, the size of the increases, approximately 70 million persons per year between 2005 and 2010, poses a continual environmental challenge. Even with declining rates of increase (see Figure 3.1), the world's human population is projected to increase from seven to more than nine billion people by 2050 and to more than ten billion people by 2100 (United Nations 2011). Virtually all of the new additions to the human population now occur in the poorer societies of the Global South, where, for the

---

[2] Originally used by natural scientists to indicate a major causal force, the term *drivers* has been adopted and widely used by sustainability scientists.

most part, they create more densely settled urban and coastal zones. Because the newborns join households that do not have the resources to protect themselves from natural disasters, their arrival adds to the ranks of the most vulnerable people on earth. The new arrivals demand more natural resources, but the increments in demand are not as large as might be expected because the new persons, although large in number, join impoverished societies in which each person consumes few resources.

Although large numbers of people do not per se impose a large environmental burden on the earth's systems, their rapid transformation in countries such as China into more affluent consumers with scaled-up demands for material goods, along with the continuing large-scale material demands of long-affluent Western consumers, does impose a heavy environmental burden on the earth's systems. It is not the size of the human population so much as the growing number of materials-intensive consumers that burdens the earth. This circumstance can best be explained through an economic Malthusian argument that features aggrandized consumer norms fostered in large part through advertising from capitalist enterprises (Foster, Clark, and York 2010).[3]

Global Capitalism

The increasing environmental burden that humans place on the global ecosystem has its origins in the human economic efflorescence of the past 200 years. Capitalism has provided a changing institutional context for this outburst of human activity. Early capitalism featured entrepreneurs who articulated a capitalist ethic (Weber 1922) and, in creating new businesses, swept away old political economic structures in acts of "creative destruction" (Schumpeter 1942). With the birth of large corporations in the twentieth century, a bureaucratic capitalism emerged. Corporate managers in these organizations used rational means to pursue goals of profit maximization (Weber 1922; Schumpeter 1934; Swedberg 2002). In the memorable words of one theorist, they "macdonaldized" the productive process (Ritzer 2003). To this end, corporate leaders embraced

---

[3] Rather than focusing on expansion in the size of a population in relation to its resource base, as in traditional Malthusian thought, economic Malthusian formulations focus on the expansion of the high-emitting, intensively consuming population. The rapid expansion in this population, in a context in which longtime high emitters in Western societies have not curbed their appetite for goods, creates severe pollution problems, most notably global warming. Because increases in economic activity, rather than population growth per se, create the environmental crisis, this line of thinking can be referred to as "economic Malthusianism."

globalization, outsourced production to low-wage countries, and opened up new markets for consumer goods in these countries. Their enterprises became engines of economic inequality, generating profits for their investors, higher salaries for their executives, and lower wages for rank-and-file workers.

Globalization also created some environmental mirages. In one of them, the burdens that people in affluent societies placed on ecosystems appeared to decline with economic development. Referred to as the "environmental Kuznets curve" (EKC) (Cavlovic et al. 2000), this line of reasoning did not count the environmental impacts of people that occurred beyond the borders of their home countries. For example, wealthier countries have seen recent increases in forest cover (Mather 1992), but the same countries that experienced the increases in forest cover also increased their imports of grains from countries that had expanded the extent of their cultivated lands, so the increases in forest cover in wealthier societies were offset to an appreciable extent by the forest losses in poorer societies (Meyfroidt, Rudel, and Lambin 2010). In effect, the wealthier countries have outsourced the production of foodstuffs, so their environmental gains are to some extent illusory. Wealthy peoples from nations that import many goods, therefore, seem to have fewer environmental impacts than a more complete accounting would indicate. Once corrected, these calculations of a population's impact on the global environment make it clear that affluent consumers and the organizations that produce for them place a heavy burden on ecosystems (Dietz, Rosa, and York 2007). The dynamics of production and consumption that generate these burdens are summarized below.

1. Producers

During the past century, business elites have satisfied consumer wants and enriched themselves by establishing "treadmills of production" that have spewed forth large numbers of durable consumer goods such as automobiles and appliances day after day (Gould, Pellow, and Schnaiberg 2008). To make mass-production treadmills more profitable, business elites reorganized their assembly lines geographically. Before World War II, the world economic order had featured clusters of economic activity organized around nation-states and their colonial dependencies. It emerged from efforts begun in the sixteenth century by western European merchants and military forces to incorporate non-western peoples and places into an embryonic world system organized around European nation-states (Wallerstein 2004).

The merchants organized commodity chains that extended from cultivators and miners in the colonies through processors in the metropole to nearby consumers. These commodity chains often did not cross political boundaries. For example, planters and peasants grew cotton in the Belgian Congo that they then shipped to Belgium, where mill owners employed workers to make clothes out of the cotton that were then sold to Belgian consumers (Likaka 1997). Even after the colonies secured their independence during the mid-twentieth century, much trade continued to follow the routes of now-defunct colonial empires, with businessmen in the former colonies trading with businessmen in the old colonial center of power. The volume of trade increased tremendously during the second half of the twentieth century, and it continued to take a vertical form in which traders in the former colonies exchanged raw materials for finished goods (Scholte 2005, 94).

Large transnational corporations, constructed by business elites, expanded and altered the spatial organization of production, distribution, and consumption during this period. Commodity chains linking production with consumption began to cross international boundaries. Designers, component manufacturers, assemblers, and consumers were sometimes located in different countries (Robinson 2004). Nike shoes, for example, would be designed in the United States, manufactured in Vietnam, and sold throughout the world (O'Rourke 2004). Wal-Mart has produced a similar strategy of outsourcing production processes to low-wage manufacturing facilities in poor countries (Perrow 2007). With the creation of these transnational production processes, world economic integration accelerated. Between 1950 and 2003, the value of international trade grew at almost double the rate of growth in the world's GDP (WSDOT 2011).

2. Consumers

The responsibility for this upward trajectory in the global demand for material goods rests in part with the leaders of already large and still growing corporations, but consumers, exposed to the blandishments of corporate advertisers, have also played a role in scaling up human activities. Since World War II, Americans have grown accustomed to "living larger." The numbers of cars owned by families and the sizes of houses have increased during the past fifty years. The acquisition of larger vehicles and bigger homes increased Americans' emissions of greenhouse gases until the economic downturn of 2008. Between 1990 and 2005, emissions of greenhouse gases in the United States increased by

16.3 percent (UNFCCC 2007). Against this backdrop, one might ask whether there are limits to personal consumption. Don't people become satiated with material goods at some point? The answer seems to be a qualified "no," at least in a culture that celebrates consumers.

An intensifying competition for positional goods explains in part the continuing desire of Americans to consume ever-larger quantities of material goods. Positional goods are those goods whose value resides largely in their exclusivity. They are valuable because their owners have them, but most other people do not (Hirsch 1978). For example, the value of a BMW car stems in large part from the car's "exceptional" nature. If everyone in a community drove BMWs, the value of the car for most owners would decline, regardless of how well the car performed on the road. Although most positional goods have a material dimension, they do not necessarily have to be material in nature. In the United States, a degree from an Ivy League university confers status on a person, even though in material terms the degree is nothing but a piece of parchment.

Hirsch argues that as societies become more affluent people no longer worry so much about acquiring basic goods, such as food, for survival. Increasingly, they focus their energies on the acquisition of positional goods that confer status. A kind of conspicuous, competitive consumption emerges (Veblen 1912; Schor 1998). People begin to experience "luxury fever" (Frank 2000). High school students want a car to drive to school, not because they have no way to get to school otherwise, but because in their social circles the possession of a car raises their status. Similarly, people purchase large homes or enlarge their existing homes not so much because they need the space but because they feel a need to have a spacious home to stay in good standing with their friends and neighbors. Corporations feed this pattern of consumption through incessant advertising (Catton 1980; Brulle and Young 2007). In this context, no amount of goods is ever sufficient to satisfy a person's status needs, even though a much smaller cache of goods could meet his or her bodily needs. Under these circumstances, the environmental impacts of people in the more affluent societies, as measured by their ecological footprints, have continued to increase (Wackernagel and Rees 1995).[4] The mean

---

[4] The ecological footprint is a summary measure that indicates the approximate amount of land it would take to meet the needs and dispose of a person's waste at the prevailing level of consumption in a society. More specifically, it adds together the amounts of basic consumer items (crops, meat, fish, wood, fiber, living space) consumed by an individual and computes the amount of the relevant natural resources required to produce that quantity of goods. Then, it sums these figures to get the "footprint" for a person (Dietz,

footprint for Americans grew from 5.0 to 9.6 acres between 1950 and 2000 (Redefining Progress 2004).

These patterns of consumption have spread to the poorer peoples of the world. In one process, dubbed "showcase modernity," national elites in the Global South reproduce the American or western European patterns of consumption to the extent to which their economic resources permit (Fajnzylber 1990). During the 1970s and 1980s, elites in Ecuador gave physical expression to this cultural ideal through well-publicized shopping trips to Miami, Florida. In more recent years, with online shopping and the proliferation of malls in Latin American cities, well-off consumers from the poorer nations do not have to go so far to reproduce the consumption patterns of the affluent societies. A worldwide consumer culture has emerged (Boli and Lechner 2001). Here, too, the never-ending competition for the latest in material goods, coupled with incessant advertising by transnational corporations (Evans 2005, 100), augments demand for consumer items, even among households with modest incomes.

Consumer demands vary with local circumstances (Stein 2008). One could even talk about an "indigenous modernity" in which new consumer goods reflect local cultural and economic realities (Fajnzylber 1990, 335). Both showcase and indigenous consumerism seem to be at work in the spread of automobile culture to poor countries. The ideal of a personal vehicle for every family seems like an import from more affluent societies, but the introduction of modestly priced, compact cars, such as the People's Car from India's Tata Motors, with a 2008 price of $2,500, reflects both the purchasing power of Indian consumers and the congested conditions of Indian city streets. The adoption of consumer goods such as cars has consequences for how people organize their landscapes. Since World War II, car-oriented American cities have expanded outward through the construction of low-density subdivisions of single-family homes on the outskirts of cities. In more recent years, sprawl has spread to other countries. Where security concerns permit, people have purchased spacious, single-family homes in Europe (Bruegmann 2005), in southern Brazil (Baptista 2008), and outside of Bangalore in India.

These increases in the scale of human activities have begun to bump up against limits imposed by the natural world (Sayre 2008).[5] When

---

Rosa, and York 2007). The 2000 per capita world average footprint was slightly more than two acres per person. For the 2000 calculations, see Ecological Footprints of Nations at www.rprogress.org/publications/2004/footprintnations2004.pdf.

[5] The "limits" in this sentence refer vaguely to the carrying capacity for humans on earth. Carrying capacities vary historically, depending on available technologies and consumer

the volume of human activities grows, it has visible effects on the larger natural world that hosts human societies, so it makes sense to talk about the amount and kind of coupling among societies and between nature and society.

Globalization, Tight Coupling, and Cascading Events

Social systems become more tightly coupled with increases in human densities and economic activities.[6] The examples of this type of tighter coupling during the past century are almost too numerous to mention. Stock markets in distant places have become more tightly coupled. The recent movements in these markets suggest a tighter coupling of world financial markets than has been the case historically. Stock brokers used to routinely suggest that investors diversify their investments across the world's large stock markets in the belief that geographical diversification across the markets would limit investors' exposure to calamitous declines in any one market. In the 2008 economic debacle, the markets, now connected electronically, fell in unison, so overseas exposure did not protect investors from large-scale losses. Large, multinational corporations are now so interwoven in their activities that windfalls or write-offs by one company have important implications for many other companies. For this reason, waves of buying or selling in one market precipitate similar waves of buying or selling in other markets around the globe. The lending activities of large, internationally active banks show similar levels of interdependence.

Populations in distant places have become more tightly coupled through air travel. The history of the SARS (severe acute respiratory syndrome) epidemic in 2002 and 2003 demonstrated how quickly contagious diseases can spread across the globe when infected people make intercontinental airplane flights. Between December 2002 and February 2003 the virus spread, with infected travelers as the carriers, from Guangdong province in southern China to Hong Kong and then overseas via airplane passengers to Toronto, Canada. Without the intercontinental air links the virus could not have spread so quickly. As Lee Clarke (2006, 33)

---

norms, so they cannot be fixed with any precision. For a discussion of the historical uses of the concept, see Sayre (2008).

[6] In this argument, the term *density* has a material meaning separate from the actual numbers of people or organisms. For example, smaller numbers of people could generate higher densities in the sense that we use the term here if they have many material possessions.

puts it, "interdependence is a disaster vector." The epidemic stopped only when health care workers and governments reduced the interdependence through quarantines and restrictions on travel.

Socio-ecological systems also became more tightly coupled as the scale of human activity increased during the twentieth century. With the tighter coupling, chain reactions become both longer and more frequent. During earlier historical periods, increases in the scale of human activities did not precipitate ecological crises because unexploited lands or seas could absorb the increased demand for goods. Now, increments in human activity precipitate crises because unexploited resources no longer exist to absorb the additional demand. In a more tightly coupled system, every increase in human pressure produces a corresponding ecological response, often in the form of a depletion crisis in a distant place.

Local economic decisions are increasingly shaped by conditions and processes half a world away (e.g., soybean production in Brazil for export to China)... [with] progressively tighter couplings at multiple scales (Liu et al. 2007b, 644).

Devising a quantitative measure of the degree of coupling between the natural system and human societies represents a methodological challenge of the first order that is beyond the scope of this book. For the purposes of the argument presented here, I present a more rudimentary, qualitative approach to measuring the degree of coupling in the global CNH that identifies two types of connectivity. One type looks at the degree of coupling between events in different but linked domains of activity. For example, a growing association between the number of fishers on the water and the size of fish stocks would indicate a tighter degree of coupling over time between these two components of a CNH. Another type of connectivity ties similar activities together. Globalization in agricultural markets would presumably increase the degree of coupling between agricultural markets in different countries. The following discussion describes recent changes in both types of coupling.

Connectivity of the first type has increased as transnational economic systems have become more tightly coupled with the reorganization of transnational production processes around "just-in-time" inventory systems. The effects of a disturbance at one node in a commodity chain radiate across borders and down the commodity chain. The supply disruption in worldwide auto production following the 2011 Fukushima earthquake, tsunami, and nuclear reactor meltdown illustrates this dynamic. Japanese auto-parts suppliers in the areas affected by the disaster had to shut down operations, which in turn created scarcities of parts that forced shutdowns of auto assembly plants far from the accident site, both in Japan and in the United States (Autotropolis 2011).

During the twentieth century a whole host of markets underwent globalization, and coupling of the second type became tighter. For example, at the close of World War II, the world's sea urchin fishery was confined to the coasts of Japan. As the market for sea urchins grew in the next three decades, the fishery expanded to include the coastal zones of the entire Pacific Ocean (Berkes et al. 2006). In the mid-1980s the fishery expanded to the North Atlantic, first off the coast of New England and later off the coasts of northern Europe. For the past two decades the activities of sea urchin fishers as far removed as New England and the Sea of Japan have been linked through the influence of their activities on market prices for sea urchins. In this way, the globalization of the sea urchin fishery after World War II has over time coupled the activities of heretofore disconnected fishers to one another. They have all become exposed to disturbances in the sea urchin fishery whenever and wherever they occur.

The preceding examples of globalization show the increased connectivity, but they do not demonstrate how events cascade through tightly coupled systems and fail to do so in the more loosely coupled systems with underutilized resources. The following comparison of two sets of cascading events triggered by the sudden demand for biofuels in the period from 2003 to 2006 illustrates how the degree of tightness or looseness in regional cropping systems affected the length of the chain reactions triggered by the demand for biofuels.

Biofuels: Two Chain Reactions

Two policy changes mandating more use of biofuels, Directive 2003:30 by the European Parliament in 2003 and the Energy Policy Act by the U.S. Congress in 2005, precipitated cascades of events that rippled to differing degrees through the globe's coupled natural and human food system. The cascading effects of the policy changes became visible in 2006 when a confluence of political economic trends increased demand for biofuels. The world price for the most widely used fossil fuel, petroleum, approached $100 a barrel for the first time. In this context, alternative fuels derived from biomass began to look like a more economically attractive way to power a wide variety of machines, including automobiles. At the same time, people showed growing concern about global warming resulting from excessive emissions of greenhouse gases in the burning of fossil fuels.

Biofuels such as ethanol looked like an ecologically attractive alternative because, in theory, they are carbon-neutral fuels. When a plant grows, it absorbs roughly as much carbon from the atmosphere as the fuel derived from the plant gives off when burned in an automobile. For this reason, a considerable number of public and private enterprises expressed an interest, shortly after the millennium, in making more use of biofuels to power their machines. In this context, the government mandates of 2003 and 2005 set in motion two cascades of events, one beginning in the United States with corn-based ethanol and the other in Southeast Asia with oil palm, that radiated to differing degrees through the CNH system. The following paragraphs present brief narrative histories of each chain reaction, beginning with the events related to corn-based ethanol.

In the United States, powerful agricultural and agribusiness lobbies pushed for and obtained government subsidies that made the commercial production of a biofuel, corn-based ethanol, financially feasible. Agricultural lobbyists secured these subsidies despite the relative inefficiency of corn compared with sugarcane or switchgrass (*Panicum virgatum*) as a source for biofuels. The demand for corn-based ethanol drove up the price of corn 52 percent between 2005 and 2007 (USDA 2007), which in turn had both direct and indirect effects on cultivators' cropland choices. In response, American farmers expanded the proportion of lands devoted to the production of corn. By 2009, more than one-third of the American corn crop was being used to produce ethanol (EPI 2009).

In a model of this chain reaction, the biofuels-induced expansion of corn acreage would trigger a reduction in soybean acreage in the United States, which in turn would raise soybean prices sufficiently to induce a large increase in soybean acreage in the southern Amazon, and in some instances a conversion of cattle pastures into soybean fields. The displaced ranchers would then carve new cattle pastures out of old-growth tropical rain forests farther to the north in the Brazilian Amazon. In theory, the loss of stored carbon through the destruction of old-growth tropical rain forests in Brazil would more than counter any reduction in emissions from the substitution of corn-based ethanol for gasoline in the United States (Searchinger et al. 2009).

Much of this hypothesized sequence of events occurred. American acreage in soybeans declined 16 percent from 2006 to 2007 (USDA 2007). This shift in the American crop mix had a predictable effect on world market prices for soy. They, too, began to climb, increasing from approximately $.25 a pound in 2006 to more than $.40 a pound in 2007. The rising soy prices persuaded Brazilian farmers to expand their acreage in soy. Some of them did so by converting cattle pastures into soybean fields, and some of the displaced ranching enterprises did reappear to the north in predominantly forested regions, where landowners carved new pastures out of the rain forests (Arima et al. 2011). The magnitude of this effect was, however, small relative to the growth in numbers of confined cattle and in stocking rates in pastures (Macedo et al. 2012). While growers converted large areas of rain forest in the southeastern Amazon basin into soybean fields and cattle ranches between 1990 and 2005 (Kaimowitz and Smith 2001; Morton et al. 2006), the state's new enforcement mechanisms against tropical deforestation and associated NGO pressure after 2005 persuaded most growers to expand their soy acreage into pastures and intensify their cattle ranching on grasslands or already cleared lands.[7] In this instance, the hypothesized counterproductive surge in deforestation did not materialize, but a chain reaction of land-use changes stemming from corn ethanol production did begin (see Figure 3.2).[8]

A longer cascade of biofuel-initiated events occurred around the production of palm oil in Southeast Asia during the same period (see Figure 3.2). Demand for palm oil had already grown substantially during the previous two decades with changes in the diets of the rapidly growing urban populations in Africa and Asia. Growing numbers of urban workers had taken to eating fried foods outside of their homes, at work, or during the commute to work. Fruits, vegetables, and starchy tubers became less important in urban residents' diets and cooking oil, including palm oil, became more important (Johns 2007).

Smallholders in Malaysia and Indonesia had already begun to establish small plantations of oil palm in the early 1970s because it produces prodigious amounts of vegetable oil. An acre of African oil palm produces roughly eight times as much vegetable oil as an acre of soybeans, sunflowers, or rapeseed (Bradsher 2008; Gibbs 2011). In this context, European demand for biofuels jumped in 2003 when the

---

[7] The resulting concentration of agricultural expansion in the Brazilian *Cerrado* raised understandable concerns about losses of biodiversity in a unique savanna zone.
[8] Figure 3.2 represents only the largest chain reactions pertaining to cultivated areas of grains. It is not meant to represent an exhaustive list of the chain reactions initiated by government biofuels initiatives. For example, one chain reaction excluded from the figures begins with the rise in the price of corn in the United States that in turn reduced the amount of land devoted to raising organic grains that could then be fed to cows producing organic milk. The resulting shortages in organic grains led to shortages of organic milk in American supermarkets during 2011. Source: *New York Times*, December 2011.

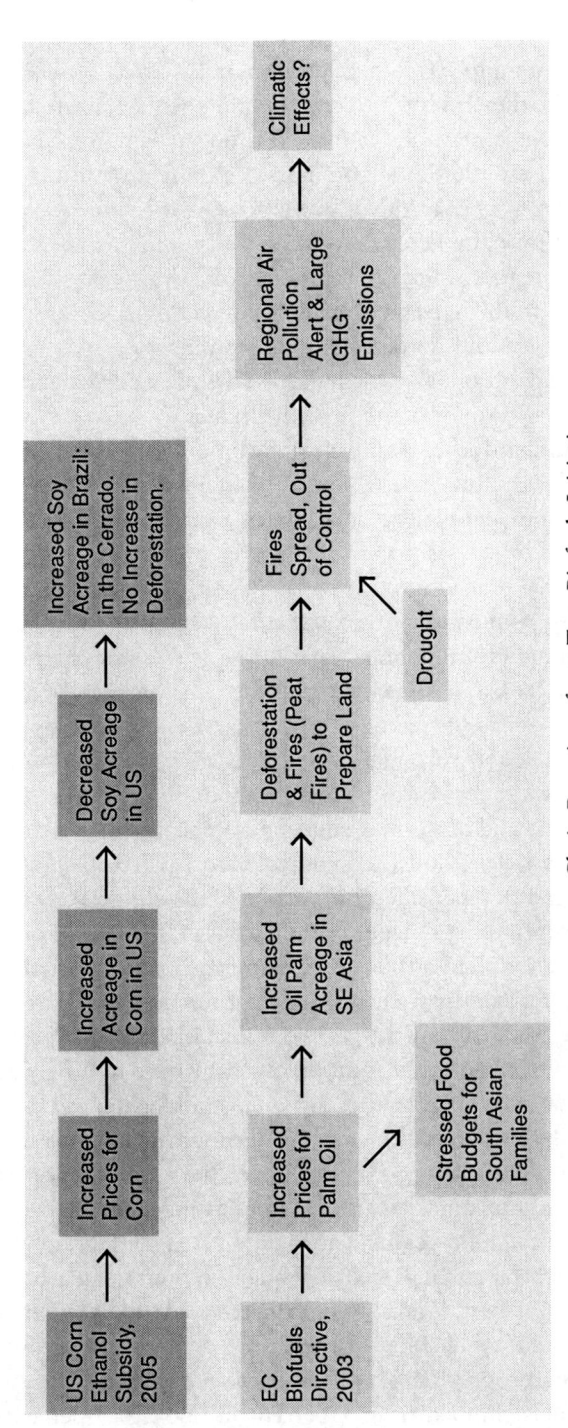

FIGURE 3.2. Chain Reactions from Two Biofuels Initiatives

European Community (EC) mandated that by 2020 10 percent of all energy used in the transport sector within the European Community must come from renewable sources (European Union 2011). The EC directive added an additional stimulus to an already rapidly expanding oil palm industry. Over a thirty-five-year period (1970–2005), planters had expanded oil palm acreage eightfold in Indonesia and Malaysia. By 2005, Indonesia and Malaysia accounted for 87 percent of global palm oil production (Gibbs 2011). Because palm oil must be processed by a mill within twenty-four to forty-eight hours of harvest, planters have also constructed mills near or on their farms. The capital demands of plantations and oil palm infrastructure have made it easier for more highly capitalized cultivators to establish oil palm enterprises, so they, rather than smallholders, now produce most palm oil.

Beginning in the late 1980s, large landowners and corporations in the outer islands of Indonesia began to log extensive tracts of rain forest and then convert these lands into oil palm plantations (Casson 2000). In so doing, these large operators often precipitated conflict with shifting cultivators by commandeering lands that shifting cultivators had historically cultivated. At the same time, the rapid expansion of oil palm plantations pushed the price of palm oil lower than the price of soybean oil. In response, poor people throughout Southeast Asia began to rely on palm oil as their primary cooking oil (Casson 2000).

Between 1990 and 2005, more than half of the new oil palm lands came from lands that had previously contained old-growth tropical forests (Koh and Wilcove 2008). A considerable portion of the old-growth tropical forest lands appropriated for oil palm plantations in Indonesia's outer islands were peatlands that had a two- to three-meter layer of partially decayed vegetative matter with particularly high carbon content just beneath the surface of the soil (Tacconi 2003). To reduce the costs of preparing the land for planting oil palms, plantation owners would routinely burn these lands. The peat would catch fire and then smolder for weeks at a time, emitting very large amounts of carbon. When drought coincided with the burning, as occurred in 1997–8 and 2006, the planters' fires expanded beyond the ignition zones, creating a long-lasting smoke haze over Kalimantan, Sumatra, and peninsular Malaysia, triggering smog alerts in Southeast Asian cities, and emitting huge amounts of carbon. By one estimate, the peat fires contributed 27 percent of all global emissions of carbon from land-use change between 1989 and 1995 (Tacconi 2003).

All told, the proportion of vegetable oil production worldwide used to make biofuels climbed from 1 percent in 2003 to 7 percent in 2007

(Bradsher 2008). In this context, the newfound enthusiasm for biofuels prompted the aforementioned rise in the price of soybean oil. The price of palm oil grew at commensurate rates, and entrepreneurs embarked on another wave of expansion in oil palm plantations, with attendant peat fires in forest-rich areas of Indonesia. The rise of palm oil prices created hardships for urban households throughout South and Southeast Asia now dependent on palm oil. The price increases also sparked plans for the expansion of oil palm plantations into old-growth rain forests. After logging the forests, planters burned the cutover districts, igniting peat fires that elevated the greenhouse gas emissions that biofuels were meant to reduce (Bradsher 2008).

The two biofuel commodity chains described here contained variable amounts of slack (underutilized resources). Farmers in the United States could not plant more corn without planting fewer soybeans because they did not have additional arable lands to cultivate, so reductions in soybean acreage in the United States, as predicted, led to expansion in Brazilian soybean acreage.[9] The cascade of events stopped in Brazil because it did contain underutilized resources. Brazilian farmers could bring less environmentally critical grasslands in the *Cerrado* into soybean production, which minimized the indirect environmental effects of the surge in biofuels production in the United States. Alternatively, cattle ranchers could confine their cows and feed them grains and forages.

Agribusinesses in Indonesia did not have less environmentally sensitive lands to bring into production when prices of palm oil rose sharply in 2006 and 2007, so they cleared old-growth tropical forests, including some peatlands, and burned these lands to prepare them for planting, igniting hard-to-control peat fires and raising greenhouse gas emissions dramatically. Poor families in India did not have savings that they could allocate to the purchase of the now more expensive palm oil. Under these circumstances, changes in one sector of a coupled human and natural system reverberated in other sectors. The EC directive on biofuels increased palm oil prices, stressed household budgets, and triggered biodiversity losses, fires, air pollution episodes, and accelerated greenhouse gas emissions. This cascade of events continued for longer in Southeast Asia because in a more tightly coupled, land-scarce regional agricultural economy there were no slack resources to absorb the additional demand

---

[9] Farmers in the United States did have some uncultivated lands in conservation reserve programs for which they received a subsidy that they would lose if they were to cultivate these lands.

created by the EC policy initiative. The biofuel event cascade in Southeast Asia, compared with the U.S.–Brazilian event cascade, underscores the connection between tightly coupled systems and periodic, sometimes massive, disruptions.

Climate Change and Cascading Events on Local and Global Scales

In the prior example, new policies triggered the cascades of events. In other instances, climate change initiates the cascades. They occur at both local and global scales. To cite one local-scale example, glaciers have melted and disappeared throughout the Andes, including the only one on the Cotacachi volcano, 4,950 meters above sea level, just north of Quito, Ecuador. With the disappearance of the glacier and a decline in rainfall, streams that had a continuous flow of water from the melting ice in the twentieth century now run dry periodically. They can no longer reliably provide water to irrigate the fields that smallholders acquired in the valley below during the twentieth-century agrarian reforms. Because the agrarian reform agency gave land to the indigenous peoples but did not assign them any water rights, the Cotacachi Amerindians sought water concessions from the *Consejo Nacional de Recursos Hídricos* (CNRH) after the glacier melted. The CNRH ruled against the indigenous peoples, who in turn responded by blockading the Pan-American highway, which runs through the valley. In this instance, the cascade of events began with increasing temperatures that led to melting glaciers, which in turn accentuated water scarcities, all of which culminated in road blockades and civil disobedience (Rhoades et al. 2008).

It becomes virtually impossible to track cascades of climatic events on the global scale because it is difficult to link discrete causes with effects. It is, however, important to note that the magnitude of the human-induced greenhouse gas emissions and their climatological effects seem to have grown in unison over time, suggesting a tighter coupling of changes in human societies with changes in nature. The scale of human activities has grown very rapidly. The expansion in the global economy between 1990 and 2006 led to a 35 percent increase in greenhouse gas emissions during the sixteen-year period (Canadell et al. 2007). Governments in many countries, as in the United States, made no effort to reduce greenhouse gas emissions. The extremely rapid growth rates in heavy industrial production in China, greater than expected in any of the global models of economic growth, generated more greenhouse gas emissions than anticipated in the models. These increases in the volume of greenhouse gas emissions and concentrations of carbon dioxide in the atmosphere paralleled increases in numbers of extreme weather events (hurricanes, tornados, floods, and heat waves) (Coumou and Rahmstorf 2012), melting of glaciers (Orlove, Wiegandt, and Luckman 2008; van den Broeke et al. 2009), and global mean temperatures (NASA 2011).

Some large-scale event cascades represent feedback effects from current global warming that would accelerate it in the future. Regional droughts, perhaps attributable to climate change, have slowed plant growth in some places, thereby reducing the carbon-absorbing capacities of the vegetation (Canadell et al. 2007). Melting permafrost has accelerated the release of methane from bogs. Finally, the melting of the sea ice during northern summers since 2007 has changed the reflective properties of the Arctic Ocean, enabling it to absorb more heat and warm the northern regions even more. The obvious growth in the number, scale, and complexity of these interactions between society and climate over the past half-century makes global warming the iconic example of a more tightly coupled natural and human system that generates cascading events.

Conclusion

The more tightly coupled configurations of nature and society generated by the increased scale and globalization of human activities bring with them an increased exposure to disturbances. The supply disruptions in the global automobile industry after the Fukushima nuclear accident in Japan, the rapid spread of SARS through air travel, and the impact of the European biofuels directive on peat fires in Indonesia all reflect a more tightly integrated global society. This narrative of change in global society and nature explains important recent events, but it is also incomplete. It misses the many small, localized ways in which individuals, households, and communities have addressed the challenges of living in a more populous, globalized, and tightly coupled natural and human system. The following five chapters describe these defensive environmental practices and the processes of human ecological succession that caused progressively larger numbers of people to become defensive environmentalists during the second half of the twentieth century.

4

Partitioning Resources, Preserving Resources?

> Yesterday and today have been sad days for Wichim.[1] We have been drawing boundaries in the forest. From today onwards, the lands of Wichim's *Achuar* are limited, reduced, and marked. Until today the *Achuar* did not need fences, locks, doors, or gates.... To have to mark boundaries means that our neighbor has become our enemy.
>
> Jose Arnalot (1977, 403)

Introduction

Humans have been carving up the earth into parcels under the control of individuals and small groups for millennia, ever since we began to rely on permanent and improved agricultural lands for sustenance (Mann 1986). Once confined to the cradles of civilization, partitioned natural resources now cover all but the most remote land areas. People typically partition a natural resource when they want to make more intensified use of it, so resource partitioning usually accelerates during periods of economic expansion. The tremendous expansion of economic activity during the second half of the twentieth century triggered resource partitioning all over the globe.

Defensive motivations, "hanging on to what we've got," drives most instances of partitioning. For example, the *Achuar* (above), an indigenous

---

[1] Wichim is an *Achuar* settlement located in the Amazonian rain forest about 150 kilometers east of the Andes in the province of Morona-Santiago. Prior to the delimiting of lands in 1977, all of the lands in the region were "public" lands. In practice, there were no boundaries between individual or community landholdings and, informally, a condition of open access prevailed.

people who live in the southeastern Ecuadorian Amazon close to the Peruvian frontier, had for centuries lived in isolated households in a rain forest without boundaries until missionaries persuaded them to resettle in villages during the middle of the twentieth century. A few years later, the *Achuar* in the village of Wichim demarcated their village lands, first with a global boundary around the village. Later, they divided the village lands into individual parcels. The *Achuar* drew these boundaries in order to strengthen their claims to the lands beneath the forest and discourage *mestizo* migrants from the Andes from lodging competing claims to the lands (Arnalot 1977).

Many human groups have delimited their lands in situations similar to Wichim's *Achuar*. Farmers along agricultural frontiers have for hundreds of years delineated the boundaries of lands that they plan to cultivate. Bottom fishermen who participate in inshore fisheries have established marine territories within which they fish. Villagers who graze livestock have established boundaries around the pastures that they habitually use. Suburban communities draw boundaries around zones of land within which only certain land uses are permitted. As the human population has grown and agents of the world economic system have incorporated previously inaccessible regions and uncontacted peoples into their economic activities, fully partitioned landscapes and partially partitioned water bodies have become common around the globe.

As the suburban example suggests, resources such as land now have multiple layers of partitions. One layer demarcates pieces of private property while a second layer, organized around a land use plan, segregates different land uses from one another. Partitioning creates boundaries around resources that either owners or communities commit to defend (Ostrom 1990). When smallholders fenced off a portion of the range in Tanzania's Shinyanga district, a luxuriant regrowth sprouted behind the fences, but only because the smallholders had committed to defending the enclosed area against herders and their flocks (Barrow, Kaale, and Mlenge 2003). In this sense, partitioning is a defensive strategy that ties users to particular parcels.

Once a peasant cuts a boundary with his machete around a heretofore unclaimed patch of old-growth rain forest just east of the Ecuadorian Andes, he ties his economic future to whatever he can wrest from that parcel of land and the forests that grow on it. The prospective dependency on the quality of the lands often spurs owners to undertake conservation-friendly behaviors such as leaving the banks of streams forested, so as to preserve sources of water on the property. In these instances, resource partitioning becomes a defensive environmentalist activity in which the landowner derives a personal benefit and the larger public benefits from preserved biodiversity and sequestered carbon.

Partitioning raises the probability of conservation without ensuring that it takes place. In an "open access" landscape where people can exhaust the resources in one place and move elsewhere without serious impediment, they have few incentives to conserve natural resources in any one place (Hardin 1968). When a household takes ownership of a tract of land, its members invest in the land and become less mobile because they want to reap the rewards from their investment. Under these circumstances, landowners often have to contend with the effects of overzealous natural resource use. Yields from continuously cultivated lands decline, and forest reserves disappear (Grafton, Squires, and Fox 2000). In a fully partitioned place, users cannot "run away" so easily from exhausted resources because unexploited and unclaimed resources no longer exist (Wilson, Yan, and Wilson 2007). The prospect of losing their livelihoods by exhausting the local supply of natural resources increases the likelihood that people in partitioned landscapes will conserve some of the natural resources under their control.

The partitioning of landscapes has caught the attention of ecologists. Odum (1969, 268) argued that over time undisturbed landscapes become more compartmentalized. As patches become more salient in landscapes, so do the partitions around them (Cadenasso et al. 2003). Partitioning reduces the competition for resources in several different ways (Griffin and Silliman 2011). Different species may over time specialize in consuming different kinds of foods, as occurred in the Galapagos Islands when one species of finches invaded an island containing other species of finches and the beak sizes of the different species diverged in the following twenty-five years (Grant and Grant 2006). Alternatively, the species may not change, but their spatial ranges may diverge. This kind of spatial partitioning is analogous to the human partitioning of natural resources.

The chapter begins by describing the historical expansion of partitioning. Then, it summarizes the theories that explain why over time changing political and economic conditions encourage people to partition natural resources and then adopt a defensive environmentalist posture in managing their natural resources. Five case studies of resource partitioning, from oceans as well as lands, from affluent as well as poor societies, then illustrate the intertwined political, economic, and environmental processes that induce groups of people to partition and sometimes preserve natural resources.

The Historical Expansion of Partitioned Natural Resources

The global partitioning of natural resources accelerated in the sixteenth century with the expansion of European states and societies into the Americas, Asia, and Africa. To secure their control over distant lands, the royal families of the sixteenth- and seventeenth-century European nations granted colonial lands to notables in their regimes. They in turn subdivided their lands, "granting" lands to colonists and surviving indigenous peoples. As the colonial regimes expanded the extent of their control within their borders, largely during the nineteenth century, large land areas became the exclusive properties of individuals, communities, and corporate entities. The most remote lands became the property of "the crown" or the state (Tiffen, Mortimore, and Gichuki 1994).

With independence, lands in remote areas became the property of fledgling states that exercised little effective control over them. In effect, many remote lands, oftentimes forested and biodiverse, reverted to open-access conditions. Forest reforms during the past two decades have reduced the extent of open-access public lands in the tropics. Burdened by the regulation of extensive state-owned lands and pressed by newly organized indigenous groups, states agreed to award ownership of state-owned forest lands to different groups of indigenous peoples and local communities, each with a new set of boundaries around their lands.

Beginning in the third decade of the twentieth century, North Americans in cities and suburbs began adding a new layer of partitions to already subdivided landscapes. In expanding urban areas, real-estate developers had subdivided farms into building lots for homes and stores. Now the new suburban residents, through their local governments, superimposed another set of partitions on the landscape, in the form of "zones" that limited lands in the same district to designated uses. These municipal land-use controls limited the intensity with which owners could exploit the natural resources on their property (Rudel 1989). In the late twentieth century, some states added another layer of partitions by designating some regions as "environmentally critical" and other regions less so. The state of New Jersey, for example, designated two areas for special land-use regulations, the largely wooded and sparsely populated Pinelands region in the southern part of the state and the picturesque Highlands region in the northern part of the state.

The partitioning has proceeded more slowly on water than it has on land. Most maritime partitioning has involved the creation of exclusive economic zones (EEZs) that establish a nation's territorial rights to an area extending from its shores. States first asserted these rights in the early twentieth century, beginning with claims to a three-mile zone. Over time the claims have grown in extent. States with extensive coast lines such as Canada pushed for a further extension of their sovereignty to twelve miles in the early 1970s. At the third intergovernmental Law of the Sea Conference in 1974, representatives approved the idea of 200-mile economic exclusion zones along the coasts of each country. Officials gave this idea legal force in the 1982 United Nations Convention on the Law of the Sea (United Nations 1982). With the adoption of laws establishing these zones, island nations, particularly in the South Pacific, gained control over immense new areas of ocean during the 1980s and 1990s.

Countries have also begun to create marine protected areas, the largest of which is the Great Barrier Reef Marine Park off the northeastern coast of Australia (National Research Council 2001). Fisheries officials have also begun to partition fishing grounds, in efforts to conserve fish stocks. To preserve stocks of ground fish (cod, flounder, and halibut), fishery managers have repeatedly closed sections of the Georges Banks off the New England coast during the past fifteen years. Some fisheries with relatively sedentary prey, such as lobsters, abalone, and sea urchins, have undergone even smaller-scale partitioning. For example, groups of lobster fishers from ports in Maine habitually trap lobsters in nearby inshore areas. They create mental maps of these waters and come to regard some areas as their own territory. When outsiders try to trap lobsters in these waters, the locals cut the ropes attached to the outsiders' traps (Wilson et al. 2007). In some places, such as the waters around Monhegan Island off the Maine coast, these territories have received legal recognition (Princen 2005). All of these examples involve "fencing the sea." In contrast, the high seas have no partitions and remain largely open in access.

With partitioning, patches of particular uses emerge within the boundaries of parcels. Some places such as California's Central Valley become centers for intensive agriculture, while other places just a short distance away, such as Yosemite National Park, specialize in a recreational land use. Places become specialized at hosting particular types of human activities, such as the agricultural districts of central California. Investments further the efficiency with which people pursue designated activities in each zone. Irrigation furthers the productivity of agricultural lands in the Central Valley while trail networks help hikers enjoy the out of doors in nearby Yosemite. In this context, it becomes appropriate to talk, paraphrasing some ecologists, about "human patch dynamics."

Over time, these investments become sunk costs that lead people to defend the use of a patch for a particular use, even in the face of mounting costs. For example, problems of salt-water intrusion, land subsidence after drainage, levee breaks, and increasing claims on the water used for irrigating fields have all called into question the exclusive focus on highly productive, irrigated agriculture in the Central Valley of California, but farmers and their supporters have persisted with these activities, in part because they and the larger society have made such a large investment in this particular land use (Service 2007). These rigidities in land use, extended across a landscape, make it difficult to site large new facilities of almost any kind. There will always be a preexisting set of users on the site committed to the existing use and willing to contest plans to change the land use. Even after disasters people will try to recreate the preexisting landscape (Vale and Campanella 2005). The efforts to rebuild on the barrier beaches of Mississippi after Hurricane Katrina illustrate this pattern. For this reason, partitioned landscapes often become defended landscapes.

Over time, these partitions increase local control, but they also create economic and environmental inequalities, privileging, for example, agricultural water users over residential water users in the southwestern United States (Reisner 1986), suburban homeowners over urban renters in North American metropolitan areas (Rudel 1989), and indigenous people over *mestizos* in the rain forest regions of South America (Cronkleton et al. 2008, 17). In defending their privileged status, these groups frequently become defensive environmentalists.

Conserving Partitioned Natural Resources: The Theories

How, then, have all of the subdividing and boundary making affected the prospects for conservation both locally and globally? Theories about the sources for collective action in natural resource management can help us answer these questions. They prove useful in assessing the likelihood of local conservation efforts, but they do not provide much help in identifying the events that precipitated the conservation efforts or in assessing the global extent of these efforts. The work of Walter Firey and Elinor Ostrom goes furthest in helping us understand how social conditions gradually emerge to support conservation efforts. Firey framed his question about the social origins of conservation in the very broad terms of an agent-based decision-making model.[2] Firey's agents take two types of actions: those that yield the largest possible personal gain and those that conserve a collective good at some immediate personal cost. Conservation occurs when people "prolong into the future the availability of certain physical resource processes by...reducing...[their] present consumption standards" (Firey 1960, 233). In this sense, conservation is like virtue, a "long range exercise in self-interest" (Plato quoted in Firey 1960, 237).

Agents are most likely to pursue the largest possible personal gain in frontier situations. Firey discusses the role that these profit maximizers play in "resource development," in particular in the rapid development of irrigated agriculture and the associated depletion of groundwater in the southern plains of the United States during the first six decades of the twentieth century. The rapid development and exploitation of natural resources have occurred over and over again in frontier situations, from tobacco farming in seventeenth-century Virginia (Craven 1965) to cocoa farming in twentieth-century Côte D'Ivoire (Ruf 2001).

In Firey's analysis, people who deplete resources or spew pollutants often have relatively little social capital.[3] They are oftentimes strangers when they first settle in an area, and they frequently plan on remaining in the region only long enough to make their economic fortune. Under these circumstances, people feel few obligations to each other or to the larger community, and they cannot be mobilized in the service of a larger cause such as conservation (Firey 1960, 207–41).

When people begin to voice a desire for the conservation of natural resources, it signals a strengthening of the local social order (Firey 1960, 208). Conservation strengthens a social order because, in conserving a natural resource, an individual foregoes some private gain in order to promote the continued existence of a natural resource from which all benefit. In effect, the resource user exhibits an "attitude of willing conformity" to the larger social order that surrounds a natural resource (Firey 1960, 235). Acceptance of these rules for resource use seems most widespread in stable social settings. In effect, Firey posits a reciprocal relationship between social capital and conservation. The one begets the other.

---

[2] In this respect Firey might be considered an intellectual precursor to today's agent-based modelers.

[3] "Social capital refers to those stocks of social trust, norms and networks that people can draw upon to solve common problems" (Sirianni and Friedland 1995).

Partitioning Resources, Preserving Resources?

Viewed historically, conservation only emerges over time as frontiers become ex-frontiers. People acquire titles to adjacent tracts of land, become more aware of emerging environmental problems, identify actions that will alleviate the problems, and begin to feel some incipient obligations to cooperate with others in solving the problems. For example, in the case of groundwater depletion in the southern plains, farmers gradually became aware of the need to avoid clustering wells, so that the drilling of new wells did not immediately begin to lower the water tables of the neighboring wells (Firey 1960, 187–90). Of course, as people begin over time to understand the dynamics of groundwater depletion, they also become acquainted with each other and begin to feel some obligations toward other resource users. In effect, as the atomized social order of a frontier setting began to give way to a more cohesive social order organized around agricultural communities, social capital began to increase in these locales and the possibilities for conservation of natural resources grew as well (Firey 1960, 237).

The conversion of resource exploiters into resource conservers can gain momentum over time. As concern about deteriorating conditions increases, people identify specific measures to address the problem and begin to advocate for these activities. In these instances, environmental concerns move beyond the expression of socially desirable ideals and become "institutionalized." People begin to believe in the value of conservation, even if it is defensive in quality. They accept the inevitability of some regulation and feel like the regulations promote both the individual and the general welfare (Firey 1960). At this juncture, arguments begin to surface among the initial opponents of regulation that acknowledge its inevitability and recommend that opponents drop their opposition to the process, if only to exert some control over the substance of the new rules (Firey 1960, 188–9).

The work of Elinor Ostrom builds on Firey's analysis by providing a more complete description of the cultural and social structural conditions that enable collective action to conserve natural resources. She points out that when people communicate infrequently, if at all, and do not subscribe to the same rules, the likelihood of joint action to conserve a resource is very low (Ostrom 2005, 131). If, however, a coupled natural and human system exhibits a substantial number of the following conditions, then the likelihood of joint action grows appreciably. Resource users must evaluate the resource as important in their daily livelihoods. In addition, they should share "a common understanding of their situation, [have] a low discount rate [i.e., they are unlikely to pick up and leave the area], trust one another, and make their own rules" (Ostrom 2005, 253). The resource must have clearly defined boundaries. A means for monitoring its condition must exist, and the prospects for improving its condition through conservation must seem plausible (Ostrom 1990).

Taken together, the work of Firey, Ostrom, and their associates establishes clear theoretical expectations about the gradual emergence over time of circumstances that favor resource partitioning as part of a defensive environmentalist strategy. Oftentimes the events that spur local conservation efforts and the partitioning of resources come in the form of unusually poor harvests. After 1950 the precipitating events increasingly took the form of proposals by highly capitalized enterprises to extract or exploit large quantities of natural resources.

Corporations, States, and Catalyzing Events in Resource-Rich and Degraded Places

Through their command of large amounts of capital, resource-extracting corporations such as oil companies shape natural resource use in fundamental ways, but the prevalent patterns of decision making in corporations are difficult to construe as any kind of environmentalism. In theory, large extractive enterprises might assume a defensive environmental posture just as the people around them do. In practice, the continuing emphasis on quarterly profits and the price of the company's stock makes most large, extractive enterprises anything but environmental in their orientations (Gould, Pellow, and Schnaiberg 2008). The extreme mobility of capital in the hands of corporate leaders makes it unusual for them to invest in the long-range sustainability of any economic activity. They always have their eye on the horizon, looking for the next big economic opportunity to come along. With this willingness to move in search of higher profits, corporate leaders rarely practice any kind of environmentalism. More frequently, the presence or discovery of valuable natural resources in a place attracts well-financed capitalists with plans for large-scale exploitation of the valuable resources. Defensive environmental reactions to these scaled-up economic operations from other resource users spur conflict and efforts to resolve the conflicts through resource partitioning.

Of course, some places attract few capitalists, either because they contain few recognized resources or, increasingly, because a mix of land users, farmers, corporations, and state enterprises have already denuded or degraded large swaths of the landscape. When resource exhaustion reduces the profit-making opportunities in these places, capitalists turn their attention elsewhere, and the resource partitioning stops. Sometimes it resumes, but in a different form, when longtime residents, with occasional state or NGO assistance, try to rehabilitate the degraded resources. The activists in these efforts, with their focus on the economic returns from rehabilitating a natural resource, are defensive environmentalists. The following pages outline this relationship between globalization, resource partitioning, and conservation using five examples: three involving highly capitalized enterprises and valuable natural resources in suburbs, tropical rain forests, and coastal fisheries, and two involving poor, rural peoples and degraded community or farm forests.

Partitioning Resource-Rich Places: Three Case Studies

1. Suburbanization and Land-Use Controls in an Affluent Society

Suburban expansion outside of cities after World War II created what one observer called a "crabgrass frontier" (Jackson 1987). Just as land companies and pioneers profited from those who came after them in frontier regions of the Americas during the nineteenth and twentieth centuries, so large landowners, bankers, and builders, with assistance from local officials and federally funded road construction crews, carved up the land in new suburbs into smaller lots and sold the "improved" land and newly constructed homes to in-migrants (Logan and Molotch 2007). Amid these rapidly changing living conditions, long-settled residents and newcomers have sought to protect themselves from noxious land uses and undesired people by creating exclusive zones of land use around their homes.

Typically referred to as "zoning" laws, the new rules imposed an additional set of regulations on a landscape already partitioned into private properties. The new laws established mutually exclusive residential, industrial, and commercial zones. By grouping similar land uses, the laws, in theory, should have reduced conflict between neighboring land users. In practice, communities enacted exacting regulations that separated people by economic status. Many land-use planners in the outer suburbs of metropolitan areas subscribed to the social philosophy of "hell is other people" (Szasz 2007). More precisely, "hell" is the condition of the community after real-estate developers have built large numbers of new homes, transforming the landscape and filling the roads with additional automobiles. To reduce the number of new homes, community land-use planners increased the minimum size of a plot of land required to build one home from as little as an eighth of acre to as much as twelve acres. They also purchased, with help from foundations, individuals, and state government, tracts of undeveloped land that they designated as nature preserves.

A threat, in the form of a large corporate entity, often triggered the planners' response. In one example, a large-scale developer of high-priced homes (Toll Brothers) proposed to build approximately 100 units in Tewksbury, New Jersey. For two centuries farm families in Tewksbury had made a living farming tracts of land in the rolling topography of the New Jersey Highlands. During the twentieth century small numbers of wealthy families from New York City, in search of an exurban experience, purchased or built single-family homes in the community. Groups of these residents showed a particular enthusiasm for horse riding, and over time they established a network of horse trails throughout the town. For them, Tewksbury represented an "equestrian way of life." The Toll Brothers development, and subsequent real-estate developments that might follow, promised to change this way of life. To prevent this now upper-class community from becoming "just another suburb," the community's planning commission initiated a review of the town's master plan in 2002, solicited opinions from the citizenry about the community's zoning law, and then decided to increase the minimum lot area required to build a home from three or five acres to ten or twelve acres, depending on the zone.

Tewksbury officials also acquired open space. On one occasion, when a landowner threatened to build a subdivision of single-family homes on a particularly visible tract of land near the central crossroads of the town, town officials, private citizens, and a foundation pooled their funds to buy the tract of land and conserve it as open space. Here, as to some degree in contemporary efforts to conserve tropical rain forests, coalitions of local citizens, some state officials, and staff from environmental NGOs came together to counter plans for development. These disparate conservation efforts in temperate and tropical locales have had an organizational link. One of the NGOs, the Nature Conservancy, that assisted in the suburban struggle to conserve the Schiff lands described in Box 4.1, has also provided funds for the conservation of tropical rain forests in Latin America.

When people undertake these anti-sprawl efforts, they do so with defensive environmentalist intent. They want to avoid the negative feedbacks of real-estate development on the local quality of life. Do these efforts at the local conservation of open space aggregate into a larger regional or even national effect? Similar conservation efforts occurred

Partitioning Resources, Preserving Resources? 63

> **Box 4.1: The Schiff Nature Preserve – A Case Study**
>
> A narrative of the events surrounding the creation of a nature preserve in Mendham, New Jersey, some thirty miles west of New York City, illustrates the sequence of events that typically culminates in the creation of preserved open space in suburbs. In 1931 Therese Schiff made a substantial contribution to the Boy Scouts of America (BSA) in memory of her son, Mortimer Schiff, who passed away while serving as president of the organization. BSA officials used the funds to purchase a tract of land that they christened the "Schiff Reservation." Then they developed it into a training camp for boy scouts. In 1979 the BSA, in the midst of relocating their headquarters to Texas, sold the land to American Telephone and Telegraph (ATT), which proposed to build a management training center on the site. Faced with persistent public opposition to their proposed facility, ATT sold the land during the early 1980s to a real-estate developer who proposed to build luxury homes on the land. At this time the Trust for Public Lands, other NGOs, concerned citizens, and officials from local and state government put together a counteroffer for the land. The developer went bankrupt and sold the land to another developer. After lengthy negotiations, the second developer agreed in 1996, in return for funds from a mix of private, philanthropic, and public sources, to build eighty houses on 180 acres and sell the remaining 380 acres to the Schiff Natural Land Trust, an NGO created to manage the reserve. All eighty homes border on the reserve, thereby adding to their value in the real-estate market. This history of open space conservation in an affluent community appears typical in both the length of the struggle with the developers and the emergence of a counter-coalition that put together an alternative to real-estate development.
> Source: www.schiffnaturepreserve.org/aboutus.htm.

with increasing frequency during the last two decades of the twentieth century across the rural-urban fringe communities in northwestern New Jersey. Anti-sprawl activists from different communities, brought together by a regional umbrella organization, learned conservation techniques from one another, and efforts to conserve natural resources spread from community to community in the New Jersey Highlands. Between 1975 and 2002 the average minimum lot area in the eighty-three Highlands communities increased from 1.49 to 2.88 acres. During the same period the percentage of conserved open space increased from 7.6 percent to 29.1 percent of the land in the region.[4]

Recent changes in building patterns in New Jersey suggest that these local actions have had an aggregate effect. In 1994 developers in northern New Jersey built 70.3 percent of all new housing units in the suburbs and 18.7 percent in the core cities of the metropolitan area. By 2007 developers built only 36.8 percent of the new units in the suburbs, and 57.3 percent in the cities. The decline in the proportion of new units built in the suburbs since 1994 may signal the emergence of a new kind of sprawl in which a smaller number of new units of increased size get built near lands recently designated for open space (Evans 2004). This shift has occurred because large-scale developers can no longer assemble the extensive tracts of land that they need to build large numbers of homes in a single development. Some developers, Toll Brothers and K. Hovnanian, for example, have begun to acquire lands and build smaller units, condominiums for the most part, in urban areas such as Jersey City, New Jersey (Rudel et al. 2011).

In effect, the success of the anti-sprawl movement in these localities has begun to force a more compact settlement form on the middle classes in New Jersey. Middle-class sprawl has been replaced by upper-class sprawl. By insisting on sparsely settled landscapes around their homes in peri-urban communities, wealthy defensive environmentalists have imposed "smart growth" on the rest of the state's population.[5] The more compact residential form, by forcing people into small homes in more densely settled communities, perhaps served by mass transit, could lower per capita greenhouse gas emissions among the middle classes. This trend also raises difficult distributive issues. With the poor and middle classes increasingly confined to more urban communities, the distribution of ecosystem services becomes more skewed. Only the wealthy get to enjoy views of sylvan landscapes on a daily basis. The delivery of affordable housing becomes more problematic because under this changing settlement pattern the middle classes now compete more directly with the lower classes for the urban housing stock.

---

[4] To calculate these figures, we obtained zoning and open space maps from the eighty-three communities, created a geographic information system for them, and used it to calculate the average minimum lot area requirements and the accumulated amounts of open space. These are regional averages (e.g., calculated by weighting each community by its land area).

[5] Landscapes organized according to "smart growth" principles feature dense, mixed-use settlements (Duany, Plater-Zyberk, and Speck 2000).

How widespread are these trends in the United States? Findings from recent census data suggest similar trends elsewhere. Residential segregation by income has increased significantly in the United States during the past three decades (Reardon and Bischoff 2012). On the other hand, the rugged topography of northwestern New Jersey has certainly influenced the observed change in settlement patterns by limiting the amount of buildable land in the region and complicating the developers' attempts to assemble contiguous tracts of land for development. In other metropolitan areas of the United States with abundant supplies of buildable land, such as Atlanta or Chicago, anti-sprawl activists would not be able to limit the supply of buildable land to the same extent, so developers might find it easier to continue building in peripheral locations. The conservation of open space has, however, proven to be very popular with American voters. In the 2004 elections they approved 120 of 161 open-space funding initiatives in a dispersed set of American communities (southern Florida, western Montana, northern Virginia, northern Vermont, and Los Angeles, California) (Rogers 2004).

Following the theoretical leads of Firey and Ostrom, the increasing age of suburban communities in America should gradually build their social capital, which in turn would lead to more community-wide efforts to preserve open space. Are these land preservation efforts examples of a defensive environmentalist practice? The residents who pursue these initiatives make their communities more exclusive, which in turn raises the value of their homes and, from their point of view, improves the quality of life in the community. These measures further stratify people in metropolitan areas. By limiting the extent of the sprawling suburban landscape, these defensive efforts by privileged suburbanites benefit the larger environment by limiting greenhouse gas emissions. For these reasons, suburban land-use controls seem like a clear example of a defensive environmentalist practice.

2. Globalization and the Expansion of Parks and Indigenous Reserves in Tropical Forests

During the past 140 years humans have partitioned a growing number of natural resource-rich areas into indigenous reserves in some places and parks in other places in order to protect either the natural resources or the peoples who earn livelihoods from those resources. Through recent forest reforms, states of the Global South have granted land tenure over more than 250 million acres to indigenous communities (Barry and Meinzen-Dick in press). By the turn of the century, local communities had acquired ownership of more than 22 percent of the world's forested land (White and Martin 2002). At the same time, the extent of protected areas continued to grow. By early 2007 the world contained more than 90,000 protected areas extending over 18 million square kilometers, approximately 13.2 percent of the earth's land area (UNEP-WCMC 2007). Do defensive environmental reactions to large-scale global actors explain the increase in partitioned and conserved resources?

The first defensive environmentalists may have been medieval royalty in Europe who preserved forests for their exclusive use as hunting reserves. More recently, the captains of industry sought homes in the country to escape the filth and pollution of cities. A plan to build a penitentiary near the country home of E. H. Harriman, a nineteenth-century American railroad magnate, disturbed him to the point where he, along with other affluent landowners in the region, prevented its construction by purchasing all of the nearby lands that could have been used as sites for the penitentiary. Harriman later purchased additional, contiguous lands. After his death, his wife donated the assembled lands to the state of New York in 1910 to establish the Harriman State Park, northwest of New York City (Botshon 2007). While Harriman's initial impulse in assembling lands around his estate was clearly an instance of defensive environmentalism, his later purchases far from the estate and his wife's decision to donate the lands to New York seem more consistent with altruistic environmentalism.

Although elites played a prominent role in the creation of the first parks in sub-Saharan Africa, they did not do so out of a defensive concern for their own landholdings. Organized initially around the Society for the Preservation of the Fauna of the Empire, conservation-minded British elites, some with interests in big game hunting, campaigned for the creation of extensive reserves for flora and fauna (Neumann 1998). After World War II, first the colonial regimes and then the newly independent states attempted to build an international tourist trade centered around the observation of sub-Saharan megafauna in their native habitats (Neumann 2002). In some instances they financed the expansion of the parks by using funds from conservation organizations to purchase landholdings from colonial settlers who were leaving Africa after independence (Neumann 1998, 2002).

Defensive environmentalist reactions did not play a role in the initial efforts to establish parks in the neotropics. Growing concern about the rapid destruction of tropical forests among global elites and a spreading conviction that all nation-states should have park systems persuaded the presidents of Brazil and Ecuador to commission well-known foreign environmentalists to design systems of national parks for their countries during the 1970s (Foresta 1991; Rudel with Horowitz 1993). Delegations of biologists from international environmental NGOs toured potential park areas in both countries and suggested areas for conservation.

The immediate circumstances that led to the creation of these new parks showed little involvement of local peoples. In an effort to avoid political conflict, politicians frequently chose almost entirely uninhabited, topographically rugged areas for protected areas. For example, in Ecuador in 1992 government officials responded to the news that Ecuador had had the highest deforestation rate in South America during the previous year by pledging to create more protected areas. To fulfill their pledge, they doubled the size of the existing Sangay Park by extending it southward into an extremely rugged and uninhabited area of the Andes. A similar dynamic of park expansion occurred in Brazil in 1995 and again in 2004 when deforestation rates peaked. This process explains why the seemingly strong conserving effect of designating lands as "protected" turns out, after controlling for topography, to be much more modest in size (Joppa and Pfaff 2011). Local peoples played virtually no role in these processes of park creation.

With increased political organization among indigenous peoples in recent decades (Yashar 2005), defensive environmental struggles have become more salient in histories of park creation. In these instances local environmentalists, indigenous people, and representatives from international environmental NGOs formed coalitions to counter well-financed entrepreneurs, sometimes international in origin, who wanted to open up remote, rain forest-rich regions for exploitation. This dynamic occurred most recently in interior Kalimantan. In 2005 the Indonesian State Plantation agency announced plans to establish the world's largest oil palm plantation, with funds from Chinese investors, in the rain forest-rich, interior uplands of the island of Kalimantan. To prevent the large-scale deforestation envisaged by this project, several large-scale international NGOs, led by the World Wildlife Fund, and working with indigenous groups, proposed to help finance the creation of a "Heart of Borneo" biological reserve that would extend across the borders of three countries, Indonesia, Malaysia, and Brunei (United Kingdom 2006; Wakker 2006; WWF 2006).

In the Ecuadorian Amazon the *Shuar* and *Achuar* have supported the creation of parks in the eastern foothills of the Andes, part of their ancestral hunting grounds, because they see the parks as a bulwark against the incursions of multinational mining companies like CANUC Resources.[6] The increased levels of indigenous organization have also led to new forms of collective action that represent defensive environmentalism. In the Brazilian Amazon indigenous peoples have limited the devastation caused by rancher-ignited fires by fighting the fires when they moved into indigenous lands (Nepstad et al. 2006a). Not surprisingly, the most effective protection of tropical forests in Ecuador occurs when an indigenous reserve overlaps with a protected area (Holland et al. in press). The thought of indigenous peoples defending the double boundary of an indigenous reserve and a park has seemed to discourage land grabbers. The long-running suit by Amerindians against Texaco, and later Chevron, represents a different type of defensive environmentalist struggle in which locals make claims for damages already done.

The defensive–altruistic environmentalist binary is sometimes not sufficient to describe the motivations of participants in conservation coalitions. For example, the local park staff took sometimes heroic measures at the Virunga Park in the Democratic Republic of the Congo and the Volcanos National Park in Rwanda to preserve the forests and populations of mountain gorillas during the 1994 genocide and subsequent years of political turmoil (Vedder et al. 2001, 558–61). They did so no doubt out of a larger sense of obligation to preserve the vulnerable populations of primates, but also out of a recognition that the death of the primates would eliminate the tourist trade that had provided them with their livelihoods.

While indigenous members of conservation coalitions clearly seem to practice defensive environmentalism, their partners in the coalitions, staff from highly capitalized international environmental NGOs like Conservation International, express an altruistic environmentalism in their mission statements and programs. The two partners learned to work in tandem, applying political pressure through what came to be known as the "boomerang effect." Locally based defensive environmentalists enlist the support of staff at international environmental NGOs, who then use their international connections and resources to exert political pressure on political leaders from outside the country. In some instances, most notably with the Kayapo in Brazil during the 1980s, these political

---

[6] CANUC Resources is a Canadian-based mining company that purchased the Nambija cluster of gold mines in the southeastern Ecuadorian Amazon from another Canadian mining company in 2007. In the summer of 2011 the first question local residents put to one fair-skinned stranger was, "Do you work for a mining company?"

pressures resulted in considerable conservation gains (Keck and Sikkink 1998).

The balance of local and global social movements in conservation coalitions may have shifted in recent years. Certainly, the attitudes of poor people living around parks in Central America have changed. An initial hostility to conservation initiatives by outsiders has evolved into an acceptance of parks that permit local people to exploit carefully defined resources (Schelhas and Pfeffer 2008). Ecotourism initiatives have generated similar stances toward preserves. During the early 1990s in a small town (Mindo) on the western slopes of the Ecuadorian Andes, four young men, born and raised in the region, began guiding visiting ornithologists on excursions into the nearby rain forests. To prevent the conversion of more forests into cattle ranches, the young men began to lobby in the national capital for the creation of a reserve. Despite opposition from cattle ranchers, the young men succeeded in getting a reserve created. Fifteen years later they continue to guide visiting bird watchers, but the stream of visitors is much larger now, and the number of local enterprises that cater to ecotourists has increased dramatically. In these settings the cultural schema of biodiversity conservation versus local livelihoods has broken down, and large numbers of local residents, adopting a defensive environmentalist posture, have begun to push for the conservation of the forests that surround the community.[7]

3. Partitioning the Seas and Fisheries Conservation

Even though people began partitioning the seas well after they began partitioning land, they had, by 2000, partitioned almost all of the oceans' continental shelves (Pauly et al. 2002). Some of the tools for subdividing the oceans, protected areas and zoning, look similar to those used on land, so they may represent another instance of defensive environmentalism and have similar conservation effects. Because the continental shelves contain 90 percent of the world's fisheries, it becomes reasonable to ask whether ocean partitioning has produced any globally observable conservation effects.

The first worldwide partitioning of seascapes occurred when nations created exclusive economic zones (EEZs) off of their shores. Because the EEZs cover the most extensive and biologically productive areas of the oceans, some advocates of extending EEZs from 3 miles to 200 miles offshore may have initially hoped to reduce fishing pressure by excluding

---

[7] Field notes, Mindo, Ecuador, July and August, 2006.

foreign fishers from coastal fishing grounds, but these hopes proved unfounded. In the first fifteen years after the extensions of the EEZs, a rapid buildup in national fishing fleets occurred. With the help of government subsidies, fishers built larger boats, and within the EEZs fishers from the same nation competed with one another in open-access fisheries.

The larger boats had an additional effect. The increase in size and speed of the boats expanded the area that fishers could exploit, sometimes dramatically. Once fishers could range the oceans, fish lost the remote refuge regions in the oceans where, in the absence of fishing pressure, fish stocks could recover and from which they could repopulate more depleted areas of the oceans. In this globalized industry Asian fishing boats began, for example, to frequent Atlantic Ocean fishing grounds. When the new fishermen discovered new species of fish to exploit, at lower trophic levels, for which there were no local regulations, unbridled exploitation of local fishing stocks became possible, and local extinctions sometimes occurred before governments could begin regulating the new fisheries. These fishers could aptly be described as "roving bandits" (Berkes et al. 2006). Under these circumstances, the EEZs did little to conserve fish stocks. Perhaps a more extensive network of marine protected areas would have had a protective effect, but, to date, partitioning through EEZs has not conserved fish populations.

Both local and national governments at all levels began establishing marine protected areas in oceans during the 1960s, and the numbers of marine protected areas have increased substantially since the 1980s. The United States now contains more than 1,500 marine protected areas, almost all in coastal waters, with a particular concentration of reserves along the densely populated northeastern seaboard of the United States. The political process preceding the creation of the Tortugas Ecological Preserve, west of Key West, in 2001 suggests how people create marine reserves. The staff of an adjacent reserve, the Florida Keys National Marine Sanctuary (FKNMS), convened a meeting of twenty-five commercial and recreational fisherman, marine ecologists, NGO representatives, and FKNMS personnel who over a long meeting stretching over several days hammered out an agreement that became the basis for the creation of the Tortugas Ecological Reserve as an extension of the FKNMS (NRC 2001). By 2012 the world's oceans contained 5,000 reserves, but they only covered 7 percent of the world's oceans. The concentration of reserves along the northeastern coast of the United States suggests that local interests, operating in a defensive environmentalist manner, play an important role in the process, but the events surrounding the creation of the Tortugas Reserve suggest that personnel from federal agencies with altruistic environmental interests also have played an important part in the creation of the reserves.[8]

Smaller-scale partitioning of the oceans has also occurred, with greater conservation effects. Groups of lobster fishers have adopted TURFs (Territorial Use Rights Fisheries), which grant exclusive fishing rights for certain species within delimited areas of the ocean bottom (McCay 2010). Other in-shore fishers have adopted catch-share systems. In these arrangements, fishers who harvest a particular resource, such as clams, form a group, and each member of the group agrees to take no more than a designated share of the total harvest. The total size of the harvest is set by some external authority whose primary consideration in setting the size of the harvest is its long-term sustainability. Other fishers who refuse to participate in the catch-share system cannot harvest the resource in question. Participants in the catch-share system can sell their "share" to other fishers. The prices of catch shares sometimes rise so much that native fishers in places like Alaska can no longer fish because they cannot afford to purchase catch shares. Conversely, the wealthy owners of catch shares can end up leasing their rights to others, becoming in effect "absentee sealords" (McCay 2010). A meta-analysis of the effects of catch shares on fisheries indicates that they prevent significant numbers of fisheries from collapsing (Costello, Gaines, and Lynham 2008). Like other instances of defensive environmentalism, catch shares stratify fishers into insiders and outsiders at the same time that they increase the likelihood of good fishing for insiders and promote the emergence of a sustainable fishery overall.

Partitioning Degraded Places: Two Case Studies

1. *Community Forests*
Cutover or degraded agricultural districts covered extensive areas of India in the mid-1980s. Loggers had extracted the commercially valuable trees and left the area. Expanding populations of shifting cultivators

---

[8] The positive association between densely populated shorelines and marine reserves only suggests that defensive environmental practices generate the marine reserves. To argue for a causal link between defensive environmentalists and marine reserves on the basis of these data ignores the possibility of an ecological fallacy (Robinson 1950) in which an association in the aggregated data proves to be spurious when we look at individual cases.

had encroached on forests and farmed the lands in short fallow cycles, leading eventually to slower and less complete regeneration of the natural vegetation (Mukjerjee 1997; Faminow and Klein 2000). The federally financed Indian Forest Service tried on numerous occasions to replant these lands, but few of their seedlings survived. These failed experiments occurred in a context of rising prices for wood driven by burgeoning demand for construction poles in Indian cities.

Much of the difficulty with government tree planting stemmed from the absence of any meaningful involvement by local rural peoples in the care of these forests. Rural peoples had no incentives to promote the restoration of forests on these sites. To involve local peoples in the restoration of these sites, the central government authorized joint forest management (JFM) schemes during the late 1980s in which the proceeds from the sale of the wood and the responsibility for maintaining the forests would be shared with villagers (Poffenberger, McGean, and Khare 1996). With a newly confirmed interest in these forests, villagers reinforced the neglected boundaries of already partitioned landscapes. The active involvement of villagers in the management of these degraded lands led to widespread forest restoration (Stone and D'Andrea 2001). By 2005, villagers working through JFM agreements managed 31 percent of the forested land in India (Mather 2007, 499). Village forest management in the middle hill districts of Nepal also proved successful in increasing both the density and extent of forest cover during this period (Nagendra 2007). A meta-analysis that compared deforestation rates in 40 protected areas and 33 community-managed forests found lower rates of deforestation in the community-managed forests, underscoring the effectiveness of local forest protection (Porter-Bolland et al. 2012).

Several factors, some anticipated in Ostrom's theory and others not, have probably contributed to the success of these forest rehabilitation efforts. Longstanding traditions of local governance in Indian villages created administrative structures that have provided a familiar means for organizing work in the forests, even though they have not equitably represented the interests of women and poor families (Colfer 2005). The ability of villagers to monitor the condition of the forests on an almost daily basis has proved crucial both for safeguarding the forests and ensuring the survival of seedlings (Agrawal 2000; Nagendra 2007). The more successful community-based natural resource management (CBNRM) programs have had more extensive interorganizational networks than less successful programs. These ties to NGOs and government agencies far from the villages provide pools of expertise and resources that village committees have been able to draw upon in addressing problems that have arisen in making forests both healthy and productive for the villagers (Berkes 2007).

Community efforts to restore or implant forests have often focused on highlands in Asia, Europe, and Latin America (Netting 1981; Nagendra 2007; Tucker, Randolph, and Castellanos 2007). The accentuated slopes make it more difficult to practice high-input agriculture on these lands, so highly capitalized cultivators look elsewhere for land. Villagers still rely on highlands, at least in part, for important resources, such as forage for animals and firewood for cooking. The individual cultivators' partial reliance on these lands makes them reluctant to try and exert exclusive control over highlands, but they are open to engaging in a collective effort with other villagers to retain control over these lands for their common use. For these reasons individual cultivators often will abandon agricultural lands in highland settings at the same time that they will participate in collective efforts to rehabilitate, restore, or protect forests on these lands.

2. Farm Forests

The most dramatic conversion of degraded lands into forests during the past fifteen years has occurred in East Asia, where small farmers in China and Vietnam have converted extensive tracts of agricultural land into forests, either by allowing trees to regenerate spontaneously on old fields or by planting fields with commercially valuable, fast-growing trees. During the 1970s, Chinese officials began mass planting of trees in shelterbelts around cities. The extent of these plantings tripled between the late 1970s and the early 1990s, but few seedlings survived. In the aftermath of the Yangtze River floods of 1998, Chinese forestry officials banned all logging in natural forests and adopted a "grain for green" program. Under the provisions of this program, officials provided small farmers with subsidies of grain if they would plant trees on a portion of their land. The grain subsidy substituted for the grain that the farmers would have otherwise grown on the lands that they now devoted to trees (Mather 2007). Between 1999 and 2003 nearly 15 million farmers participated in the program. China accounted for 54 percent of the worldwide increase in forest plantations between 2000 and 2005.[9]

---

[9] Many of the Chinese plantations created during this period stretched the definition of a forest plantation. Plantations of rubber trees were, for example, counted as forest plantations.

After policy reforms during the early 1990s, government officials in Vietnam began to return both hill and valley lands to smallholders. In addition, the government paid smallholders a small subsidy if they would allow trees to regenerate on the upland portions of their land. At the same time, lowland agriculture intensified in response to growing demand for foodstuffs from urban consumers and road improvements that provided better access to urban markets. The intensified demand for crops such as rice produced in irrigated valley fields pulled farm laborers off of the marginal hillside lands, which then reverted to natural forests. The same improved network of roads, coupled with growing consumer demand for wood, convinced some cultivators to convert a portion of their land into tree plantations in order to meet the demands for wood in burgeoning urban markets (Mather 2007; Meyfroidt and Lambin 2008).

Smallholders have also created agro-forests, by planting tree after tree in their backyards, especially in smallholder-dominated districts surrounding cities in sub-Saharan societies where people have secure claims to their land. By 1990, in Kenya's Machakos district, just outside of Nairobi, small farms contained an average of fifty-nine fruit trees per hectare, compared to twenty-one fruit trees per hectare on larger landholdings (Tiffen, Mortimore, and Gichuki 1994). Smallholders planted the fruit trees, along irrigation ditches and in small clusters, with the intention of selling some fruit in urban markets and consuming the rest of the fruit at home. People have planted agro-forests in other densely populated sub-Saharan regions, in the western highlands in Kenya (Holmgren, Masakha, and Sjoholm 1994), in Rwanda before the genocide (Kampayana 1992), in the Western Usambara mountains of Tanzania (Barraclough and Ghimire 1996), and in the coastal plain outside of Mombasa, Kenya (Ng'weno 2001).

Only farmers with the smallest lots refrain from planting trees out of a concern that the shade from the trees will impair food production from household gardens. For those who can plant trees, agro-forestry brings additional benefits. Because the stands of timber require little labor, they free up the farmer to earn an income in non-farm pursuits. This complex of practices constitutes what R. Mac Netting (1993) called the "ecology of small scale, sustainable agriculture." These practices have provided the popular foundation for a campaign to plant a billion trees launched in 2006 by Kenyan activist and Nobel Peace Prize winner Wangari Maathai (Alter 2006). As the billion-tree campaign suggests, smallholder tree farms sometimes bear the marks of a globalized commerce. In smallholder agro-forests in the Dominican Republic, a common fast-growing species is an exotic tree, *Acacia mangium*, and the agents promoting its use are staff members of an international environmental NGO, Environment and Development Alternatives (Rocheleau et al. 2001).

Another example comes from the Sahel. French colonial policy prohibited tree cutting. The intent of the French policy was to protect trees, but, because the law conveyed the impression that the trees belonged to the state, it in effect dissuaded farmers from planting trees or caring for spontaneously generated trees on their farms. The legacy of restrictive French colonial policies regarding trees persisted into the first few decades of the postcolonial period, but, beginning in the 1980s, with the growing weakness of the state in Niger coupled with several grassroots, NGO-supported tree planting initiatives, smallholders began to realize that the trees on their farms belonged to them.

This altered understanding of tree tenure gave smallholders the confidence to embark on additional resource partitioning, distinguishing the ownership of individual trees as well as the ownership of individual parcels of land (FAO 1999; Reij, Tappan, and Smale 2009; Bilgur 2011). While the externally funded NGOs provided the initial impetus to plant thousands of seedlings in shallow water collecting pits, the tree planting spread when local farmers turned it into a social movement. As Reij put it, "This isn't a big project with a cloud of money. It's a movement with a bunch of people with their noses (pointed) in the same direction" (quoted in Bilger 2011, 121).

Seedling survival was enhanced by increased precipitation during the first years of the tree planting movement. Controlled comparisons between changes in tree cover in adjacent areas of Nigeria and Niger that received equivalent amounts of rain indicated that more reforestation occurred in Niger than in Nigeria, which in turn suggests that the institutional changes in Niger made a decisive contribution to the greater-than-expected tree growth. The tree growth, by providing shade for crops such as sorghum, also increased the yields from these crops (Reij and Tappan 2008). Taking note of the program's successes, the United Nations has now launched the Great Green Wall project, a multinational program to promote afforestation among smallholders across the Sahel (SSO 2008).

Fast-growing trees increase the returns to farm forests and encourage smallholders to plant. After the larger logging firms exploited the swamp forests of the *varzea* outside of Belem, Brazil, they left the area. Natives of the region (*caboclos*) set up small logging operations on these lands, salvaging abandoned machinery left by the larger logging firms and using it to establish small sawmills. The *caboclos*' income comes from the sale of a fast-growing tree, *Calycophyllum spruceanum*, that reaches commercial size in only eight years (Pinedo-Vasquez et al. 2001). The resurrection of small-scale enterprises in these cutover districts led people to reaffirm the partitioning of the resource. In this context, the departure of the larger logging firms restored local control over natural resources, stabilized the social order, and provided the impetus behind a new type of plantation forestry in the region. As Zimmerman (1951) has pointed out, people only plant trees when they think that the local institutions are sufficiently stable to allow them to harvest and market their timber ten to fifteen years later.

Conclusion

Economic development has fostered resource partitioning under a variety of conditions during the twentieth and twenty-first centuries. Accelerated economic exploitation of valuable natural resources by highly capitalized investors in suburbs, tropical rain forests, and coastal fisheries prompted defensive environmental efforts to preserve local natural resources that often led, after political conflict, to a partitioning of the resources. In just as many instances economic groups devastated natural resources, and, as the value of the resources declined, the impetus to partition them diminished, and boundaries between properties became soft, not worth defending. When economic development resumed, albeit in a reduced form, in these cutover, fished out, or abandoned sites, fledging enterprises, revived community forest councils or individuals interested in reaping benefits from trees on their farms, attempted to reassert control over now degraded but not entirely worthless resources. To do so, they put into place new partitions, distinguishing trees to be preserved from those to be cut. In all of these settings people partitioned natural resources when the prospect of economic development or environmental degradation made the resources valuable enough to want to control. As levels of political organization increased during the twentieth century among local people with long-term, defensive interests in threatened natural resources, partitioning led to increased natural resource conservation.

5

Advantaging Offspring, Limiting Offspring

> In the U.S.... a... "good mother" sacrifices whatever she must to unfailingly respond to her children's needs round-the-clock.
> Elizabeth Soliday (2009, 49)

Introduction: Costs of Children, Defensive Environmentalists, and Population Declines

The cultural ideal of intensive mothering and parenting, articulated above by Elizabeth Soliday, often makes itself felt for the first time in the lives of young people in a seemingly disconnected way. They decide to continue going to school and to postpone marriage and childbearing until they achieve some economic security. More education, with a corresponding delay in entering the labor force, will probably improve their chances of landing a secure job, but, by delaying childbearing, young adults run the risk of having no children or, at the very least, fewer children than they would have had otherwise (MacDonald 2006). Assumed, but sometimes not stated, in these mental calculations is the underlying assumption that raising a child is a resource-intensive, competitive activity that adults do not want to undertake until they are in an optimal position to do so. This line of reasoning figures prominently in explanations for the dramatic declines in human fertility over the past century. It also represents a defensive environmentalist practice in that the intensive parenting featured in this strategy usually benefits the child and therefore the family at the same time that the declines in fertility benefit the global environment by reducing the numbers of high greenhouse gas emitting humans in the next generation.

Natural scientists who study life histories have noted similar reproductive strategies in other species (Reznick, Bryant, and Bashey 2002). MacArthur and Wilson (1967) stimulated this line of research when they argued for a relationship between density dependence, reproduction, and evolution.[1] In theory, the predominant reproductive strategy shifts from r-selected to K-selected species over time as biomass accumulates in a place. R-selected species pioneer the revegetation of disturbed places by producing large numbers of offspring. As other plants occupy these sites, competition between plants increases, and the characteristics of the predominant plants change. K-selected species become more common. They produce fewer offspring that compete more effectively against the other plants that occupy the site. Low-fertility human societies seem, at least superficially, like K-selected populations.

Pianka (1970) enumerated the attributes associated with r and K strategies, but field researchers during the 1970s and 1980s found it difficult to identify ecological communities characterized by r and K life histories, so the use of the dichotomy declined. Ecologists continue, however, to affirm that density dependence, the availability of resources, and the extent of environmental fluctuations, all variables that figured centrally in the r and K selection arguments, play important roles in shaping life histories (Reznick et al. 2002).

Few social scientists have gone so far as to use the terminology of r and K selection to describe recent trends in human behavior, even though its heuristic value would seem to be undeniable, at least when applied to recent changes in human reproduction and consumption strategies.[2] The growing prevalence over time of K-selected strategies would signal the adoption of a defensive environmentalist strategy that benefits their families and, unwittingly or not, the larger environment. Several journalists (MacKibben 1998; Wiseman 2007) have argued that we could reduce the scale and severity of global environmental problems dramatically if we would limit our fertility to one child per family. Few social or natural scientists have explored this possibility. Most analysts of global environmental change focus on near-term increases in the global

---

[1] In density-dependent relationships, the population densities of species explain important aspects of their behavior. Explanations that feature urbanization as a primary driver of change would be a substantively similar kind of argument in social science.

[2] For an exception, see Margolis (1973). She argued that people in frontier settings, in her case in southern Brazil, could be understood as r-selected foragers who quickly occupied sites and had large numbers of offspring. Later arrivals in these places could be more accurately typified as K-selected foragers who occupied particular occupational niches in a growing regional economy.

population and project population-induced increases in greenhouse gas emissions that are roughly proportional to the size of the population increases (Rosa, York, and Dietz 2004; O'Neill 2010). In other words, a 20- to 30-percent increase in human population by 2050 would generate an equivalent increase in greenhouse gas emissions.

Because populations in the most emissions-intensive societies have recently seen their fertility rates drop below replacement rates, it is at least theoretically possible that relatively small population losses could occasion larger than proportional declines in global greenhouse gas emissions. A simulation of different projected rates of fertility over the next forty years found that the lowest fertility path would generate 15- to 30-percent declines in greenhouse gas emissions, largely through absolute declines in population (O'Neill et al. 2010). The following pages investigate the empirical origins of below-replacement fertility in order to assess whether or not it represents a defensive environmental practice with the potential for producing global environmental benefits.

Fertility Declines and the Costs of Children

1. *Patterns of Decline*

Most analyses of the projected human environmental impact on climate overlook the recent sharp declines in human fertility. For example, Pacala and Socolow (2004) describe how we can counter global warming through wider use of existing technologies, but they do not include contraceptives in their list of familiar technologies that, if used more widely, would reduce climate change. This oversight seems hard to understand because social scientists now acknowledge that with urbanization, industrialization, and increasing levels of education, humans have begun to limit child bearing to below replacement levels. Figure 5.1 outlines changes in fertility across nations, beginning in 1960. It shows dramatic declines in total fertility rates (TFR) over a forty-seven-year period.[3] Total fertility for the global population declined from 4.47 children per woman during 1970–5 to 2.55 children per woman in 2005–10 (United Nations 2007). By 2007, societies with slightly more than one-half of the human population exhibited below-replacement fertility. Replacement fertility is 2.1 children per woman. The societies exhibiting below-replacement fertility include more than just the long-affluent Western societies in Europe and North America. Societies as varied as those in Chile, China, Iran,

---

[3] The total fertility rate (TFR) is the number of children that a representative woman in a society will bear over the course of her lifetime.

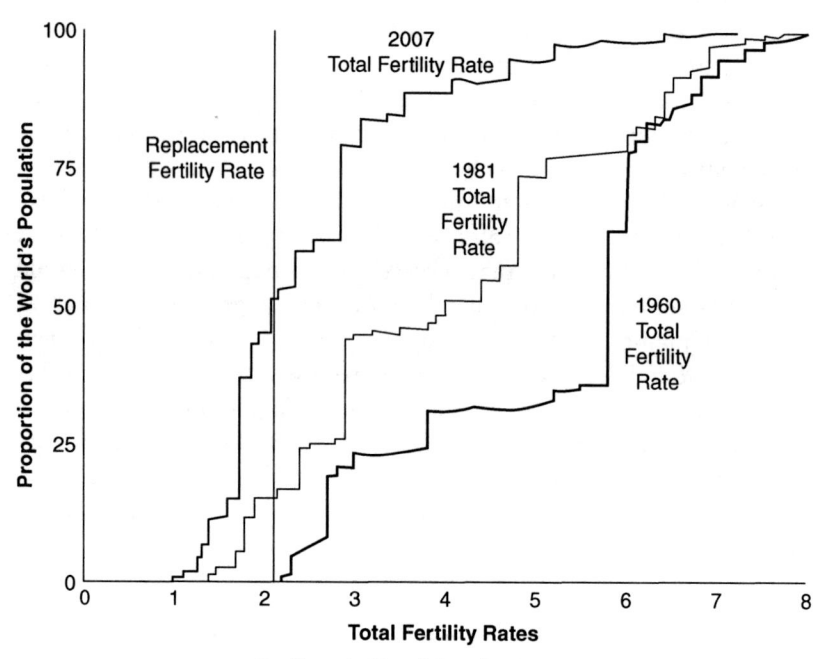

FIGURE 5.1. Declines in Total Fertility Rates, 1960–2008

and Sri Lanka exhibited below-replacement fertility in 2007. Even in a country such as India with high overall rates of fertility, more than 350 million people live in states with either replacement or below-replacement levels of fertility (Vithayathil 2011). Countries such as Germany, Japan, and Russia have begun to experience absolute, year-to-year declines in population that are attributable, at least in part, to below-replacement fertility (UNPD 2007).

These trends do not imply an immediate end to global population growth. Above-replacement fertility in the preceding decades built "positive demographic momentum" into populations, so that those cohorts of women just entering their childbearing years are larger than the older cohorts of women exiting their childbearing years. Even though younger women may have children at a lower rate, they are more numerous and for that reason will give birth to more children than the less numerous older women. In addition, although virtually all societies now exhibit declining fertility, societies with above-replacement fertility rates, particularly in sub-Saharan Africa, deviate from replacement levels (say, 6.0 compared to 2.1) much more than societies with below-replacement rates (1.5 compared to 2.1). As a result, the total fertility rate for the global population in 2007, 2.55 births per woman, still exceeds the replacement rate.

Nevertheless, the sharp declines in fertility are unmistakable. These declines do not stop at replacement levels. Typically, the rates decline to below-replacement levels of 1.3 to 1.7 children per woman before stabilizing (Morgan 2003). The most precipitous declines occur when young people decide to postpone marriage, which depresses period-specific fertility rates. When the age at first marriage stops climbing, the TFR increases a small amount, from 1.2 to 1.4 offspring. The reversal in the direction of change in the TFRs does not, however, signal a change in the overall pattern of fertility. The TFRs remain well below replacement levels for almost all European societies (Goldstein, Sobotka, and Jasilioniene 2009). Eventually, with declines in fertility to below-replacement rates, negative demographic momentum begins, with each successive cohort of women having smaller numbers. Under these circumstances, even a small upward increase in fertility rates will not stem an overall decline in population. For example, at a slightly higher (1.35 births) than currently observed (1.2 births) fertility rate, the population of Italy would still decline by 30 percent by 2050 (Morgan 2003, 591). European populations overall began to experience negative demographic momentum in 2000 when, as a consequence of sharp fertility declines sixteen years earlier, the numbers of young people in each succeeding childbearing cohort began to decline (Lutz, O'Neill, and Scherbov 2003). The size of eventual population declines in these countries will depend in part on the size of the immigrant populations that they admit (Sobotka 2004).

Regional variations mark the overall pattern. In southern Europe, young women postpone fertility until later years, and larger numbers of women (15–19 percent) end up childless (Perelli-Harris 2005). In northern European societies, fertility rates have fallen to below-replacement levels (1.8–1.9), but they have not reached the low levels observed in southern Europe, Eastern Europe, and East Asia. In East Asia, young people tend to remain single for longer periods than they do in Europe. At current rates between 10 and 20 percent of an Asian cohort may never marry (Jones 2007). These regional variations provide clues that should help us tease out the forces that have driven the larger global decline in fertility.

2. *Explanations for the Decline*

An examination of the social and economic forces that have driven recent declines in fertility makes clear the defensive quality of the behaviors. The persistence of these social and economic forces and their likely spread into high-fertility societies make it conceivable that below-replacement fertility could reduce the global population. To assess this likelihood, the following pages examine the explanations for recent declines in fertility to below-replacement levels.

During the past fifteen years demographers have begun to distinguish between first and second demographic transitions. The first transition to lower levels of mortality and fertility began in Western Europe during the late eighteenth century and spread gradually throughout Europe, later to North America, and then to several Asian societies (Japan and Taiwan). After a brief increase in fertility following the end of World War II, total fertility rates resumed their decline after 1970. In their post-1970, "second transition" form, the declines characterized a wide range of societies, some such as the United States that had low mortality rates and had experienced an increase in fertility after World War II, and others in the developing world that had had both high mortality and fertility rates prior to 1970.[4] Between the late 1950s and the late 1970s fertility began to decline significantly in societies containing 80 percent of the world's population (Caldwell 2001, 93).

The wide variability in the social circumstances surrounding the declines and the near-simultaneity in the onset of the declines argue for a common set of driving forces across societies. Certainly, the widespread declines in childhood mortality rates after World War II provided an indispensable precondition for the subsequent declines in fertility. The introduction and widespread availability of oral contraceptives after 1960 also provided a crucial means to lower levels of fertility. The simultaneous emergence of a world economic system in which children did not confer an economic advantage on their parents also contributed to the declines (Caldwell and Schindlmayr 2003, 257).

Global capitalists may have inadvertently impeded human reproduction through their relentless pursuit of profits. The growing demands of the workplace discouraged activities outside of the workplace such as childbearing and child rearing. Work cultures, as in Japan, that required long hours at work made it difficult for parents to care for their children;

---

[4] The United States represents a case that is hard to summarize. For decades it has exhibited slightly below-replacement fertility; 2.06–2.09 children per woman during the 2000–7 period. These rates are higher than total fertility rates in other affluent societies. Explanations for the higher fertility rates in the United States stress the higher fertility rates among recent immigrant groups and the higher rates among low-income minority groups (Frejka 2004).

this circumstance may have even deterred them from having children in the first place (Boling 2008; McDonald 2009). Neo-liberal regimes that have supported large capitalist enterprises may have magnified this effect by providing few supports for young households during their childbearing years, thereby discouraging childbearing.

The cultural ideal of intensive mothering, described by Soliday, has probably worked in tandem with unsympathetic employers to discourage childbearing. Intensive mothering and parenting imply a commitment to the child that knows no bounds. It cannot be combined with a similar commitment to work. A 2005–7 survey of Singapore residents showed that parents committed to the ideal of intensive parenting were less likely than other parents to have children in the future (Straughan, Chan, and Jones 2009). Of course, intensive parenting has usually meant intensive mothering. Fertility declines have been especially sharp in southern European and East Asian societies that have combined the insecurity of employment in a neo-liberal labor market, a commitment to gender equity in schools, and a continuing emphasis on patriarchal arrangements in families (MacDonald 2009). These conditions have placed contradictory demands on young women in the workplace and at home. They should work hard at their places of employment and shoulder most of the burden of child rearing at home.

Under these circumstances, populations in urbanizing and industrializing societies may not reproduce themselves. Other analysts have recast this line of reasoning, highlighting the rising costs of children in urban and industrial contexts (Becker 1991; Azarnert 2010). In this view, fertility declines because parents spend liberally on education in order to produce "quality" (highly educated) offspring. In so doing, the parents increase the likelihood that the next generation of their family will prosper. With child mortality rates at low levels, families may prefer to have small numbers of children and pour familial resources into these children in an effort to advantage them in later competitions for spouses and for high-income positions in the labor force (Mace 2008). In terms that resonate well with the analyses of community ecologists, Mace (2008, 765) argues that

in post-industrial urban societies over the long-term, reproductive strategies based on having few, higher quality offspring could be more successful than strategies based on having more, lower quality offspring.

In societies where large numbers of parents pursue this strategy, a competitive process develops in which parents engage in "a runaway process of ever-escalating levels of investment in... children that... drive(s) fertility ever lower" (Mace 2008, 766). In the United States, the ratio between upper-class and lower-class expenditures on children increased from 5 to 1 in 1972 to 9 to 1 in 2007 (Kornrich and Furstenburg in press). Success in this competition does not usually take the form of enhanced transmission of genes to the next generation. Rather, it comes in the form of status and wealth in both current and subsequent generations (Richerson and Boyd 2005).

This line of thinking envisages a growing number of couples with desires for one as opposed to two or more children, and it sees fertility rates sinking to below-replacement levels. This trend is apparent in China, where the implementation of the one-child policy actually varies by region and by family background. Only the populations in the relatively affluent coastal provinces must limit their childbearing to one child. In Jiangsu province in the interior, where couples are allowed to have two children, only 40 percent of the adults surveyed in 2006 wanted to have two or more children (Gu 2009). Similarly, when only children marry in China, they are allowed to have two children, but only 18 to 24 percent of married only children in the survey wanted to have two or more children (Jones, Straughan, and Chan 2009). In Eastern Europe and Russia, large numbers of women marry and have their first child at an early age, but in many instances they do not go on to have a second child, in part out of economic insecurities (Perelli-Harris 2006). Forty-five percent of survey respondents in the Ukraine report having had abortions, with a mean number of 2.5 abortions per women. In India, in the province of Kerala, women marry and have their first child at a relatively young age. Increasing numbers of them then get sterilized, and the state subsidizes the costs of the procedure. Kerala now has below-replacement fertility (1.7–1.9 range) (Vithayathil 2011). In Japan, the proportion of married couples having a first child has increased in recent years while overall fertility rates have continued to decline (Ogawa, Retherford, and Matsukura 2009).

In the absence of large-scale societal restructuring, this shift in fertility behaviors should, at least theoretically, be enduring (Reher 2007). The highly educated girls in one cohort become a decade later highly educated young women who experience high opportunity costs when they leave the labor force to have children. If full-time employment is difficult to find and requires advanced education, then young people will stay in school and postpone starting a family. If the demanding work culture of full-time employment is not supplemented by well-remunerated part-time positions and adequate child-care facilities, then the commitment to have children becomes even more costly.

Does the recent empirical evidence of fertility declines support this line of thinking? Fertility declines have almost always begun in cities, both in nineteenth-century Europe and twenty-first-century sub-Saharan Africa. When fertility rates in Europe reached below-replacement levels in the 1970s and 1980s, analysts argued that most of these period-specific declines could be explained as postponed fertility that women would later "recuperate" through higher rates of fertility at later ages (Sobotka 2004). Analyses did show increases in the ages when children left the home, married for the first time, and had their first child, particularly in southern Europe (Billari and Kohler 2004). Studies also showed small increases in fertility rates in the latter years of childbearing, but these increases have not been large enough to bring total completed fertility up to replacement levels. After an initial decline, total fertility rates rose to 1.71 children per woman in Europe. In Taiwan, South Korea, and Hong Kong little recuperation occurred after the initial decline in fertility (Tu and Zhang 2007; Jones et al. 2009). In Taiwan and Hong Kong, declines in fertility in the early childbearing years led to declines in total fertility to rates of approximately 1.2 children per woman.

When asked about having children, Asian respondents frequently say that having a child "is too difficult to cope with right now." Underlying these sentiments is an ideological position, consistent with the ideal of intensive mothering, that good parents only have a small number of children because they must devote so much time and expense to each child (Morgan 2003). Survey data from Britain underscore the class dimensions of these decisions. Women from poorer households were more cognizant of the increased costs for the household of going from one to two children, whereas women from wealthier households were more sensitive to the increased costs of going from two to three or more children (Lawson and Mace 2010). In East Asia, the most pronounced increases in age at marriage and in the proportion never married has occurred among lower-income males (Ogawa et al. 2009).

The Japanese involvement with "cram," or Juku, schools embodies the type of parental investment that makes young women hesitate at the prospect of having children. Between the 1970s and 2000 the number of Japanese households enrolling their children in "cram" schools increased from 38 to 61 percent of all households with middle-school-aged children. These schools charge tuition, so enrolling a child in a Juku school creates an economic burden for heads of household. Perhaps more importantly, enrolling a child in a Juku school requires an additional commitment of time by a parent (usually the mother). She must research the schools prior to selecting one and then monitor her child's schoolwork (Rosenbluth 2007b).

The parents take on these responsibilities in the belief that attending a Juku school will improve their children's academic performance to the point where they will be able to attend a prestigious university and secure employment later in life commensurate with their academic achievements (Hirao 2007). In effect, this type of parental investment promotes "lineage mobility" (Caldwell 2001, 96), but it comes at a considerable cost. According to one estimate (Jones 2007), the cost for a middle-class Japanese family of having a child and raising him or her to maturity may well exceed $1 million. Under these circumstances, young women will often postpone childbearing until they feel financially secure, a condition that they may not achieve, if ever, until they are more than thirty years old. This rationale for limiting fertility seems to apply much more generally. Among Germans, those couples who chose not to have children cited financial concerns most frequently as their rationale for choosing childlessness (Stobel-Richter et al. 2005).

The attitude of a twenty-year-old male student in Singapore attests indirectly to these pressures. In his words, "I am not interested now in love relations because I want to continue my studies. If I concentrate on love relations, I won't be able to concentrate on my studies." Public officials in Singapore, which has a completed fertility rate considerably below replacement, focus on the same circumstances but express a different point of view. At a news conference in 2008, Yu-Foo Yee Shoon, the minister of state for community development, youth, and sports, said, "We want to tell students, 'don't wait (to start a family) until you have built up your career. Sometimes, it is too late, especially for girls'" (Mydans 2008). In both Asia and Europe adult children may continue to reside in the parental home after finishing their schooling. In Japan observers refer to these adult children as "parasite singles" because they frequently spend their income on entertainment and do not contribute to the parental household budget (Yamada 2001). In China, unmarried singles in their late twenties and early thirties refer to themselves as "leftover" girls or boys.

Institutional structures in capitalist economies that favor full-time over part-time workers contribute to fertility-limiting behaviors, at least indirectly. In hiring full-time workers, Japanese companies have favored males over females out of a concern that women will leave the company and the labor force when they have a child (Rosenbluth 2007a; Boling 2008). In this instance, the company loses its investment in a young employee. At least in Japan, but most likely in Germany as well, women have responded to these constraints on their opportunities by redoubling their efforts at work, often choosing not to have children. The long working hours and the persistence of traditional divisions of labor between spouses create an unpalatable set of choices for prospective mothers. They can choose to have a child, but this course of action brings with it either a poorly compensated part-time job or economic dependence on a male breadwinner who, required to work long hours for a company, contributes little to the household beyond his salary. Divorce for a woman in this circumstance can lead quickly to poverty. Alternatively, women can secure their financial independence by remaining in the labor force and opting not to have children.

States pursuing neo-liberal policies often compound the problems faced by would-be parents. Out of a concern for the financial health of corporations and their owners, governments tax corporations at low rates, do not provide social services such as day care centers, and do not mandate parental leave policies for companies (Caldwell and Schindlmayr 2003; Rosenbluth 2007a; Ogawa et al. 2009). State policies in the Scandinavian countries differ from this pattern. Their fertility rates, while still below replacement levels, are significantly higher than fertility rates elsewhere in Europe and East Asia (1.9 versus 1.4). Female employment is high, but governments in these societies provide generous social benefits to families with children. In Sweden, female participation in the labor force concentrates in the public sector, where organizations look more favorably on maternal leaves.

These new institutional patterns have altered the relationship between female labor-force participation and fertility, at least in Europe. Female labor-force participation and fertility exhibited an inverse relationship until 1990 in most places. Societies with large numbers of women in the labor force had low fertility rates. After 1990, this pattern changed in the affluent OECD countries. Societies with governments that pursued neo-liberal economic policies tended to have informal barriers that discouraged women from pursuing full-time, lifelong employment. Because many women in these societies have chosen not to accept economic dependency on males, they have sought more education, have entered the labor later in life, married at relatively late ages, and had small numbers of children. Conversely, the wealthier Scandinavian countries, with more fertility-supporting social services such as child care, have begun to exhibit higher female labor-force participation rates and higher fertility rates (Billari and

Kohler 2004). The same pattern has begun to emerge within regions of the same country. For all of the twentieth century, northern Italy, more affluent than southern Italy, exhibited higher rates of female labor-force participation and lower rates of fertility than southern Italy. Beginning in the 1960s, the differences in total fertility rates between the two regions began to narrow, and since 2004 the TFR for women in northern Italy has exceeded the TFR for women in southern Italy (Caltabianco, Castaglioni, and Rosina 2009).

Because the patriarchal, neo-liberal pattern that has characterized the southern European countries is much more prevalent in developing countries than the egalitarian, service-rich Scandinavian pattern, the southern European pattern of very low fertility appears more likely to spread to poorer societies in Africa, Asia, and Latin America (Caldwell and Schindlmayr 2003, 257). More than half of the Latin American societies now have total fertility rates near replacement levels, and this group includes the four most populous Latin American countries: Brazil, Mexico, Colombia, and Argentina. Recent associations in Latin America between increases in higher education for women, delayed childbearing, and increased childlessness recalls the European pattern of declining fertility during the second half of the twentieth century (Rosero-Bixby, Castro-Martin, and Martin-Garcia 2007). These dynamics are more evident in urban than in rural communities. In China, for example, total fertility rates had reached 1.13 for urban women in the late 1990s, compared to rates above replacement for rural women during the same period (Zhao and Guo 2009). Hong Kong, with an entirely urban population, had the world's lowest TFR, .93 in 2004 (Yip, Law, and Cheung 2009).

While total completed fertility declined across Europe throughout the last two decades of the twentieth century, individual aspirations for families remained largely unchanged. People wanted families with slightly more than two children per household. Only in the 2001 Euro barometer survey did the ideal family size drop to below-replacement levels (1.7 children per woman) among the German-speaking populations in Europe (Goldstein 2003). The expressed preference for only children among Chinese and Japanese families suggests a similar regional trend in East Asia (Gu 2009; Jones et al. 2009). Some analysts have conjectured that these changes stem from an increased emphasis on self-actualization among younger cohorts (Van de Kaa 1987; Lestaeghe and Neidert 2006). Because children require sacrifices from parents, the presence of children would hamstring adults' attempts to "find themselves." Other analysts deemphasize these factors. Either way, the recent declines in desired family size suggest that European and East Asian fertility levels will not rise to replacement levels in the near future.

Short-term economic fluctuations have often provoked sharp changes in fertility rates that figure in the longer-term trends. During the first six years of the depression during the 1930s, crude birth rates dropped by 21 percent in fifteen European countries (Caldwell 2006). Similarly, in the aftermath of the revolutionary changes of 1989 in Eastern Europe and the Soviet Union, cash benefits for childrearing declined, subsidized or free child care disappeared, access to public housing became more difficult, disposable income declined, and fertility rates dropped sharply (Macura 2004; Perelli-Harris 2006).

Following the 1997–8 Asian economic crisis, couples in South Korea postponed marriage and divorced at higher rates than they had prior to the crisis. The decline in marriages after the crisis was most evident among less-educated Koreans (Kim 2009). In post-1998 Hong Kong, young couples postponed marriage until a more advanced age and waited longer after marriage before having their first child (Yip et al. 2009). More recently, crude birth rates in the United States dropped by 2 percent between 2007 and 2008 as the "Great Recession" took hold. The largest declines in numbers of births occurred in states such as Arizona that were most affected by the economic downturn. In surveys, poorer American women (9 percent) more than wealthier women (2 percent) cited economic conditions as a reason for postponing a birth (Stein 2010). In all of these instances, economic insecurity increased sharply, and fertility rates plummeted.

At the same time that these social structural dynamics during the last three decades of the twentieth century increased the demand for contraceptives, family-planning programs increased their supply (Bruce and Bongaarts 2010). The effectiveness of these programs may explain why the more recent fertility declines consistently began to appear at lower levels of economic development in Asian and African societies than they did earlier in nineteenth- and twentieth-century European societies. The post-2000 decline in international support for family-planning services may explain in part the more rapid than expected growth in sub-Saharan Africa's population over the past five years (United Nations 2011). Demographers also ascribe the continuation of high fertility rates among women in Sub-Saharan Africa to their lack of autonomy in their relationships with men. This conclusion underscores a presumption in analyses of defensive environmentalism that practitioners have a certain measure of autonomy or freedom of action to choose defensive courses of action.

In some notable instances the contraceptives came with coercion. China introduced its coercive, one-child policy in 1979, and, even though the policy seems to have become less effective after 2000 (Zhang and Cao 2009), it played an important part in driving Chinese fertility rates to below-replacement levels (1.6 children per women in 2007) between 1980 and 2000. Perhaps surprisingly, the fertility declines in China have historically paralleled fertility declines in other Asian societies with different forms of governance (Caldwell and Zhao 2009). This circumstance points to the influence of urbanization on fertility declines in Asia. Like other Asian societies China has urbanized at a rapid rate. The urban proportion of the population increased from 36.2 percent in 2000 to 49.7 percent in 2010 (Hvistendahl 2011).

The coercive policies in some countries, the religious opposition of Catholic prelates, and the eugenic overtones of programs aimed at poor households in developing countries made family-planning programs controversial during the late twentieth century (Connelly 2008). A shift in the focus of family-planning programs toward maternal and infant health after 1994 strengthened moderate voices and allowed some observers to acknowledge the potential importance of population control in combating climate change without asserting that growing families are as important as corporate producers and affluent consumers in destabilizing the climate (Petroni 2009; Kissling 2010; O'Neill 2010).

Countervailing Trends: Urbanization, Aging Populations, and Declining Household Sizes

The magnitude of the eventual environmental dividends from fertility declines depends in part on the strength of several countervailing trends that have accompanied the declines in births. The continuing stream of migration from rural to urban areas in Asian and African societies, with the projections of a global population that is 70 percent urban by 2050 (United Nations 2011), should strengthen the social forces that contribute to fertility declines. At the same time, urbanization encourages increases in household energy consumption because it promotes economic growth and, in so doing, allows newly affluent households to increase their consumption of fossil fuels (Dzioubinski and Chipman 1999).

The declines in fertility and the aging of populations set in motion other trends that affect greenhouse gas emissions. In aging, low-fertility societies, households decline in size and change in composition. These demographic changes can be quite dramatic. Between 1985 and 2000 the numbers of Chinese households grew three times as fast as the population, and the mean household size declined from 4.5 to 3.5 persons (Liu and Diamond 2005). Between 1970 and 2000 the average household size in affluent countries declined from 3.2 to 2.5 persons (Keilman 2003). Because smaller households consume more natural resources per capita than do larger households (Liu et al. 2003), declines in their size retard any corresponding decline, generated by declining numbers of people, in the magnitude of the human impact on the global environment

The declines in household size have several different sources. The aging of the population creates more "empty nest" households consisting of one or two persons. The older children leave home to form new households, and one of the spouses may die. Societies undergoing urbanization, with attendant increases in female labor-force participation rates, see increased numbers of divorces. When couples divorce, two households form and the same number of people then inhabit two houses. The new residences require more raw materials to build, more energy to heat, and more wood for furniture than the previous dwelling that the family shared, so per capita consumption of raw materials increases. In a study that compared resource consumption among divorced and married households in twelve countries, divorced households had between .8 and 1.2 more rooms per capita and spent between 46 and 56 percent more on utilities than did married households (Yu and Liu 2007).

The aging of populations also increases the numbers of retired persons in populations, and while these smaller households consume more natural resources per capita, the adults also work less. Because workers have higher incomes than retirees and use more energy than do retirees, the increase in the proportion of retirees in a society reduces per capita expenditures of energy and per capita emissions of greenhouse gases (MacDonald, Forgie, and MacGregor 2006). With this shift in the age composition of the population, societies dematerialize to some extent, and greenhouse gas emissions should decline.

Population declines may also induce efforts by politicians, concerned with a decline in their nation's relative political standing, to reverse the decrease in population. To date, there is little evidence to suggest that people in affluent, low-fertility societies will demand pronatalist policies from their politicians or that these policies, once implemented, will prove effective in reversing population declines (Jones et al. 2009). Discussions in the popular press in Western Europe show only moderate levels of concern with low fertility rates. Frequently, commentators will discuss low fertility as a factor that contributes to another social problem rather than as a problem in its own right. When governments in Western Europe and East Asia have implemented family-friendly policies in deliberate attempts to reverse downward trends in fertility rates, the policies have not produced substantial increases in fertility rates (Stark and Kohler 2002, 2004; Kim 2009). This record suggests that pronatalist government policies, even if enacted, are unlikely to stem declines in birth rates in the coming decades.[5]

Projecting Changes in the Human Population

In trying to assess the aggregate effects of defensive, micro-level decisions of couples on global environmental change, it is useful to review the projections about the future size of the human population that so frequently inform assessments about the magnitude of global environmental changes. Modelers project that the world will have more than 9 billion persons by 2050 and 10.1 billion persons by 2100 (UNPD 2007, 2011). Juxtaposed against the dramatic historical changes in fertility evident in Figure 5.1, the United Nations projections seem like an insufficient guide to our demographic future because, as projections, they ignore the volatility of human fertility rates. Projections are not forecasts, although commentators often treat them as if they were forecasts.

Demographers have tried to deal with the demographic uncertainties associated with volatile fertility rates by producing projections based on different fertility rates. These projections come in three variants that assume either high, medium, or low fertility rates in the future. All three variants assume declines in fertility, but the rates at which fertility declines and the level at which it stabilizes vary from projection to projection. The choice of one variant over another produces big differences in projected population sizes. The high, medium, and low projections yield, respectively, populations of 10.8, 9.2, and 7.8 billion people in 2050. They assume that total fertility will stabilize, respectively, at rates of 2.35, 1.85, or 1.35 children per women for the high, medium, and low projections.

---

[5] Many Europeans associate pronatalist appeals with Nazi population policies during the 1930s, so they have particularly negative connotations. Given that most of the research on pronatalist appeals and policies has been done in Europe, it is possible that in other parts of the world pronatalist arguments and policies will prove more effective because people do not associate pronatalism with horrible historical events.

As Lee has noted, projections of fertility are the most "error prone" component of population projections (Lee 2011). Comparisons of the twentieth-century historical record of population projections with actual population changes demonstrate that the medium variant projections have consistently erred on the high side. In the case of projections for countries, demographers did not anticipate how rapidly fertility rates would fall (Bongaarts and Bulatao 2000). In the case of cities, demographers did not anticipate the degree to which fertility would fall among urban residents (Montgomery 2008). In most instances, growth in the use of now more available contraceptives, rather than changes in ideal family sizes, drove most of the rapid and unanticipated declines in fertility after 1970 (Feyisetan and Casterline 2002).

These errors in the projections seem understandable given the volatility of recent fertility rates. Demographers have frequently noted the recent acceleration in rates of fertility decline (Bongaarts and Watkins 1996), but they have not really explained it. Both increased social integration attributable to a growing ease of communication and "catch-up" efforts by committed elites appear to be plausible explanations (Rudel and Hooper 2005). Regardless, the increased volatility in the fertility rates would appear to heighten the uncertainty associated with population projections and associated greenhouse gas emissions. Given the dramatic changes in human fertility during the twentieth century, humans will most likely experience some demographic surprises during the twenty-first century.

This cautionary note notwithstanding, the explanations for recent declines in fertility do provide some basis for assessing the plausibility of the high, medium, and low projections for the size of future human populations. Given continuing streams of rural-to-urban migrants in most Asian societies, including China, a majority of their people will be living in cities by 2030. Montgomery (2008) projects that 86 percent of the world's growth in population between 2000 and 2024 will occur in cities of the developing countries. Urban societies in which large capitalist enterprises provide the most sought-after employment seem likely, for reasons outlined earlier, to promote continued declines in fertility rates. Given this shift toward a more urbanized population beset with capitalist-engendered economic insecurity and saddled with the high costs of raising "quality" children, it seems implausible, for example, to project that China's total fertility rate will increase from 1.6 to 1.85 children per woman, as required by the medium variant of the UNDP projections (Zhao and Guo 2009). The low variant with projected total fertility rates of 1.35 may seem like an extreme projection, but certainly total fertility rates substantially below replacement in large parts of the world would be consistent with what we know about the historical drivers of human fertility in recent years.

Conclusion: Defensive Environmentalist Practices and Population Declines in Affluent Societies

Defensive environmentalists exert control over close to home environments, and the number of children in a household plays a major role in the quality of life in homes, so in a context in which child rearing is very expensive it makes sense that defensive environmentalists would seek control over their fertility as an important component of control over their own lives. For this reason, below-replacement levels of fertility coincide frequently with defensive environmental postures among people The subsequent declines in these populations occur in a context in which rising levels of personal consumption in populous, developing countries seem inevitable, so declines in the populations of the affluent societies may not make much of an impact on overall greenhouse gas emissions, barring thoroughgoing public policy initiatives. Nevertheless, the sharp declines in fertility rates since 1960 do provide some basis for hoping that, if the low fertility rates persist, they will reduce greenhouse gas emissions within the next forty years.

The association between fertility declines and greenhouse gas emissions provides the basis for these hopes. Fertility rates have declined to below-replacement levels, for the most part, in the affluent societies where per capita greenhouse gas emissions are high.[6] In contrast, above-replacement fertility rates characterize societies with low per capita greenhouse gas emission rates. These patterns explain why, for example, the average human ecological footprint, by one measure, has fallen in recent years even as our aggregate footprint has grown rapidly (Redefining Progress 2004, 7).[7] If, as demographic theory might lead us to believe, fertility rates have fallen farthest in societies with already high greenhouse gas

---

[6] There are, of course, exceptions to this generalization. Some of the highest per capita greenhouse gas emission rates occur in oil-rich Middle Eastern societies that also have relatively high fertility rates.

[7] By the original measure of the ecological footprint (Wackernagel and Rees 1995), the average per capita footprint has fallen. With a second-generation measure of the footprint that includes additional components, per capita footprints have not changed much in recent years. For details, see Redefining Progress (2004).

emissions (e.g., Europe) or rapidly expanding greenhouse gas emissions (e.g., China), then policies that facilitate fertility declines may provide an effective means of accelerating declines in greenhouse gas emissions in these societies. This is a "fewer mouths to feed" argument, but unlike the "population bomb" arguments of the 1970s, the policy implication here is not "birth control for other people's kids," but birth control for ourselves and our children. It is a policy for expediting population decline among those people who do the most damage to the environment. Affluent countries that commit to declines in greenhouse gas emissions as part of a global climate compact could, conceivably, meet some of their commitment for emissions reductions through declines in their populations.

6

Choosing Foods, Saving Soils

> Our highest shopping goal was to get our food from so close to home, we'd know the person who grew it.
> Barbara Kingsolver (2007, 10)

Introduction

The large, urbanized human populations of the twenty-first century depend for their sustenance on the copious amounts of foods produced by industrialized agricultural enterprises. The production of all of this food has generated problems for both consumers and producers. Traces of toxic substances from the chemicals used to boost production often contaminate the produce that we consume. The continuous cultivation of fields over time leads to soil erosion, soil degradation, and smaller harvests. Both of these dynamics represent instances of reflexive modernization (Beck, Giddens, and Lash 1994; Beck 1999) in which people have come to enjoy the individual benefits of modernization at the same time that they have had to cope with new threats to their health and their food supply that have arisen as a byproduct of society's material successes. To defend themselves from a buildup of toxins in their bodies, consumers have begun to choose foods produced without chemical fertilizers, pesticides, and herbicides. Some farmers have responded to this shift in consumer sentiments by adopting the chemical-free strictures of organic agriculture. At the same time, farmers' markets have become more popular and widespread as consumers have found, in weekly face-to-face meetings with farmers, a way to allay their concerns about the quality of the foods that they consume.

Other farmers, concerned about soil erosion and labor costs, have begun to practice conservation (no-till) agriculture, in which they eliminate or reduce the number of times they plow their land each year. Another kind of conservation agriculture has emerged among small-scale cattle ranchers in the Ecuadorian Amazon. Concerned about the declining productivity of their pastures after forty years of continual use, they have allowed silvopastoral landscapes to emerge, with the hope that litter from the trees will fertilize their pastures and the eventual sale of the wood from the trees will provide additional income for the household. All of these participants in alternative food systems – the organic consumers, the buyers and sellers in farmers' markets, the no-till farmers, and the silvopastoral cattle ranchers – have adopted defensive environmentalist practices.

Like the other defensive environmentalist practices, alternative agriculture has analogs in ecological processes. Over time as their net additions to biomass grow, biological communities become more efficient at recycling nutrients from waste into substances that feed plants (Vitousek and Reimers 1975). Long-standing, still-growing tropical forests exemplify this tendency. Virtually all of the nutrients in this biological community are bound up in the biomass, in various stages of growth and decomposition. Through various channels, the nutrients in the decomposing matter cycle quickly back into plants, leaving the soils that underlie the forest relatively free of nutrients and, in this sense, impoverished (Terborgh 1992).

Agro-ecologies such as organic and conservation agriculture also emphasize the recycling of nutrients to new plants through microbial processes from decaying plants via soil organic matter. This emphasis minimizes energy and resource use (Altieri 1995). Under this type of regimen, topsoils, rich with organically derived nutrients, provide a productive base for the growth of new crops. The high soil fertility, in turn, makes it easier for farmers to cultivate crops without using chemical fertilizers. Agro-ecologically oriented farmers focus on the recycling of nutrients because, from a defensive environmental point of view, it maintains the quality of their soils at the same time that it offers long-term efficiencies in the production of food for humans.

This chapter begins by describing the defensive environmentalist rationales behind recent changes in food choices and agricultural techniques. It then describes the growing prevalence over time of alternative agricultural practices such as organic farming, direct marketing, minimum tillage agriculture, and silvopastoral cattle ranching. An explanation for the growing prevalence of these practices follows. The chapter concludes with a discussion of the role of the food movement in the spread of alternative agricultures.

Defensive Environmentalist Rationales for Food Choices and Farming Techniques

Rachel Carson's depiction in *Silent Spring* (1962) of the ravaging effects of DDT and other pesticides as they accumulated in birds made it seem likely that the same toxic compounds could accumulate in the bodies of humans. In this context, consumers began to express a preference for organic foods, prepared from crops grown without the toxins found in pesticides, herbicides, and inorganic fertilizers. To cultivate crops without chemical supplements, organic farmers focused on building nourishing organic matter in their soils through crop rotations, cover crops, animal manures, and crop residues (Faye 2003; Kasperczyk and Knickel 2006). Most organic farmers may have chosen to farm organically because it increased their agricultural income and reduced their exposure to toxic compounds, but, in so doing, they adopted agricultural practices that, by increasing biodiversity and carbon sequestration in agricultural landscapes, benefited the larger world. This combination of personal benefits coupled with global environmental gains defines defensive environmental practices.

Out of concern about the quality of their foods, consumers like Barbara Kingsolver, quoted at the beginning of this chapter, have become more involved with farmers during the past two decades, largely through farmers' markets. Many, but not all, of the farmers who sell at farmers' markets practice organic agriculture. They share with consumers a desire to relocalize agriculture, so producers and consumers in a place come to know one another through local food markets, creating in effect a "civic agriculture" (Lyson 2004). Consumers at farmers' markets are also defensive environmentalists. The prospect of fresh, high-quality produce for their families attracts them to farmers' markets at the same time that their participation in the markets reinvigorates local agriculture and, in so doing, reduces the greenhouse gas emissions associated with foods that travel long distances from farm to market.

The growing numbers of farmers who engage in conservation agriculture are also defensive environmentalists. No-till farmers leave crop residues in the fields and plant leguminous cover crops to restrict weeds and restore fertility to their soils (Hobbs 2007). They use seed drills to insert seeds and fertilizers in the soil and, if they practice no-till, they do not plow their land at all. By eliminating or minimizing plowing, minimum tillage farmers reduce their expenditures for fuel and labor. These practices also reduce soil erosion and in so doing increase soil organic matter, so farmers stand to benefit directly from the adoption of no-till practices. At the same time, no-till increases carbon sequestration in agricultural soils and reduces the runoff of chemical residues into rivers, so it produces global ecological benefits (Soil Association 2009). In this sense, conservation agriculture, like organic agriculture, qualifies as a defensive environmentalist activity.

Because minimum- and no-tillage farmers often use herbicides to prevent weeds, they do not practice organic agriculture. Although they differ in tillage practices and herbicide use, both organic agriculture and conservation agriculture increase organic matter in the soils and rely on the recycling of nutrients through microbial activity to restore the fertility of soils after cultivation. In this way they reduce soil erosion and prevent nutrients from "leaking" into nearby streams.

Defensive environmental practices have also spread in some parts of the Global South. In the long-settled cattle ranching zones of the Ecuadorian Amazon, cattle ranchers have begun to create silvopastoral landscapes. Sun-drenched tropical pastures with a few palm trees have gradually become populated with dense stands of young trees while remaining in use as cattle pastures. Young farmers, working small cattle ranches of 30 to 50 hectares each, have begun to allow spontaneously sprouting seedlings of commercially valuable species to grow into trees. Over time, these trees come close to creating a closed canopy of trees without eliminating the shade-tolerant pasture grasses below. The sprouting trees provide tangible benefits to the cattle ranchers, ranging from litter to fertilize the pastures to income from the sale of wood. The trees also make the pastures more biodiverse and sequester carbon, so they provide benefits for the wider world as well.

Like organic agriculture, the various forms of conservation agriculture need to be viewed in a context dominated by conventional agricultural techniques that "burn soil organic carbon" by destroying soil microbial life through pesticide applications and plowing (Holland 2004). An end to these practices, a buildup in soil organic matter, and an associated increase in soil carbon would offset a small but still significant portion of societal greenhouse gas emissions (Burras et al. 2001). For example, if California farmers adopted more organically minded agricultural practices, the carbon sequestered in this manner could offset up to

1.6 percent of annual emissions from the burning of fossil fuels in California (Kroodsma and Field 2006).

The Spread of Alternative Agricultures: An Historical Account

Organic Agriculture

Organic agriculture is both very old and quite new. For centuries farmers with little land have practiced what amounts to organic agriculture. In densely settled places with permanent fields the recycling of organic wastes became a crucial component in the emergence of small-scale, sustainable agriculture. Smallholders in southern China constructed one of the most enduring examples of this agro-ecosystem. Beginning as early as 2000 years ago, Chinese smallholders recycled organic materials in a wide variety of ways. Cover crops, mulches, and crop residues fertilized soils. Manure from both humans and livestock stimulated biotic activity in the soil. Crop rotations, agro-forestry, and mixed crop–livestock operations enhanced nutrient cycling in soils (Netting 1993).

Large numbers of intensive, small-scale, sustainable agricultural operations continue to exist. Smallholders recycle organic wastes in a diverse set of places around the world. Dairy farmers in the Swiss Alps, Kofyar peasants in central Nigeria, and religiously conservative farmers in the North American corn belt all recycle extensive amounts of organic waste as part of a small-scale, intensive agricultural regimen (Netting 1993; Salamon 1995). Some of these cultivators, especially in the Global South, practice "organic by default" agriculture (Scialabba and Hattam 2002). They produce organic crops, but they are not certified as "organic," so their crops cannot be sold in high-priced organic markets.[1] It is only with the spread of commercially produced pesticides, herbicides, and chemical fertilizers after World War II that prehistoric, organic agriculture became the exception rather than the rule in farming.

The modern movement to promote organic agriculture had its origins in Europe during the 1930s and 1940s when Rudolf Steiner and Lady Eve Balfour (Trewavas 2001) began to promote a holistic approach to agriculture that stressed how healthy soils (with much microbial activity) promoted healthy animals and healthy people. By the 1950s, these

---

[1] "Certified" organic croplands have undergone an inspection by a nongovernment organization that specializes in ascertaining whether or not a cultivator follows the rules for cultivating in an organic manner. Farmers must pay a fee to the certifier. For that reason, many poor farmers are reluctant to undergo certification, even though it may enable them to sell their products for a higher price.

ideas had attracted a small core group of enthusiasts. Changes in agricultural technologies during the same period inadvertently reduced the degree to which farmers routinely recycled organic matter in their cultivation of the land. The widespread adoption of chemically intensive agriculture created a linear process of cultivation that reduced reliance on recycled organic materials. Over time, extensive external inputs in the form of fertilizers, pesticides, and herbicides, along with deep primary plowing, destroyed soil organic matter and made future harvests more dependent than ever on external inputs (Holland 2004). These cultivation routines also maximized the greenhouse gas emissions from agriculture by destroying organic matter in the soils. This trajectory of change characterized agriculture in postwar Europe and North America, and it has recently spread to agriculture in eastern and southern Asia, where farmers increased the use of chemical fertilizers between 40 and 60 percent between 1995 and 2005.

The growth of a worldwide environmental movement during the 1960s and 1970s intensified the search for a more sustainable agriculture, which in turn rescued organic agriculture from obscurity (Kristiansen and Merfield 2006). At first, the growth in organically managed lands occurred primarily in Europe, but since 1990 the growth has been concentrated outside of Europe, and many of the new organic products are being grown in poorer countries and shipped to more affluent countries (see Figure 6.1).[2] To an appreciable degree, the growth of the organic market has followed the established paths of the globalized food markets created by twentieth-century entrepreneurs.

Consumers' concerns about growing conditions and product freshness have drawn organic producers and consumers together. The geographical distribution of organic farms in the United States underscores this link. The farms cluster in three areas: in the interstitial rural areas between cities in the Northeast, in rural areas of the upper Midwest, and in agricultural districts along the West Coast (USDA 2007). All three locations

---

[2] The data used to describe recent trends in organic and conservation agriculture come from a number of different sources and vary in quality from country to country. The data on the changing global extent of organic agriculture come from a biannual survey conducted by researchers at the International Federation of Organic Agriculture Movements (IFOAM). They compile data submitted by national organic agriculture organizations. In some countries the data come from agricultural censuses carried out by governments, while in other countries the data come from membership surveys. In still other countries there are no data. These variable data constraints from country to country also characterize the international agricultural data sets created by the Food and Agricultural Organization (FAO) of the United Nations.

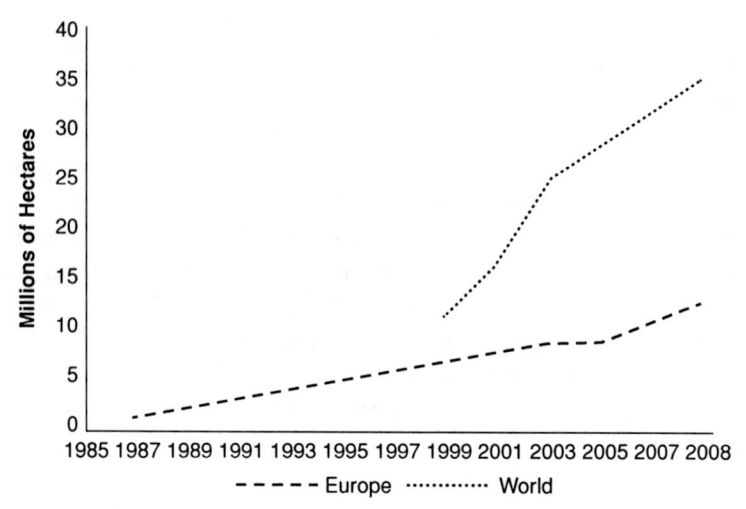

FIGURE 6.1. Trends in Certified Organic Agricultural Lands: Europe and the World

provide organic farmers with proximity to large populations of affluent, urban "foodies" who will pay extra money for organic crops because they appreciate the chemical-free practices of the farmers.

The increase in the numbers of farmers' markets stems from a similar desire among consumers, as Kingsolver puts it in the epigraph, to know who grows their food. Farmers' markets are, like organic agriculture, both very old and quite new. The direct sale of produce from farmers to residents in nearby towns and cities predates the industrial revolution. In many predominantly rural areas of the Global South, farmers and local residents still congregate weekly in plazas at open-air markets where they exchange produce for money. With the globalization of agricultural markets and the introduction of more processed foods, commodity chains from primary producers to consumers have gotten longer. Most recently, supermarkets have replaced direct marketing to consumers as the primary way that urban consumers in Latin America obtain food (Reardon et al. 2003). For consumers at the end of these long commodity chains, the stores sell sometimes stale foods produced under unknown circumstances.

In response to these conditions, farmers and shoppers have begun to show new interest in farmers' markets. Farmers like direct sales to consumers because they capture more of the consumers' dollars. Consumers like the markets because they obtain fresh foods produced under familiar conditions. Buoyed by these sentiments, farmers and consumers in the

United States have founded farmers' markets in large numbers during the past two decades. Farmers' markets in the United States have increased in number from 1,755 in 1994 to 6,132 in 2010 (USDA 2011a).

The sale of locally grown produce occurs in other ways as well, at roadside stands and through community-supported agriculture (CSA). In 2007, the United States had more than 12,000 CSA farmers who sold their produce to subscribers who lived nearby (USDA 2009). Consumers who belong to CSAs receive fresh produce and a sense through the CSA that they are participating in the food movement, a social movement with larger concerns for the community. A recent survey of farmers in the state of Washington indicates that approximately 20 percent of all farmers in the state engage in some kind of direct marketing through roadside stands or farmers' markets. The farmers who marketed their crops directly were drawn in overwhelming numbers from the vegetable and fruit sectors of the farm economy. Beef and grain producers rarely, if ever, engaged in direct marketing (Ostrom and Jussaume 2007). The geographical distribution of farmers' markets follows a regional pattern similar to the pattern for organic agriculture across the states. Farmers' markets are numerous in urban, affluent states such as California, New York, and Massachusetts, but they can also be found in large numbers in Iowa, a state with a large population of farmers (USDA 2011a).

The spread of alternative agricultural practices has occurred incrementally, one locale at a time. Neighbors who use the new techniques facilitate the spread of these practices. Neophytes benefit from just being in close proximity to other organic farmers (Risgaard, Frederiksen, and Kaltoft 2007, 452).

So, when you are driving around, you can keep an eye on what the neighbors are doing in their fields. How did he do it? How did it turn out? And then you may use the experience yourself. This is essential. You use your neighbors to keep yourself updated.

Conversations with the neighbors also help.

It is nice to hear from those with more experience that there is no need for sleepless nights because there are weeds in the fields.... We really looked up to the pioneers and learned from their experiences. I did. And I do.

A similar dynamic has driven innovation in a very different agricultural context, the Iowa corn belt. Iowa farmers who minimize chemical inputs have opened their farms up to other interested farmers once a year for "field days" in which the farmers give tours of their farms and explain particular organic farming practices to the visitors. Small groups of organic farmers also visit each other's farms periodically and give each other advice about how to solve nettlesome production problems (Bell et al. 2004). In effect, organic producers have formed conservation "cells."[3] The members of these groups provide vital social and technological support for farmers who are thinking about converting to organic practices. As one farmer put it (Bell et al. 2004, 184),

I probably wouldn't have taken that step [converting to organic] if I hadn't had... some people there to hold my hand.

Some networks of innovators have included NGOs and scientists. In California's Central Valley, an agro-ecological partnership of almond growers, a growers' association, and scientists from land-grant universities achieved an 80 percent reduction in pesticide use between 1992 and 2000 when they devised biological controls that disrupted mating among important agricultural pests (Warren 2007). The network achieved the declines in pesticide use through a process of social learning in which farmers monitored pest conditions in their fields and adjusted, with the help of scientists, their countermeasures accordingly (Coughenour 2003; Warren 2007, 224).

Interestingly, the California cultivators cooperated readily because they saw almond growers in other countries, not each other, as their chief economic rivals (Warren 2007, 215). Certainly, cultivators in the capital-poor, labor-surplus conditions of the Global South have found the prospect of organic agriculture attractive given the higher prices, the absence of expensive, manufactured inputs, and the higher, but still supportable, needs for additional labor. For this reason, organic growers have increased rapidly in number over the past fifteen years in Africa and Latin America (see Figure 6.1). The developing world now contains approximately one-third of the world's organically managed agricultural lands. While the conversion to organic practices may have produced some localized ecological gains, the many food miles between farms and markets reduced the global ecological gains from this trade.

During the past ten years certifiers have begun designating "wild collection lands" as organic lands. Landowners reserve these tracts for the collection of wild edible products such as berries, mushrooms, and herbs

---

[3] The analogy to the communist "cells" of the early twentieth century is deliberate. These tight social groups help sustain adherents' beliefs in the face of indifference to their cause by large numbers of people around them.

that, if the landowners manage these lands for wild collectibles, can be designated and marketed as "organic." While wild collection lands remain a rarity in North America, they are common elsewhere and have increased at very high rates since 1998. By 2006, the world contained almost as many wild collection lands (31 million hectares) as organic agricultural lands (35 million hectares) (Willer and Kilcher 2010). In most instances, certification as wild collection lands did not actually change land uses so much as ratify preexisting land uses. The real transformations in land use have occurred on croplands.

The recent declines in the use of synthetic fertilizers in the more affluent countries may reflect the growing prevalence of organic practices. Between 1995 and 2005 fertilizer use by European farmers declined 23 percent from very high levels of fertilizer application per hectare. In some instances, European governments imposed limits on farmers' use of nitrogen fertilizers in attempts to prevent the creation of further "dead zones" in coastal waters that are caused by algae blooms attributable to agricultural runoff (International Fertilizer Industry Association 2012).

Despite the rapid growth in the organic sector during the past two decades, organically managed lands only account for .81 percent of all agricultural lands worldwide. Two-thirds of the organic lands are pastures. Organic lands comprise 4 percent of all agricultural land in Europe and less than 1 percent of the agricultural land in Asia, Africa, and the Americas (Willer and Kilcher 2010). Given the still small extent of organic lands, organic foods now represent a small but growing global niche market. Whether or not organic agriculture can continue to expand during a period in which globalization and global climate change have encouraged the spread of invasive species, including pests, remains an important, unanswered question.

Conservation Agriculture

The spread of conservation agriculture during the past four decades also signals the growing appeal of defensive environmental rationales in natural resource management. The techniques of conservation agriculture, ranging from minimum-tillage corn cultivation to silvopastoral cattle ranching, all manipulate landscapes less than conventional practices. Minimum tillage reduces the intensity with which farmers manipulate the soils in a variety of ways. Farmers employing no-till or minimum-tillage techniques reduce the number of times that they plow their fields during each growing season. They plant seeds by drilling a hole in the soil. Farmers cultivate cover crops whose roots and residues provide nutrients for the soils. They leave crop residues from the previous year's harvest on the land because they too fertilize the soils with decaying organic matter (Smil 1999; Holland 2004). These techniques make it possible for fields to absorb rather than emit greenhouse gases.

Farmers first began experimenting with no-till techniques in the early 1960s in Kentucky. The first field demonstrations by the no-till pioneers attracted hundreds of farmers to the innovators' western Kentucky farms. The interested farmers often had experienced a particularly bad storm that had made them more aware of the soil erosion problem on their lands. As with the field days on Iowa farms mentioned earlier, the field demonstrations of no-till techniques brought together farmers who in many instances went on to create networks of no-till farmers elsewhere in the Midwest. Network members provided each other with support and advice about how to implement no-till practices on their farms. When no-till spread over longer distances, across state boundaries, extension agents and specialists from the land-grant colleges played more important roles in adoption and diffusion processes (Coughenour and Chamala 2000). A patchy geographic pattern of adoption in the northwestern United States, largely coterminous with county lines, suggests that the attitudes of county agricultural extension agents toward no-till may have encouraged or discouraged the creation of geographic clusters of no-till farmers. Federal subsidies for direct seeding provided additional incentives for farmers to practice no-till agriculture after 1976 (Kane et al. 2011).

The spread of no-till agricultural practices during the 1990s stemmed in large part from two government-initiated changes. First, the passage of the Food Security Act of 1985 required that farmers would have to develop conservation plans for their farms to continue receiving price support payments from the federal government. This mandate encouraged farmers to consider and then adopt no-till practices on their farms. Second, scientists at agricultural experiment stations produced a series of small improvements in no-till techniques that made it easier for farmers to adopt no-till in a wider range of agricultural regions (Coughenour and Chamala 2000). Highly capitalized farmers with improved management tools were best positioned to adopt these improvements in conservation tillage.

While organic agriculture may seem like no more than a niche technique, albeit a growing one, conservation agriculture, in particular no-till techniques, shows signs of becoming a widely accepted practice among larger farmers. By 2009, farmers had increased the worldwide extent of minimally tilled lands to 106 million hectares, more than ten times the

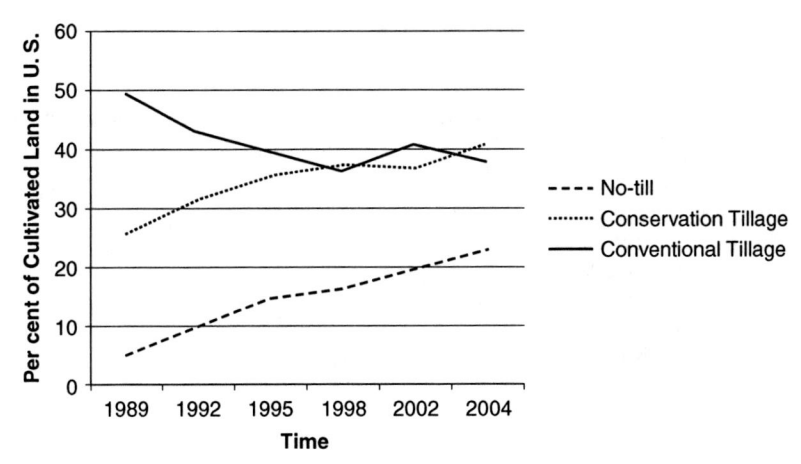

FIGURE 6.2. Trends in U.S. Tillage Practices over Time

extent of organically managed croplands (Kassam et al. 2009). The rates of increase have been particularly rapid in North America. Between 1991 and 2001, Canadian farmers increased the extent of their minimum-tillage lands from 33 to 61 percent of all Canadian cropland. As documented in Figure 6.2, the percentage of American cropland cultivated with no-till techniques increased from 5.0 to 22.6 percent between 1989 and 2004 (Montgomery 2008; Conservation Technology Information Center 2011).

Farmers in the Americas have adopted conservation tillage out of a desire to limit the costs of inputs, in particular labor and fuel, and preserve the quality of their soils. Conservation tillage retains soil moisture better than conventional tillage, and in semiarid zones water retention in the soils can make a crucial difference in the size of harvests. In Europe, farmers have adopted conservation tillage out of a concern with soil moisture, a desire to cut input costs, and as a response to European consumers who want to eat foods cultivated in environmentally friendly ways (Holland 2004). With the spread of these techniques, farmers, at least in the affluent societies, have become more proficient in recycling the organic matter in their soils.[4]

---

[4] It is important not to interpret the absence of an organic market in rural areas of the Global South as disinterest in organic foods. In rural Ecuador, some people maintain organic gardens in their backyards, but they do not have the income to purchase organic products in the market, so markets for them never appear.

TABLE 6.1. *The Changing Extent of Conservation Tillage in the United States*

		1996	1997	1998	1999	2000	2001–2	2004	2005–6
Corn	Crop Residue (% acres)	29	29	25	26	28	27		31
	# of Tillage Operations	3	3	3	3	3	3		3
	Cultivated for Weed Control	33	55	42	48	38	37		15
Soybeans	Crop Residue (% acres)	39	37	38	37	38	41		49
	Tillage Operations	3	3	3	2	2	3		1
	Cultivated For Weed Control (% acres)	29	28	26	22	17	13		10>
Winter Wheat	Crop Residue	19	20	20		23		36	
	Tillage Operations	5	5	4		4		5	

Source: Successive Agriculture Resource Management Surveys (ARMS), 1996–2006, United States Department of Agriculture. Accessed at http://www.ers.usda.gov/data-products/arms-farm-financial-and-crop-production-practices.aspx.

Trends in the tillage practices of American farmers who cultivate three major grain crops provide another indicator of the growing popularity of conservation agriculture. While the specific patterns of change have differed from crop to crop since the mid-1990s (see Table 6.1), in each instance cultivators have found a way, within the agro-ecological constraints of their crop, to reduce plowing.

The adoption of no-till, ridge-till, and stubble-mulch agriculture among American farmers has occurred in spurts.[5] Farmers in Kentucky began to experiment with no-till in the late 1960s. They reduced or eliminated plowing and hoped that yields would not fall. When the yields remained roughly the same, the farmers knew that they had found a way to both cut costs and improve their soils by reducing erosion. Rapid

---

[5] Ridge-till farming reduces tillage operations by limiting them to raised beds arranged in rows across a field. Stubble-mulch farming leaves the crop residues from the previous growing season on the surface of the soil. By leaving the stubble in the soil, stubble-mulch farming also reduces the number of times that farmers till their soil each season.

adoption of conservation agriculture in the border states, particularly in Kentucky, occurred during the 1970s, followed by a pause during the 1980s and a further increase during the 1990s (Coughenour and Chamala 2000). While the principles of conservation agriculture may seem simple, they have been difficult to implement given the different micro-ecologies of farms. As one farmer put it, "it (conventional tillage) takes a lot less thinking. It takes a lot less planning.... With no-tillage, you are continually learning" (quoted in Coughenour and Chamala 2000, 150).

The recent spread of silvopastoral cattle ranching among family farmers in the Ecuadorian Amazon illustrates the wide range of situations in which cultivators adopt defensive environmental practices. The common element that links large-scale grain farmers in the American Midwest with small-scale cattle ranchers in the Ecuadorian Amazon is the continual use of the land for long periods of time, 150 years in the Midwest, 40 years in the Ecuadorian Amazon. Under these circumstances, environmental degradation began to concern both sets of farmers. Episodes of soil erosion began to trouble grain farmers, and degrading pasture grasses caused concern among cattle ranchers.

In response, young cattle ranchers in Ecuador have consciously begun to allow spontaneously sprouting tree seedlings to grow in their pastures, so tree densities have increased in the region's pastures. The cover photo for this book comes from one of these working pastures with trees in the Ecuadorian Amazon. Because the predominant pasture in the region, *Panicum purapurascens*, tolerates shade well, the increased number of trees in pastures has not negatively affected the productivity of the pastures for raising cattle. The pastures with the highest densities contain large numbers of young trees, so the trend toward more silvopastoral landscapes seems to have developed recently as farmers sought new sources of income from the sale of trees in pasture and new ways to combat pasture degradation, in this instance through the accumulation of litter from the trees in pastures. In this sense, the growing extent of silvopastoral landscapes signals the spread of another defensive environmental practice.

What Has Driven the Conversions to Alternative Agricultural Practices?

Organic Foods, Organic Agriculture, and Farmers' Markets

Food-focused defensive environmentalists usually come from urban communities in affluent countries (Wier et al. 2008). The sales of organic foods in North America and Europe comprised 97 percent of the world's organic food sales in 2008 (Willer and Kilcher 2010). Within Europe, organic consumers cluster in the wealthier nations, in Scandinavia and in the Alpine countries. In Asia, the wealthier countries, Japan, South Korea, Taiwan, Hong Kong, and Singapore, contain the largest numbers of organic consumers. Even in much poorer West African societies organic consumers come disproportionately from households with above-average incomes (Bouagnimbeck 2010). Chinese government officials in high positions receive organic vegetables from farms that produce only for them (Demick 2011). Organic food production and consumption in China, as elsewhere, stratifies people even as it repairs agricultural landscapes.[6]

While economic affluence enables the consumption of organic foods, fears of food contamination drive people to consider purchasing it. Even in poor countries, such as Vietnam, widely publicized episodes of food contamination increase consumers' interest in organic foods (Linh 2010). A cluster of these events occurred in the spring of 1989 in the United States. A month after a cyanide-laced grape was sent to the United States from Chile, the Alar scare occurred, followed several weeks later by the Exxon Valdez oil spill. The discovery that the skins of apples contained residues from Alar, a pesticide, aroused particular alarm among American consumers, in part because parents had been packing pesticide-laced apples in their children's' school lunch boxes. Surveys underscore the importance of these incidents. About two-thirds of all American consumers cite health concerns as the primary reason for their enthusiasm about organic products (Dimitri and Greene 2007). Survey results from elsewhere in the world reveal a similar set of motives (Roitner-Schobesberger et al. 2008). The purchasers of organic products throughout the world tend to be disproportionately young, female, and from affluent households (Lea and Worsley 2005; Aguirre 2007; Dimitri and Greene 2007). Frequently, they cite a concern for their children as the reason for the purchase. For example, one mother bought organic produce because, as she said (Diamond 2006, 223),

I've already screwed up my health enough... but I am much more regimented about what he [her son] eats... he gets like a very rare treat of candy or cookies. It's more that I want him to have healthier eating habits than I [do].

---

[6] The stratification occurs in multiple ways, in terms of body burdens, as emphasized here, but also in terms of culturally constructed hierarchies in which the consumption of culturally preferred foods enhances a person's standing in a community (Johnston and Baumann 2010).

Not surprisingly, organic products have captured their largest market shares in baby food markets; they constitute 30 percent of the market in England and 60 percent of the market in Germany (Faye 2003). The ideology of intensive mothering outlined in the epigraph to the preceding chapter (Hays 1996; Soliday 2009), so prevalent in lower-fertility societies, would reinforce mothers' concerns about childhood nutrition. The unconditional commitment of mothers to the welfare of their children implies a concern with the quality of the foods that a child eats.

Low fertility probably intensifies the concern with children's exposure to contaminants. With so much of themselves invested in the survival and prosperity of one or two children, with histories of protecting both themselves and their children from diseases, and with knowledge about the special vulnerability of fetuses and young children to toxic substances (Agin 2009), parents have reacted viscerally to the threat of toxins in food and water as these threats became apparent (Norah MacKendrick, personal communication). While extensive knowledge about these environmental threats to the young undoubtedly concentrates among highly educated parents, concerns about these connections between local environments, foods consumed during pregnancy, and childbearing and rearing have been widely disseminated for decades in childbearing handbooks such as *What to Expect: Eating Well When You're Expecting* (Murkoff 2010). In this context, affluent consumers have developed a new appreciation for foods that farmers have cultivated without the aid of chemicals.

Increasing numbers of consumers have come to believe that they could "shop their way to safety" (Szasz 2007). Once imbued with this belief, they seem to do so systematically. A survey of consumers in Great Britain found that 10 percent of consumers accounted for 60 percent of the organic purchases (Hallam 2003). Not surprisingly, organic consumers have tended, at least in the United States, to be highly educated, although in the most recent surveys this difference between consumers of organic and conventional products was less pronounced (USDA 2010). In recognition of this new niche market, supermarkets in the United States, Europe, and, most recently, Latin America have begun to stock their shelves with increasing numbers of organically produced foods (Garibay and Ugas 2010), making it easier for consumers to purchase them.

While the increased concern about foods produced with pesticides, herbicides, and fertilizers stems from specific historical episodes in which people ate contaminated foods, this concern has been augmented by a growing recognition that people's bodies accumulate toxic chemical compounds over the life course. Referred to as "body burdens," these accumulated chemicals are sometimes carcinogenic and have been detected in children as young as eighteen months (Miller 2007). In an effort to shield their children and themselves from exposure to these chemicals, parents have developed a "not in my body" sensibility, and, to this end, they have looked for uncontaminated sources of food and drinking water for themselves and their children (Depuis 2002).

The search for uncontaminated foods has led consumers to organic foods, and in this instance it appears that their concerns about contamination have been well founded. Conventional produce in grocery stores contained pesticide residues more frequently (75 percent as opposed to 23 percent of the samples) than organic produce from the same stores (Baker et al. 2002). Children who consumed conventional produce had six times the concentration of contaminants in their bodies compared to children who primarily ate organic produce (Burros 2002; Lu et al. 2006; Szasz 2007, 181). In their search for pure water, American consumers have begun to drink privately bottled water out of the frequently mistaken belief that it is less contaminated than publicly supplied tap water (Szasz 2007, 105–33). In all of these instances consumers profess and practice defensive environmentalism.

Most conventional farmers who converted to organic agricultural practices during the 1980s and 1990s did so in order to obtain the higher prices for organic products (Guthman 2004). For example, growers in the United States have regularly sold organically grown broccoli and carrots for more than double the price of conventionally grown broccoli and carrots. Between 1985 and 2005 the price differentials between organic and conventionally grown vegetables showed no signs of declining as the volume of organic produce grew and consumers made more purchases of organic products at conventional supermarkets (Dimitri and Oberholtzer 2007). When these price differentials narrowed, as they did after 2005 with the increased demands for biofuels, fewer farmers converted from conventional to organic cultivation (Kasterline 2010).

The numbers of organic farms and farmers' markets have grown in tandem, with expansion in one contributing to expansion in the other. The higher profit margins available to farmers who sell directly to consumers explain the coincidence of the two trends. Because organic farmers refrain from using pesticides, they can experience sharp fluctuations in the volume of their harvests. In difficult years they may have small harvests. In this context, the higher return that farmers obtain when they sell directly to consumers becomes especially important to organic farmers. For this reason, high proportions of the organic farmers in a region will participate in farmers' markets, if at all possible.

Conservation Agricultures
The first farmers to experiment with minimum tillage found it appealing because, by reducing or eliminating plowing, it promised to reduce fuel costs, labor costs, and soil erosion on their lands (Coughenour 2003). To practice no-till, farmers had to purchase seed drills to implant the seeds and fertilizer in the ground. The purchase of the new machinery represented an "up-front" cost for farmers, but in the long run minimum tillage reduced the farmers' need for machinery by reducing the number of times that they had to plow their land (Coughenour and Chamala 2000). The focus on reducing labor and fuel costs increased the likelihood that only farmers who owned medium and large amounts of cropland and paid large sums of money for fuel and hired labor would practice no-till. Smaller-scale farmers often found the initial cost of purchasing a seed drill more than they could afford (Kane et al. 2011). Most of the new recruits to minimum tillage have come from the ranks of younger, more educated farmers who work relatively large farms. Growers who work rented land may have had fewer incentives to practice minimum tillage (Corolan 2005).

Conservation-minded cultivators differ from conventional cultivators in the importance they attach to controlling the costs of agricultural inputs as opposed to maximizing the volume of their harvests (Kane et al. 2011). The no till farmers focus on maintaining already productive farms with selective changes in the way they farm. They cluster in the world's five large grain-exporting nations, all of which have significant numbers of big, mechanized farms. The United States, Brazil, Argentina, Canada, and Australia contained 93 percent of the world's minimum-tillage lands in 2005 (Hobbs 2007).

Many farmers have gravitated toward a flexible, site-specific kind of integrated farm management in which they adopt low-input strategies such as integrated pest management and no-till agriculture whenever conditions permit (Trewavas 2001). This strategy limits the use of increasingly expensive fossil-fuel–based chemical inputs on farms. At the same time, these farmers limit pesticide and herbicide applications, in part to conserve soil organic matter, which, other things being equal, raises crop yields. If the use of genetically modified varieties of crops reduces the range and volume of pesticides used on farms, as for instance it does in the case of cotton (Pray et al. 2002), low-input integrated farm management could involve the use of genetically modified seeds.

Conservation agriculture in the Ecuadorian Amazon has a similar set of origins. It stems from deliberate decisions by smallholder cattle ranchers to allow spontaneously sprouting seedlings to grow in their pastures. As with grain farmers in the American Midwest, cattle ranchers in Ecuador were much less likely to practice conservation agriculture on rented lands (Corolan 2005; Lerner et al. 2012). When asked why they allowed these silvopastoral landscapes to emerge, landowners offered a mix of reasons. The seedlings of commercially valuable secondary forest species such as *Pollesta discolor* can be sold ten to fifteen years later to local sawmills and furniture makers; the litter from the trees fertilizes the degrading pastures; and the trees protect water sources in pastures that in times of drought become an important source of water for the cows, which normally get all of their water from waterlogged pasture grasses. In these varied ways shade-filled pastures provide smallholders with tangible environmental and economic benefits at the same time that they promote biodiversity and sequester carbon.

Alternative Agriculture: A Social Movement with Transformative Potential?

While individuals' concerns about themselves, their families, and their land have shaped their involvements with alternative agriculture, altruistic concerns have sometimes played an important role in the commitments that people make to alternative agriculture, in particular to organic agriculture. Some participants, either as consumers or producers, have professed an "ecological citizenship" in which they share with others a personal commitment to sustainability, even if it inconveniences them personally (Seyfang 2006). These concerns for the larger collectivity have reinforced individual searches for safely produced food. The ecological benefits of organic agriculture – fertile soils, erosion control, and contaminant-free produce – have spawned a social movement to promote its spread. Recruits to the movement include people who use contacts they make through an environmental NGO, WWOOF (Worldwide Opportunities on Organic Farms), to volunteer to work on organic farms throughout the world.[7] Other recruits include a small segment of

---

[7] WWOOF volunteers represent a new kind of migrant labor.

the American baby-boomer generation who chose an alternative lifestyle during the 1970s and set up small farms to practice organic agriculture (Jacob 1998).

With the pesticide-related health scares of the 1980s, NGOs such as the Rodale Institute began to experience more success in promoting organic agriculture as an alternative to a conventional agri-food system that featured ever larger farms, more globalized markets, and more numerous supermarkets (Hart 2003; Reardon et al. 2003). In the early 1990s, the United States Department of Agriculture and land-grant universities began to recognize the growing importance of organic agriculture and established small programs designed to promote applied research on organic agriculture. One organic consumer underlined the link between his concerns and these larger transformations (Diamond 2006, 246):

If somebody wants to treat their land better, then I'm for supporting them. And if somebody wants to treat their animals [better], I'm all for supporting them. It's more like if I can support somebody who is doing it the way that I feel that it should be done, then maybe other people will say hey, this guy is making a living doing it this way, maybe I can do it also.

The alternative-agriculture NGOs and the CSAs that link consumers and farmers all seek to expand organic agriculture in North America. Similar organizations, such as Slow Food International, link organic farmers and consumers in affluent European societies (Halberg, Alroe, and Kristensen 2005). With a rank and file composed of consumers and farmers who derive personal benefits from organic products and want to promote an environmentally friendly transformation of modern agriculture, these people constitute a transnational food movement.

While most no-till farmers focused on incorporating minimum tillage practices into the agro-ecology of their own farms, a small group of the leaders in the no-till movement in the United States showed a concern similar to that of organic advocates for the larger benefits of minimum tillage practices. The early no-till farmers in Kentucky held many "field days" to demonstrate the economic and environmental advantages of no-till. Countless times they showed off productive but unplowed fields to visitors in impromptu tours of their farms. Some extension specialists dedicated their working lives to researching and promoting minimum-tillage techniques among farmers (Coughenour 2003). Movement infrastructure has also appeared, in the form of research centers, magazines, and associations devoted to the promotion of conservation agriculture. A comparable set of enthusiasts work to promote silvopastoral landscapes internationally. While not as radical, visionary, or large in scale as the organic movement, both groups of activists have promoted institutional reforms to facilitate conservation agriculture.

While the shift toward alternative agriculture is unmistakable, the ecological benefits attributable to it depend crucially on changes in its form as it expands to include larger numbers of farmers. Organic agriculture usually takes on some of the characteristics of conventional agriculture in the same place. Just as Argentine farms are large, so organic operations in Argentina are large, averaging more than 1,000 hectares. Conversely, in Indonesia, Senegal, and Benin, where small farms predominate, organic farms average less than one hectare in extent (Parrott et al. 2005). High land prices in a place force a common set of procedures on conventional and organic farms. With debts for land or inputs to repay, both types of growers must engage in labor- and capital-intensive practices to get good harvests out of a given amount of acreage.

Under these circumstances, the geographic patterns of organic production and trade began to resemble the production and trade patterns for conventional agriculture. Trade in the organic sector shows signs of becoming another form of vertical trade in which the developing world furnishes wealthier countries in Europe and North America with important natural resources. Similar patterns exist at smaller spatial scales. Within Europe, the most rapid expansion in organically managed lands has occurred in Eastern Europe, where newly converted farms produce largely for consumers in the wealthier European societies (Willer and Kilcher 2010). For example, large mark-ups in the prices of organic products have encouraged growers in places like Chile to produce (organic grapes) for export to affluent markets in distant places. For this reason, despite the advent of community-supported agriculture, most organic consumers cannot be described as "locavores."[8]

Marketing considerations sometimes add "food miles" to the itineraries of organic products before they arrive in consumers' kitchens. Because high-priced organic milk sells slowly relative to conventional milk, a carton of organic milk must have a long shelf life. Processors can extend the shelf life of milk through a process of ultra-high-temperature pasteurization (Diamond 2006, 188). Few plants can carry out ultra-high-temperature pasteurization, so organic milk must travel long distances to these plants and then travel long distances again before it comes to rest in the cold sections of supermarkets. In these instances,

---

[8] A "locavore" is someone who primarily eats locally produced foods.

ecological gains in sequestered carbon and reduced soil erosion come from pasturing free-range dairy cows rather than growing row crops to feed confined dairy cows, but these gains dissipate when organic products travel many food miles before they reach consumers.[9]

These convergences have spawned political conflict over standards for certifying commodities as produced through organic processes. Large dairies that confine their cattle and large farms that burn their lands but cultivate using biological controls see certification as "organic" as the way that they can earn the trust of the consumer of organic goods and gain access to a lucrative, fast-growing market. Dairy farmers with smaller free-range herds and grain growers who do not burn their lands oppose these more inclusive definitions of "organic" products. Under these circumstances, heated discussions have erupted over the certification standards used within the organic-industrial food complex (Pollan 2001; Guthman 2004). When the National Organic Standards board of the USDA solicited comments on organic standards in the early 1990s, it received more than 220,000 comments, the largest public response to proposed USDA rules ever (Allen 2004, 196). At stake in these debates is the ability of large-scale producers to alter the meaning of "organic" in a way that will allow them to use economies of scale to squeeze small producers out of the organic market.

Projections of future growth trajectories for conservation and organic agriculture would seemingly depend on political economic trends that are difficult to predict. Food inflation, present since 2005 and spurred by continuing demand for grains to produce biofuels and feed livestock, has narrowed the price premium enjoyed by organic products and slowed the conversion of farmers to organic production, at least in the United States (Sahota 2010). The use of no-till techniques might actually increase under these conditions because no-till represents one of the few practices that conventional farmers can use to reduce erosion on sloped, hard-to-farm lands that farmers have withdrawn from the Conservation Reserve program in order to expand their acreage under cultivation. Similarly, the post-2005 surge in commodity prices for wood should promote the spread of silvopastoral landscapes in the Amazon.

A countervailing trend, the growing real costs of fuel, coupled with new policies to reduce greenhouse gas emissions from landscapes, such as REDD+ (Reducing Emissions from Deforestation and Degradation),

---

[9] To apply the label "organic" to their milk, farmers must pasture their cattle rather than confine them to feeding stalls in buildings.

should provide competitive advantages to farmers who practice alternative agriculture, with its lower fuel costs and carbon-sequestering agricultural practices (Hinrichs and Barham 2007). Finally, consumer demand for organic products slumped only slightly during the economic recession of 2008–9, but it became more difficult for farmers to finance the conversion from conventional to organic operations, so the net effect of the recession on organic expansion was negative (Sahota 2010).

Extensive conversion of agricultural lands to alternative forms of agriculture, although unlikely, might not alter already tight food supplies that much. Yields would decline in the high-yielding conventional agricultural districts in affluent countries, but they would increase in the currently low-yielding agricultural districts in poor countries (Badgley et al. 2007). The impact of these shifts on the availability of foodstuffs would depend, at least in part, on unrelated changes in the agri-food sector. If people consume more meat as their incomes grow, as they have in China and India in recent years, the feed demands of growing herds of livestock will create additional price pressures in addition to the environmental burdens of increased greenhouse gas emissions from the animals (Steinfeld et al. 2006).

It is worth recalling at this point that the spread of organic agriculture, farmers' markets, and conservation agriculture has occurred with only small amounts of help from the state (Scialabba 2007). Only China, with its Chinese Ecological Agriculture (CEA) initiative, prioritized alternative agriculture, and its initial attempt at promotion largely failed. A later effort beginning in the 1990s to promote "green foods" produced by environmentally conscious collectives has had more success (Sanders 2006). With the environmental benefits of alternative agriculture now more widely known, other Asian states have begun to reconsider their laissez-faire policies, and they have begun to prioritize alternative agriculture in their national plans for agricultural development (Wai 2010).

Certainly, there is no shortage of ways in which governments could promote alternative agriculture. Many local activists find themselves mired in the day-to-day tasks of keeping a "buy fresh, buy local" campaign or a local CSA afloat, so they cannot find the time or resources to scale up their efforts.[10] Concerted state and federal efforts to promote the expansion of carbon-sequestering forms of agriculture could articulate well with these local efforts. The knowledge-intensive nature

---

[10] Personal communication, Clare Hinrichs, Pennsylvania State University.

of conversion to both organic and conservation agriculture advantages farmers who have access to government-supported agricultural extension agents familiar with alternative agriculture (Risgaard et al. 2007). Government-supported initiatives could subsidize the costs of certification for small farmers. Programs of publicly funded research might place a higher priority on developing productive agricultural regimens that combine the minimum tillage of conservation agriculture with the low synthetic inputs of organic agriculture to create a no-till, organic, and cover-crop approach to alternative agriculture.

The spread of alternative agriculture, at least during the mid-twentieth century, occurred in tandem with the growth of the larger environmental movement. The publication of *Silent Spring* animated the organic movement much as it did the larger environmental movement. In more recent years, as the larger environmental movement has struggled politically in the United States, the trends toward these defensive environmentalist activities seem to have taken on a life of their own, driven largely by changing costs of production in the case of conservation agriculture, by the lengthening of agricultural commodity chains in the case of farmers' markets, and by the continuing accumulation of knowledge about human exposure to carcinogens in the case of organic agriculture. In each instance, an organizational infrastructure has emerged, with advocates who promote the further spread of these defensive environmental practices.

7

Removing Rubbish, Recovering Resources, Creating Inequalities

> It is no coincidence that the age of ecology corresponded with the rise of environmental inequalities.
> Andrew Hurley (1995, 172)

Introduction

Cleaning up after oneself might be an iconic example of defensive environmentalism. People dispose of waste that has accumulated in their immediate environment, in the kitchen, the house, or the yard, for a variety of sanitary as well as cultural reasons. In theory, well-organized waste disposal would seem to be an instance of defensive environmentalism in that it produces immediate benefits for the disposer and, if done well, it could benefit the global environment by limiting the accumulation of pollutants in the larger environment.

Historically, waste streams have not received much attention from students of environment–society relations, although, with the sustained attention devoted to environmental degradation during the past four decades, some analysts have recently begun to focus on waste streams and the problems that they present for societies (Jensen and McBay 2009; MacBride 2011). Much of their attention has been focused on municipal solid waste, even though it represents only a relatively small segment of the overall societal waste stream. Consumers never see the largest volumes of material in the waste stream (MaKower 2009). They are generated by industrial and mining enterprises, dumped as sludge or slurry at the site of the activity, and subjected to little, if any, regulation (McBride 2011).

In practice, most waste disposal is only defensive environmentalism in a very limited sense. While it certainly benefits the immediate environment of the people performing the cleanup, it usually does so at the cost of degrading the environments of other people near where the waste is dumped. For this reason, the most salient aggregate effect of waste disposal is the creation of environmental injustices (Pellow 2004). Perhaps tellingly, the New York City Department of Sanitation Web site describes in great detail the city's procedures for removing waste from residents' homes, but it says nothing about where the waste goes.[1]

People who practice the "three Rs" (reducing, reusing, and recycling) qualify more clearly as defensive environmentalists. Their practices produce benefits for their immediate environment and for the larger environment by reducing the use of unexploited natural resources. The following pages review the history of these efforts, with particular attention to the type and tempo of forces driving recent increases in the amount of recycling.

With the increased scale of human activities in the twentieth century, flows of waste have expanded tremendously, raising questions about where to dump it or how to process it into something that humans can use. The increased attention devoted to this issue is consistent with the observations of community ecologists that, as patches of relatively undisturbed vegetation gain biomass over time, litter accumulates, and organisms in detritus cycles become a more prominent aspect of food webs (Facelli and Pickett 1991, 8–9). These organisms feed on the waste of other organisms, extract nutrients from the decomposing matter, and return them to the plant community. In this sense, ecological processes involving detritus become more salient in late successional communities.

The material dimension of human societies has changed during the past two centuries in ways that mimic this pattern of ecological change. We have created an "industrial ecology" (Graedel 1994; Desrochers 2002). Just as biomass increases in biological communities as they age, so the material scale of human communities has grown tremendously during the industrial efflorescence of the past 200 years. The increased numbers of people and livestock represent one dimension of this material increase. The growing skylines of cities with high-rise buildings capture in a glance another dimension of this material increase. The large numbers of people, animals, and habitations packed into small places (cities) generate large volumes of waste that others become specialized in removing and

---

[1] Available at www.nyc.gov/html/dsny.

processing. Waste workers occupy the same position in human societies that organisms in detritus cycles occupy in ecological communities.

Does this local impulse to clean up the environment around us have implications for reducing our global environmental impact? Al Gore thought so. At the end of *An Inconvenient Truth*, when Gore implores us to take action, he tells us to "recycle!" People recycle when they convert the waste from the consumption of one product into raw material for the production of another product (Hershkovitz 2002, 44). In this sense, recyclers recover resources. Visions of sustainable societies invariably feature large numbers of people who recycle materials. The following pages provide an historical narrative of recycling during the transition from an agrarian to an urban-industrial society and, more recently, during the past four decades, as societies have grappled with what to do with all the waste generated by our newfound affluence. The recent history focuses on trends in two commodities: aluminum and paper. An explanation for the forces behind these trends follows. The last section looks at the impact of the recently emerged environmental justice movement on waste management and resource recovery.

Waste, Urbanization, and the Rise of Recycling: Historical Patterns

In agrarian societies the size of populations played a crucial role in waste management. In sparsely populated regions inhabited by small groups of shifting cultivators and nomadic pastoralists people typically expended little effort on waste management. Shifting cultivators would abandon fields and nearby residences after two or three years of cultivation and residence. They would only return to these places after a long fallow period during which the decay of secondary growth had restored some fertility to the soils (Conklin 1957) and absorbed other human wastes. People had few personal possessions, so their activities produced few piles of trash. Even so, small groups of Amerindians along the Atlantic coast in the northeastern United States did over time create "middens," piles of discarded shells from the shellfish that they consumed during repeated short, seasonal visits to the seashore (Cronon 1983). In more densely populated settings where people cultivated permanent fields, recycling did occur when cultivators spread all kinds of household waste back on their fields in an effort to maintain soil fertility (Netting 1993).

When peasants began to move to cities in large numbers during the seventeenth and eighteenth centuries, the accumulation of people and animals in cities created unsanitary, unsightly piles of waste, and the numbers

Removing Rubbish, Recovering Resources, Creating Inequalities 123

of people involved in recycling waste multiplied. In 1912, for example, teams of workers for the city of Chicago removed 10,000 horse carcasses from the city streets (Strasser 1999, 124). In mid-nineteenth-century London, poor people, often recently arrived from rural areas, scavenged for all kinds of wastes. They removed bones, rags, horse manure, and human excrement from sidewalks, latrines, and rivers. Peddlers went from house to house and business to business gathering scrap materials and selling them to newly established factories for reuse (Zimring 2005). Collectively, they removed waste from the cities for a price, but inevitably much waste remained, and it contaminated local water sources, increasing the vulnerability of urban residents to water-borne diseases, most especially cholera (Johnson 2006).

Organized trash removal may have begun in nineteenth-century cities, but urban residents at the time produced comparatively little trash and reused materials extensively. People became "stewards" of material goods, extending their useful life through frequent repair. Women mastered the arts of sewing and knitting not only to make new clothes but also to repair old clothes (Strasser 1999, 21–67). The wealthy differed from the poor only in that they employed someone else to do the repair work. With the mass production of material goods, this pattern changed. The wealthy purchased newly manufactured goods. The new article of clothing or the new tool became a positional good, defining its holder as a person of higher status (Hirsch 1978). Used or recycled goods became associated with poorer people. People felt "cleaner" using newly produced goods, so, as they became more affluent, they purchased more new goods and threw away more old goods.

Governments and manufacturers facilitated this shift in consumer habits. Once late-nineteenth-century governments assumed the responsibility for carting away trash and cleaning the streets, people had fewer qualms about throwing away used materials. During the first three decades of the twentieth century manufacturers encouraged people to purchase new goods and dispose of old goods by coming up with newly designed goods each year. Initially, these changes in fashion applied primarily to (women's) clothing, but in the 1920s they began to apply to a wider array of goods, most notably automobiles. General Motors led the way, introducing new models of cars each year (Strasser 1999, 193). The manufacturers of new products celebrated the value of new goods through advertising. In so doing, they reinforced the not-so-subtle connection between the reuse of goods and poverty. A "throwaway culture" began to emerge in which "the growth of markets for new products came to depend in part on the continuous disposal of old things" (Strasser 1999, 15).

Government officials in the United States responded to citizens' demands to cart away trash in part because they could find places to dump it. The construction in the United States of the Interstate Highway System after World War II opened up large areas outside of cities, oftentimes abandoned quarries but sometimes prime farmland, as possible trash disposal sites. Starting small, these landfills have in some cases grown to very large sizes as the never-ending stream of solid waste has grown in volume (Bailey 2005). Between 1960 and 2007, the volume of solid waste that Americans sent to landfills each year increased from 88 million tons to 252 million tons. Since 2007, the overall volume of solid waste going to landfills has declined slightly. The per capita generation of solid waste climbed from 2.68 pounds per day in 1960 to 4.74 pounds per day in 2000 before declining to 4.34 pounds per day in 2009. At the same time, the recycling rate for municipal solid waste in the United States climbed from 5.6 percent in 1960 to 33.8 percent in 2009. The largest increases occurred during the 1990s (USEPA 2010).[2]

During the same period, the numbers of operating landfills in the United States declined dramatically from more than 20,000 during the 1970s to 7,924 in 1988 and 1,754 in 2006. The size of the remaining landfills increased, but so did the costs of dumping (see Figure 7.1) and the distance necessary to travel to reach an operating landfill.

Corrected for inflation, the data on tipping fees at landfills in Figure 7.1 indicate that they increased 221 percent in real terms between 1985 and 2009. The national trend in tipping fees masks some regional disparities. Few landfills remain open in the Northeast. Tipping fees (the cost to dump) in this region grew dramatically during the 1980s (Repa 2005b) and regional governments built incinerators, now dubbed "waste to energy" facilities. The cities and suburbs in the Boston to Washington metropolitan corridor now cart the bulk of their trash, at considerable expense, to distant landfills in Virginia, Pennsylvania, and Ohio (Repa 2005a). Recycling became mandatory in these communities, and local officials began to promote recycling as a way of reducing waste disposal costs. To reduce the out-of-pocket costs of waste disposal, governments had essentially bartered the labor of their citizens for the fiscal relief

---

[2] Business cycles affect the sizes of the solid waste and recyclable streams. They both decline in size during recessions, which may account for the downturn in the volumes of both streams since 2007.

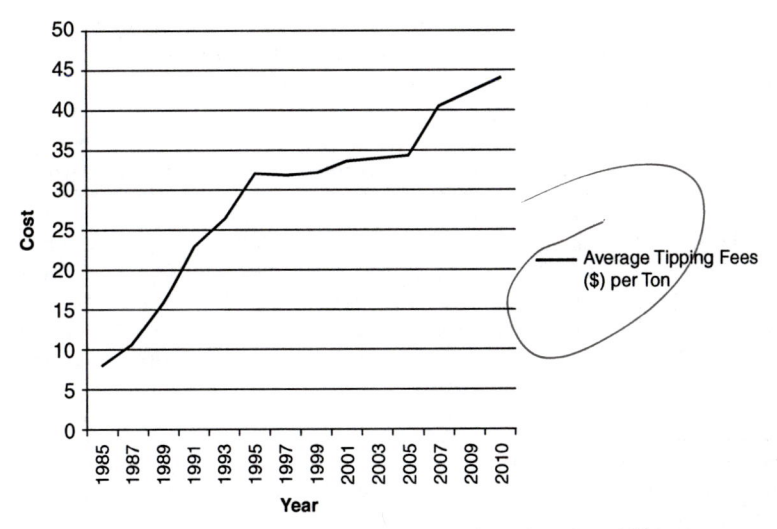

FIGURE 7.1. Trends in Average Tipping Fees at American Landfills, 1985–2010

represented by recycling. The recycling also represented a form of environmental relief, so in this respect the municipalities and, indirectly, their citizen recyclers became defensive environmentalists.

1. One American Suburb's Solid Waste and Recycling Story

Events in Metuchen, New Jersey, a densely populated suburb on the coastal plain southwest of New York City, exemplify the historical dynamics that have accompanied the emergence of recycling as a defensive environmental practice. Viewed from the sea, the ridges that run across this region's western horizon are high points in the county landfill, prompting the observation that, at least in New Jersey, "people are like termites."[3] They build large piles of waste. The county landfill that takes Metuchen's trash had approximately nine years of capacity left in 2011 at current rates of deposit. Metuchen's garbage trucks currently pay a $64 tipping fee per ton of garbage to dump at the landfill. The town, like most other communities in New Jersey, does not charge residents by the volume of garbage that they produce. In the words of one observer "most people in [Metuchen and] the state are on an all-you-can-eat buffet system for garbage" (Sucato 2008). On average, each individual in the county produces about one and a half tons of garbage per year.

[3] James Fairhead, personal communication.

TABLE 7.1. *Proportions of Households Participating in Recycling in Different Neighborhoods of a New Jersey Community*

Neighborhoods	Number of Homes	November	December	January	February	Average % of Homes Participating
Amboy	4	25%	25%	25%		25%
Beacon Hill	28		79%	82%		81%
Beechwood	13	69%		23%		46%
Bounty	21		54%	46%		50%
Carlton	21	67%	50%	70%	38%	56%
Harvard	27		37%		48%	43%
Home	27	63%	70%		63%	65%
Voorhees	22	41%	68%	50%		53%

Sources: Walking surveys of numbers of homes with recycling containers at the curb at 8 AM on the morning of a scheduled pickup of comingled recyclable items in different neighborhoods in the community.

With the rise in environmental concern and the growing cost of dumping ever larger streams of garbage, recycling became a "cause célèbre" of the environmental movement during the 1960s and 1970s (MacBride 2011). Recycling campaign literature played on people's altruistic environmental impulses, exhorting them to "do something for mother earth!" Environmentally concerned residents in Metuchen and other communities established voluntary recycling centers where residents could take recyclable goods. This altruistic strain of recycling remains visible in the activities of the Zero Waste Alliance, which advocates for more reuse and recycling in residential communities.

The motivations for recycling changed during the 1980s in the northeastern United States. In 1987, New Jersey legislators made recycling programs mandatory for communities in the state. In so doing, the state committed the community's Department of Public Works and its residents to time-consuming recycling activities, what MacBride (2011) has called "busywork." Metuchen has mandated curbside pickup of mixed papers and comingled containers every week. Walks through the town's different neighborhoods on the morning of a recycling pickup indicate that households participate at variable rates across neighborhoods (see Table 7.1), which in turn suggests that distinct subcultures of recycling have emerged in different neighborhoods. In some neighborhoods, the evening before a suspected recycling day, residents who have not memorized the recycling schedule look to see what the most fastidious of their neighbors are doing, and, to be above reproach, they do likewise.

As a result, in some neighborhoods more than 80 percent of the households put out items to recycle. In another neighborhood, a mile away, no more than 35 percent of the households recycle.[4] The municipal government used to refuse to pick up solid waste that contained recyclable items. The men on the back of the garbage trucks carried out the inspections. When the municipality changed to single-person waste trucks to save on labor costs, the enforcement of recycling ended, so it now continues only because it has become part of neighborhood cultures.

Nonetheless, the economics of solid waste in this region have made it imperative that communities continue to recycle. It has become so expensive for a town to dump recyclables along with the solid waste that it saves large sums of money when it diverts recyclable goods from the municipal solid waste stream, earns a small sum of money for selling the recyclables, and, most importantly, lessens the volume of waste that it sends to landfills. Like New York City and other large communities in the region, the town has mobilized the labor of its citizens and its workers for recycling efforts that reduce the community's waste disposal costs.

Where do the recycled goods go? Metuchen's comingled recyclables (five kinds of plastics, aluminum, steel cans, glass, and mixed paper) go to China and Indonesia in the otherwise empty holds of ships returning to the Far East to pick up a fresh cargo of Chinese manufactured goods for American consumers.[5] Workers and machines sort through the comingled recyclables in China. Any accounting of the environmental impact of this recycling program might want to consider that the "recyclables" do not add to the miles that the ships would travel. Nevertheless, the 12,000 miles the recyclables travel before sorting seems bizarre. It is a byproduct of globalized circuits of trade.

2. International Patterns

Figure 7.2 outlines the central tendencies in streams of waste across contemporary societies. People in the poorest societies generate the smallest solid waste streams because they consume so little. They do without all

---

[4] The survey data were collected by members of the Metuchen Environmental Commission using a single protocol on a series of mornings during the winter of 2010–11. The absence of a recycling container out by the curb does not necessarily mean that the people in a household do not recycle. They may not have accumulated enough recyclables for that week's pickup of goods for recycling. To neutralize this effect, we did repeated surveys.

[5] The same kind of imbalance in cargos characterizes trade between Asia and Europe. Ships go from Asia to Europe loaded, on average, to 100 percent capacity. They return to Asia with loads that average 60 percent of their capacity (Chinese Shipping 2008).

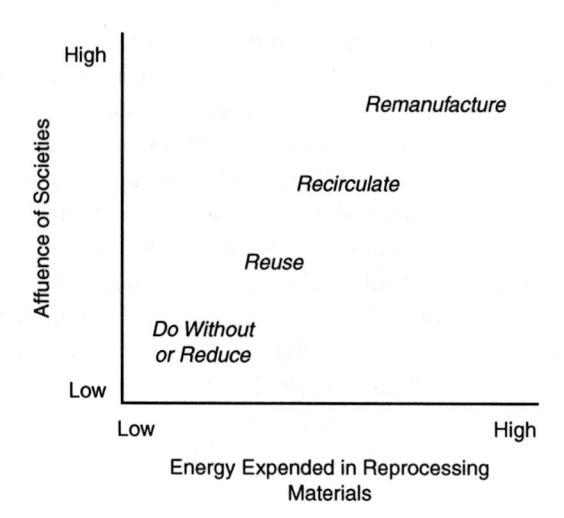

128 *Defensive Environmentalists and the Dynamics of Global Reform*

```
Affluence of Societies
High │
     │            Remanufacture
     │
     │         Recirculate
     │
     │       Reuse
     │
     │   Do Without
     │   or Reduce
Low  │
     └─────────────────────────
       Low                High
       Energy Expended in Reprocessing
                 Materials
```

FIGURE 7.2. Doing Without, Reusing, and Recycling across Societies

manner of material goods, "reducing" their consumption to match their limited means. People in slightly wealthier societies "reuse"; they have had the income to make the initial purchase, but, to live within their means, they have to extend the lives of their possessions, so they repair consumer goods and reuse them. In still wealthier societies, people recycle goods in two separate ways.

In some instances, people recirculate goods. When someone trades in an older car while purchasing a newer car from an auto dealer, and the dealer then sells the older car to another buyer, the older car recirculates. Sometimes enterprises remanufacture goods. The production of energy by burning waste represents remanufacturing where the product changes form. In most instances of remanufacturing the same good gets reproduced. For example, a household head recycles an aluminum can; the owners of an aluminum smelter then melt down the can and use the melted aluminum to make a new can. In the wealthiest, advertising-saturated societies where consumers place a premium on new products, corporations remanufacture goods in order to give them the appearance of being "new." These remanufacturing processes are often energy-intensive, so the conservation gains from remanufacturing are the smallest of all recycling processes (Weinberg, Pellow, and Schnaiberg 2000). Reducing, reusing, recirculating, and remanufacturing activities coexist within the same society, but the pathways traveled vary from good to good and change over time. Companies remanufacture aluminum cans; households tend to recirculate cars, and, as suggested by Figure 7.2, the relative frequency of these activities shifts as poor societies become wealthier.

The most affluent societies generate the most solid waste.[6] For example, Americans generate a little more than four pounds of waste per capita per day, one pound of which may be recycled. Spaniards generate two pounds of waste per capita per day, and they recycle about one-half pound of their waste (Keene 2007). In poorer societies, such as Senegal, individuals generate less waste and households recycle or reuse everything of economic value, even items as small as orange peels (useful in the manufacture of perfumes) (BBC 2005). Scavengers, oftentimes gathered around municipal dumps, do much of the recycling in cities of the Global South (Moore 2008). In rural areas, store owners recycle commodities. Before the advent of cheap plastic containers in rural Ecuador, anyone who wanted to purchase a soda in a small store had to present an empty bottle that he or she could then exchange for a full bottle. Under these circumstances, it is difficult to quantify the extent of recycling because so much of it occurs in the informal sector.

Among the affluent societies, Japan, Sweden, and Switzerland have the highest recycling rates (Planet Ark 2004; BBC 2005), averaging around 50 percent of their entire waste stream. These high rates of recycling have several origins. A scarcity of land to devote to landfills, coupled with high incineration costs, has spurred European governments to set tipping fees that are double the most expensive tipping fees in the United States (Kelleher 2007). These societies have also adopted thoroughgoing recycling reforms that re-engineer productive processes around the need to use recycled materials in the construction of "new" products. Through the redesigned production processes, governments, activists, and business leaders, particularly in Europe, have reduced their use of raw materials.

Some individuals and corporations have reduced the size of waste streams from their activities by reforming the activities that produce the waste. The producers of paper plates, plastic bottles, and aluminum sheets

---

[6] An absence of data and the uncertain quality of existing data hamper the following analysis. There are no central repositories for data on recycling. The Organization for Economic Cooperation and Development (OECD) collects and standardizes data on recycling from twenty-five to thirty member states. FAO collects recycling data on paper products. Industry associations for aluminum and fertilizer collect data on the worldwide consumption of these commodities. Given these disparate sources of data, comparing recycling statistics across nations or across commodities must be done in a cautious way that only draws inferences from very large differences between countries or commodities in recycling rates.

have all made their products 20, 30, or 40 percent lighter during the past thirty years. These efforts reward them economically by reducing their expenditures for raw materials and diminishing the impact of their products on the environment. The gains are limited because the articles themselves do not change much in form, even though they weigh less. The bottles, for example, still have to be recycled or thrown out.

The most transformative of the recycling reforms establishes "extended producer responsibility" (EPR) systems in which producers become responsible for the disposal or recycling of their products when their useful life ends. In so doing, EPR gives producers an incentive to keep extraneous material such as packaging to a minimum because otherwise they will have to pay for its disposal. These EPR schemes "close the loop" in the flow of materials for producers much in the same way that an agro-ecosystem does for farmers. Producers who design easily recyclable products gain at the end of the product cycle. Similarly, farmers who recycle soil organic matter through their cultivation practices achieve higher levels of productivity in subsequent years through the buildup of organic matter in their soils.

Although EPR schemes for beverage containers have been the focus of extensive political struggles since the 1970s in the United States, EPR did not become law at a national level until the German federal government enacted an EPR policy in the early 1990s that required manufacturers to take responsibility for the disposal of the packaging that accompanied new products. Producers either had to designate a third party to manage the recycling or disposal of the used product, or they had to take back the product and use its components to produce a new product. In perhaps the most widely noted example of the second option, BMW (Bavarian Motor Works) redesigned the parts in their current car models so that they can take back these cars when they are old and use the parts to manufacture new BMWs. Other nations in the European community, in addition to some Asian and Latin American nations (Japan, Korea, Taiwan, Brazil, and Peru), have recently adopted EPR programs (Hanisch 2000). The environmental effects of EPR have now been documented in several European countries. In Germany and Sweden, EPR produced declines of 13 to 20 percent in per capita consumption of packaging materials. While almost all EPR systems have required legislative action, some companies, often consumer-oriented companies such as Starbucks or Xerox, have begun to recycle their own products after discovering that they may be able to cut costs if they incorporate recycled materials

Removing Rubbish, Recovering Resources, Creating Inequalities 131

into their production processes. In some Starbucks stores, for example, the company now collects used paper cups that then become the raw material for the manufacture of napkins for the stores.

Restrictive recycling cultures sustain high recycling rates in land-scarce settings such as Germany and Japan. "Salvage stewards" exhorted their fellow citizens to recycle in Britain during World War II (Riley 2008). More recently, Germans have berated foreigners living in Berlin for not separating recyclables from their trash (BBC 2005). The Japanese, with little landfill space, exert strong cultural controls over recycling activities. Depending on where the residents of Japanese cities live, they may have to sort their garbage into as many as ten or more categories. In the city of Yokohama, self-appointed "garbage guardians," often retirees, inspect the clear plastic bags with identification numbers in which people put out their garbage and recyclables for pickup. When they find an offender, someone who has sorted recyclables and trash incorrectly, they inform the offender about the error of his or her ways. When offenders have continued to resist recycling, garbage guardians have taken their complaints to the offenders' landlords and asked that they be evicted from their apartments (Onishi 2005). In other contexts, the appointment of "block captains" has raised recycling rates (Porter, Leeming, and Dwyer 1995). Children who have learned about recycling in school have proven to be particularly effective in enforcing cultural norms about recycling; they exert "pester power" over their parents (Victoria Nielsen, personal communication). Those parents whose children participated in recycling activities at school recycled significantly more material than the parents of children who did not participate in the school program (Porter, Leeming, and Dwyer 1995). When communities make recycling mandatory, as Seattle recently did, rates of resource recovery often jump.

Local cultures can also work the other way. A recently transplanted Englishman related the following interchange with the caretaker of his building in Rome, Italy (BBC 2005).

When I moved here five months ago, I asked the caretaker of my building whether I should separate my family's rubbish. He laughed and looked incredulous. "Are you joking?" he said. "This is Rome."

These cultural inclinations sometimes lead to remarkably low recycling rates, as in Greece (3 percent) (BBC 2005). Under these circumstances, it may take a political crisis, such as the uncollected garbage that piled up in the streets of Naples in the spring of 2008 (Fisher 2008), before a culture and political structure shift enough to accept and institute waste management through a recycling regimen.

3. Global Dynamics in Resource Recovery

Commodity-specific analyses like those that follow make it easier to appreciate the effects of resource recovery on a global scale. The magnitude of the recovery efforts can be assessed against a global backdrop of increasing demand for the product generated by worldwide economic expansion. To assess the balance of these forces, the next several pages describe the effects of recycling on the flows of materials used to produce aluminum and paper.

The volume of aluminum production from primary materials (bauxite) has increased substantially during the past forty years, from an average of 27,000 metric tons per day in 1973 to 70,000 metric tons per day in 2008 (International Aluminum Institute 2008). Per capita consumption of aluminum cans varies dramatically from wealthier to poorer societies. Americans use 340 cans per year, compared to 35 cans for the average European and 10 cans for people in the emerging economies of China and India (Gitlitz 2006).

Of all of the commodities, aluminum presents perhaps the clearest case of energy savings from recycling. The recycling of an aluminum can for use by another consumer involves an energy-intensive process that heats the used container to 600 degrees Fahrenheit, melts it, and recasts it as a new can. When a smelter with recycling capacity exists nearby, all of the original metal from an earlier can reappears on the shelves of stores as a new can about sixty days after someone throws the original can in the recycling bin. The expenditure of energy in remanufacturing represents only about 5 percent of the energy expended to produce a comparable can from primary materials (Reuters 2008).

Recycled aluminum commands a price on the market that far exceeds the prices for other recycled materials, and for this reason companies as well as consumers recycle it and explore ideas for recycling even more of it, such as aluminum foil. Recovery rates for aluminum in buildings and cars have ranged from 60 to 90 percent between 2003 and 2007 (International Aluminum Institute 2008). The recovery rate for aluminum cans in the United States was 52 percent in 2006, considerably less than recent recycling rates for aluminum cans in Sweden (86 percent) and Brazil (95 percent) (Planet Ark 2004; Reuters 2008). Alcoa (Aluminum Company of America) recently initiated a campaign to raise the American recovery rate to 75 percent. Company executives want Alcoa to remain a leader in the technology for reprocessing aluminum, and to that end they have expanded capacity at a recycling smelter in Tennessee. An increase in the local recycling rates would ensure that the smelter has an adequate supply of materials to process.

While the global growth in aluminum recycling is visible, the size of the stream of recycled materials has not grown large enough to reduce the extraction of primary materials. Overall consumption of aluminum in the United States declined 13.5 percent between 2003 and 2007, but consumption elsewhere in the world increased considerably, so despite recent increases in recycling rates, the volume of aluminum production from primary materials has continued to increase. From 1990 to 2008 it increased 84 percent (International Aluminum Institute 2008). To accommodate the increased demand for aluminum in automobiles, among other things, companies and countries have continued to construct new smelters, primarily in Asia. These trends in smelter capacity reflect a situation where the increases in the consumption of aluminum in developing countries have far outstripped the small declines in consumption that have occurred in the already affluent societies.

The production of paper and paperboard has more than quadrupled in the last half-century. World production increased from 77 million tons of paper and paperboard in 1961 to 352 million tons in 2005. Per capita consumption of paper more than doubled over the same time period, from 25 to 54 kilograms per year. The tremendous increase in the volume of electronic communications since 1995 appears to have induced a small but still significant decline in paper consumption in North America. Yearly consumption of paper declined from 321 kilograms per capita in 1995 to 291 kilograms per capita in 2005, a decline of just under 10 percent. These trends occurred in a global context marked by stark contrasts in levels of paper consumption. In recent years, North Americans consumed around 300 kilograms of paper per capita per year, compared with 40 kilograms per capita in China and only 6 kilograms per capita in sub-Saharan Africa (WRI 2008).

Compared to paper produced from virgin materials, recycled paper achieves savings in energy expenditures that range from 26 to 45 percent depending on the type of recycled paper. In addition to these savings, a reliance on recycled paper preserves important ecosystem services in forests that would have otherwise been destroyed or degraded to produce wood for the paper mills. These ecosystem services include averting greenhouse gas emissions, species preservation, flood prevention, and nutrient cycling provided by the still-standing forests. In addition, the recycled paper reduces the volume of waste going into landfills, thereby conserving landfill capacity and reducing landfill emissions. Recycling also reduces the volume of waste going into incinerators, thereby reducing the air pollution from burning garbage.

Paper products account for more than one-third of the solid waste generated in the United States each year. As with other materials, the recovery rate for paper products has grown considerably since 1960, from 16.9 percent in 1960 to 51.6 percent in 2006 (USEPA 2007). Between 1989 and 1999, recycled paper increased from 25 to 37 percent of the raw material used by paper mills in the United States. In many instances, the companies blended recycled papers with primary products in making new paper. Overseas demand for recycled papers grew rapidly during the same period as companies constructed new mills or retrofitted old mills to process recycled paper. In 2006, American recycling firms sent about 16 percent of all recovered paper to mills overseas.

The global pattern of paper production and recycling appears to have shifted in recent years. From 1961 to 1997 global paper production from both primary and recycled materials increased each year, but the annual increases in primary production outstripped the increases in recovered papers by about 3 million tons each year. Because paper and paperboard manufacturers made up these differences by purchasing more primary materials (wood), these trends increased demand for wood from loggers and timber companies. After 1997 the gap between the two streams of material dropped to 1 million tons annually. After 2001 a slowdown occurred in paper production from primary materials and from recycled materials (FAO 2006). Perhaps the much-anticipated "paperless office" began to make a belated appearance (Sellen and Harper 2002). The historical coincidence of trends in paper production, information technologies, and paper recovery makes this interpretation plausible. Taken together, recycling, driven by defensive environmentalist sentiments and coupled with reduced demands for paper by affluent, computer-enabled consumers, may have begun to reduce human demands on forests. Recycling of paper contrasts with resource recovery from aluminum recycling, which has not been sufficient to reduce the production of aluminum from primary materials.

These contemporary differences in resource recovery across commodities and between societies have emerged in a dynamic historical context in which rates of resource recovery have changed dramatically. In China the production of solid waste by industrial facilities has risen very rapidly, but after 1999 the actual amounts of solid waste shipped to landfills declined because enterprises recycled so much of their waste (Liu and Diamond 2005). Taiwan, which has the world's second-highest population density among nation-states, instituted mandatory recycling in 1990. With increasing affluence, per capita production of solid waste per day in Taiwan had increased from .63 kg in 1983 to 1.14 kg in 1997. From 1998 to 2002, after the introduction of mandatory recycling, per capita production of solid waste declined from 1.14 kg to .81 kg (Lu et al. 2006). In addition to making recycling mandatory, the Taiwanese adopted a "pay as you throw" system in which the fee for garbage collection increases with the amount of garbage generated by a household. This system creates incentives to reduce the overall amount of waste generated by producers.

As the earlier description of recent recycling in a New Jersey community suggests, the international trade in recyclables has grown with the rise in recovery rates. International trade promotes higher recovery rates by opening up more markets for the sale of recycled materials (van Beukering and Bouman 2001). The global structure of the recycling business reflects disparate regional trends in the manufacturing sectors of economies. The burgeoning manufacturing economies of South and East Asia create demand for recycled materials that cannot be satisfied with local sources of supply, so entrepreneurs create large-scale recycling enterprises that purchase recycled materials from the slow-growing, materials-abundant economies in Europe and North America. Workers from industrializing regions have even traveled to old industrial regions to dismantle factories, transport the parts to their own country, and then reconstruct the factories in new industrial complexes, as the Chinese recently did with a German steel mill (Kahn and Landler 2007). The international shipbreaking trade exhibits similar dynamics. Shipbreaking enterprises locate along wide beaches in two South Asian locations, one in Bangladesh and the other in India, pay the owners of the ships for the opportunity to salvage the mostly metal products in the ships, and sell the resulting scrap in domestic markets. To do so, the salvagers will beach a ship. Then, large numbers of poorly paid workers swarm over the ship and, using primitive tools in hazardous situations, disassemble the ship's hull and superstructure. Bangladesh meets 80 percent of its annual needs for steel from these shipbreaking activities (Rousmaniere 2007).

In contrast, African nations have less robust manufacturing sectors, so fewer recycling industries spring up to serve them, and countries receive fewer recycled materials from overseas. They are more likely to become a destination for dumping toxic materials that cannot be recycled (Oh-Jung Kwon, personal communication). This regional division of labor creates noxious, new environmental inequalities.

The Driving Forces Behind Recycling

Many municipal recycling programs in the United States began during the surge of environmental concern among Americans during the late 1960s and early 1970s when communities established recycling centers where residents could drop off recyclables if they chose to do so. Although visible, these initiatives generated very small streams of recyclables. The volume of recycled materials only began to increase during the 1980s, when what began as an environmental fad became an economic necessity for communities in the northeastern United States. Multiple landfill closures and difficulties in siting new landfills in the region caused dramatic increases in tipping fees (the fee per ton paid by a truck to dump at a landfill) at the landfills that continued to operate in the region. Similar dynamics have begun to occur elsewhere in the United States (see Figure 7.1).[7]

With the rise in tipping fees, the value of recycling to communities increasingly depended on the ability of recycling regimens to cut the flow of waste to expensive landfills, rather than on the actual price that the recyclables could command in resource-recovery markets. With incineration deemed dangerous, many communities in affluent, densely populated parts of the United States had few options for their waste streams, other than to reduce their size through recycling, reuse, or reduced use.[8] To ensure that communities explored their recycling options, urbanized states like New Jersey made recycling mandatory for all communities in the state.

---

[7] Despite the dramatic declines in the numbers of landfills in the United States from 20,010 to 1,970 over the past forty years, the overall volume of landfill space did not decline. The operating landfills grew larger. Because the remaining landfills were on average farther from the communities where the waste originated, transportation costs for the waste and the overall costs to communities for waste disposal rose at a faster rate than the tipping fees. As the numbers of operating landfills declined, the open landfills may have assumed the position of oligopolists in regional waste markets, which in turn might explain some portion of the increases in tipping fees.
[8] Incineration or what came to be known as "waste to energy" projects became a popular option for waste disposal during the 1970s and 1980s. Concerns about the health effects of incineration and its economic viability have slowed the growth in the numbers of incinerators in the United States over the past thirty years. European societies continue to incinerate large portions of their waste streams.

Source reduction in the form of EPR schemes did not become widespread in part because manufacturers fought hard to avoid being saddled with the responsibility of reusing, recycling, or disposing of their own products. In this respect, industries have largely escaped any waste regulation. Industrial producers do not have to report flows of nontoxic wastes generated on-site during the production of products, and they are not responsible for taking back the residual elements of their products such as packaging and containers after use by consumers (MacBride 2011). These streams of waste often end up accumulating near disadvantaged human communities.

While American industries may have stymied efforts to regulate how they manage their waste, consumers, animated in part by defensive environmentalist sentiments, paid increased attention to waste issues during the second half of the twentieth century. Two associated trends prepared the ground for recycling programs: growing affluence, which induced people to throw away more used goods, and urbanization, which precipitated declines in landfill space near cities and facilitated the pickup of recycled goods. The international patterns in recycling suggest a similar set of pressures in other countries (Berglund, Soderholm, and Nilsson 2002). The societies (Switzerland, Germany, and Japan) that have generated, proportionally, the largest streams of recycled goods have had affluent, urbanized populations and little space to devote to landfills. These material conditions have contributed to the growth of restrictive recycling cultures in these places. In poorer places like nineteenth-century American cities, the expense of material goods, coupled with inexpensive labor, contributed to high levels of informal recycling by peddlers and private waste haulers. This dynamic would also explain the poorly documented but widespread reuse of all kinds of goods in rural parts of the Global South.

More generally, the prevalence of organized recycling in so many settings suggests an explanation that begins with processes of industrialization and urbanization that over time generate defensive environmentalist postures in people. Recycling removes wastes from places of intense human activity, so from this perspective it should be thought of, first of all, as a waste removal activity that happens to benefit the participating individuals, their communities, and the larger environment. So, while people have initially endorsed recycling programs in part out of concerns about global environmental deterioration (Ackerman 1997, 15), they have continued to support recycling because it promotes NIMBY (not in my backyard) conditions. The salient role of the public sector in

138 *Defensive Environmentalists and the Dynamics of Global Reform*

recycling efforts should come as no surprise, given that urban residents have constructed elaborate organizations for local governance. Citizens have given their governments mandates to address waste problems generated by consumers, but they have largely exempted corporations from oversight unless they handle toxic wastes.

Environmental Inequalities and the Environmental Justice Movement

With their focus on cleaning up after themselves through waste removal and recycling, defensive environmentalists have inadvertently generated environmental inequalities. In turn, an environmental justice movement has emerged to eliminate the inequalities. The inequalities and the environmental justice movement have both had important indirect effects on resource recovery efforts. The more affluent households in societies generate the environmental inequalities through defensive behaviors. Out of a desire to be closer to nature, to reduce their exposure to noxious pollutants from nearby factories, and to avoid contact with lower-class people, middle-class city dwellers in the United States began moving to the less densely populated, less industrialized suburbs after World War II. Once settled in the suburbs, the new residents tried to wall themselves off from sources of pollution through efforts to close nearby landfills or through resistance to plans for new polluting facilities, including landfills, near their new homes.

Poorer households could not afford the higher-priced housing in the suburbs, so they continued to reside close to the urban point sources for the pollutants. By preventing the creation of new commercial and industrial facilities in many suburbs, suburban residents contributed to the emergence of a societal siting policy, identified by the acronym CLAMP (concentrating locations at major plants), which expands the capacity of already existing repositories for waste (Greenberg 2009). For example, nuclear waste under this type of policy just accumulates in the existing nuclear plants. CLAMP creates enduring environmental inequalities, with the poor living close to major polluting facilities and the more affluent residing in distant, pollution-free communities. As suggested by the quote that prefaces this chapter, the "age of ecology" had generated enduring environmental inequalities (Hurley 1995).

With the globalization of recycling markets, the international dimensions of these environmental inequalities quickly became apparent. Used computers, by the millions, went to China, where poorly paid workers disassembled them, extracting the lead parts by hand and thereby exposing themselves to lead poisoning (Grossman 2006). Inexperience or lax regulatory oversight made it possible for companies to pump oil in the Ecuadorian Amazon without using established practices to safeguard local populations, such as injecting waste water back into the underground cavities created by the wells. Instead, waste water accumulated in unlined holding ponds that overflowed and exposed downstream populations of Amerindians to carcinogenic wastes (Kimerling 1991).

These inequalities first became apparent to people of color in the United States, after the surge in environmental concern during the 1960s and 1970s. Building first around networks of civil rights activists based in churches in the southern United States, people began to protest the unequal exposure of blacks and other minorities to toxic wastes in the United States. The activists came together quickly and created an environmental justice (EJ) movement (Pellow and Brulle 2005) dedicated to closing or cleaning up existing plants or dumps and preventing the siting of noxious new industrial facilities and dumps in minority communities. To protest the international dimensions of these environmental injustices, the EJ nonprofits have expanded their activities overseas during the past two decades (Pellow 2007). With their focus on helping communities of disadvantaged people resist the siting of noxious facilities near their homes, EJ movement activists have empowered disadvantaged defensive environmentalists.

Movement activists, coupled with local activists in wealthier communities, contributed to the accelerating closing of landfill sites in the United States during the 1980s and 1990s. The famous *Mobro* and *Khian Sea* garbage barge incidents during the late 1980s dramatized the difficulties faced by some communities in finding places to dispose of their waste. The boats, the *Mobro*, loaded with 3,100 tons of trash, and the *Khian Sea*, loaded with ash from incinerated trash, visited multiple ports of call in the western Atlantic Ocean, where governments, either immediately or eventually, refused to accept the waste. Unable to find sites to dump their cargo, the ships eventually had to return to their points of origin, Long Island for the *Mobro* and Philadelphia for the *Khian Sea*, for further processing and final disposal of the waste (Katz 2002; Pellow 2007).

These incidents dramatized how the acceptance of someone else's trash identified a community or a country as somehow inferior to the sending community. This framing made it difficult to ship waste across domestic and international boundaries. For factory owners these circumstances encourage resource recovery, which, by reducing the size of waste streams, may enable waste producers to avoid the difficult dilemmas of the long-distance waste trade. Perversely, the same circumstance may encourage producers to dump on-site. In this sense, the EJ movement, by limiting new opportunities for waste disposal among poor peoples, works indirectly to strengthen both resource recovery efforts and CLAMP, the dumping of wastes in already established sites usually located in poor communities. Resource recovery has its origins in essentially defensive environmental activities. Its continued expansion probably depends in part on the ability of EJ activists to make it more difficult for wealthy communities to dump their waste beyond their boundaries.

Conclusion: Resource Recovery in Historical Perspective

Waste disposal problems come with prosperity, and recycling resolves a small proportion, literally, of these problems. It represents another component in the large-scale, long-term dynamic of material efflorescence, reflexive modernization, and close-to-home defensive environmentalist practices. While the initial surge of attention directed at recycling by activists during the 1970s benefited from sentiments of altruistic as well as defensive environmentalism, the subsequent expansion of these programs seems to have responded primarily to changes in the local cost–benefit calculations that concern defensive environmentalists. Changes in these incentives might explain the recent increases in the numbers of source reduction programs by corporations. Rising real costs of raw materials make resource recovery and reduced reliance on primary materials more attractive at the same time that EJ activists make it harder for wealthy communities and corporations to dump their waste in places inhabited by poor people. This historical pattern of expansion in recycling suggests that defensive environmentalist actions can grow in frequency even during "business as usual" political conditions.

8

Saving Money, Conserving Energy

We shape our tools, and thereafter our tools shape us.
Marshall McLuhan (1964)

Introduction

The challenges presented by the human use of energy during the twenty-first century are daunting. To contain the inevitable human-induced changes in climate within manageable limits, we must reduce the volume of greenhouse gas emissions by 80 percent by 2050 at the same time that billions of poor people in the Global South begin to adopt the energy-intensive lifestyles that have long characterized the inhabitants of the more affluent societies in Europe, Japan, and North America (Holdren 2007). The scale of the necessary changes is immense. A conversion from fossil fuels to renewable energy in the European economy could require the creation of wind farms the size of countries like the United Kingdom. A similar conversion in North America could involve the creation of solar farms the size of the state of Arizona (MacKay 2008).

To be sure, people in some households and organizations have reshaped their daily activities and power sources to reduce their energy expenditures and greenhouse gas emissions. Isolated households have gone "off the grid," generating all of their own electricity. After an initial payback period to defray the installation costs of the new technologies, these consumers save money at the same time that they reduce global emissions, so they practice defensive environmentalism.

In an historical context marked by the spread of energy-intensive lifestyles across borders, the role of defensive environmentalists in curbing energy expenditures seems critical to effective, global-scale environmental reform.

Energy flows have changed during the course of industrialization in a way that parallels the changes in flows of energy and stocks of biomass that occur as undisturbed biological communities age. Older, undisturbed communities support increased stocks of biomass from a given flow of energy (Margalef 1968). In this sense energy efficiency increases with growth in stocks of biomass. A comparable pattern has characterized human societies during the course of industrialization. As noted by industrial ecologists (Grubler 1994), energy use per unit of production declined across a wide range of human societies during the twentieth century. Some analysts have construed this reduction in energy flows per unit of production as a kind of "ecological modernization" (Mol, Spaargaren, and Sonnenfeld 2009) because it has reduced both the resource depletion and waste generated by each unit of production.

This chapter describes the historical processes that have both stopped and on occasion spurred ecological modernization. It begins by describing the long-established, seemingly contradictory, global trend of simultaneous increases in energy efficiency and energy consumption, a pattern that sustainability scientists call "Jevons paradox." Then it describes, first, the historical complex of social forces that has slowed the adoption of more energy-efficient technologies and, second, the extraordinary historical conditions that have periodically induced enterprises to adopt clusters of new, more energy-efficient technologies. The chapter concludes with a discussion about the ways in which recent changes in energy consumption in China illustrate the historical dynamics that accompany defensive environmentalist patterns of behavior.

Jevons Paradox: Global Trends in Energy Efficiency and Energy Consumption

Innovations that made more efficient use of energy did not reduce human pressure on the environment during the twentieth century. As Bunker (1996) pointed out, "economies become more efficient in their use of resources as they develop, but growth in production outstrips savings from efficiency," so energy consumption increases and greenhouse gas emissions from energy use grow. Figure 8.1 captures these countervailing trends, charting the overall increase in human energy consumption

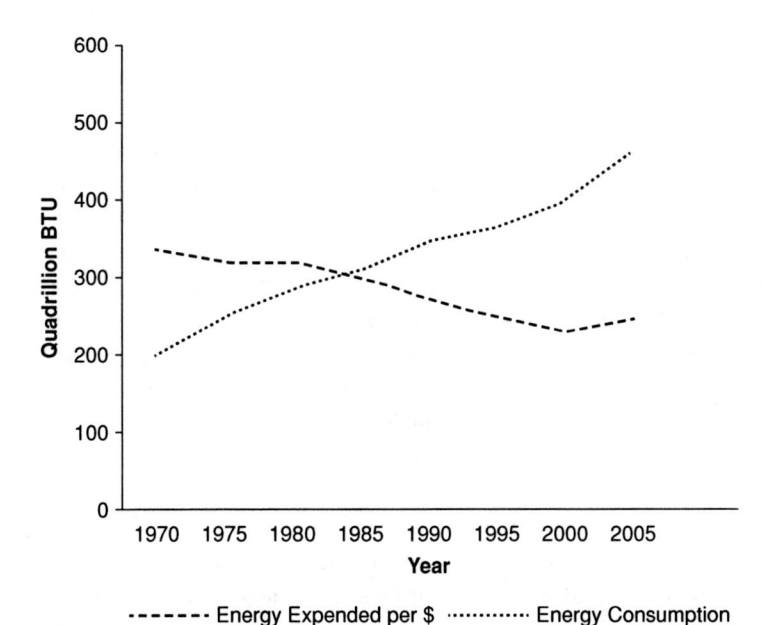

FIGURE 8.1. Global Trends in Energy Consumption and Energy Efficiency, 1970–2005

against the declines in energy intensity, the amount of energy required to produce a dollar of output.[1] The overall pattern, more efficient use of energy, coupled with increases in the amount of energy consumed, is often referred to as the "Jevons paradox." William Stanley Jevons, a nineteenth-century English economist, noted that although the increasingly efficient use of coal in Great Britain during the nineteenth century might have been expected to reduce overall coal consumption, in fact people used more of it because their growing appetite for goods produced with coal more than offset efficiency-induced declines in coal consumption (York 2006). The Jevons pattern continued to characterize human societies throughout the twentieth century (Foster, Clark, and York 2010).

---

[1] Energy intensity is a widely accepted measure of energy efficiency, but there are different metrics for it, and they do not all agree about recent trends in energy efficiency. One measure, tons of oil required to produce a given amount of goods, used by the World Resources Institute (WRI), shows continued increases in energy efficiency through 2005. The other widely used measure, from the Energy Information Agency (EIA) of the United States Department of Energy, tracks the number of BTUs expended per unit of production. It shows little improvement in energy efficiency after 2000. The energy efficiency trends reported in Figure 8.1 come from the more widely used EIA trend data.

"Periodic jumps to new technological regimes" over short periods of time have punctuated the long-term trend of increased energy consumption (Turner 1995). The innovations, along with the new sources of energy, have come in "clusters." Grubler defines a cluster as "a set of interrelated technological, infrastructural, and organizational innovations driving output and productivity growth during particular periods of time" (1998, 117). European and North American societies adopted a cluster of innovations – the steam engine, railroads, and large steel mills – in the mid-nineteenth century. In this dynamic, new technologies beget new technologies. For example, the proximity of coal deposits near seaports in England, coupled with new technologies of steel production, made it possible for the English to build large, ocean-going, iron-clad, coal-powered ships during the second half of the nineteenth century (Cottrell 1955).

While improved communications accelerated the spread of information about the new technologies from place to place, decisions to adopt these technologies often hinged on local experiences and considerations. Most manufacturers would adopt a new technology only after others in their social network had done so. Consistent with Turner's (1995) idea of discontinuities in technological regimes, the pace of adoption varied over time. Initially, it would be slow because only risk-taking pioneers would invest in the new technology. Then, the pace of adoption would accelerate as the pioneers' experiences confirmed the value of the new technology and the more reluctant adopters felt the need to keep up with the technological leaders. Eventually, it would slow again when the new technology had "saturated" the local market for it (Grubler 1998).

After widespread adoption of a new fuel and related technologies, populations become politically "locked in" to the new fuel (McLuhan 1964). The forces for stasis come in multiple forms. Routines figure centrally in the resistance to change, but so does the exercise of political power. Initial concentrations of wealth aid in the development of the new technologies, but over time the elites that sponsored the development of a new technology become pressure groups that work to ensure the continued dominance of "their" energy source (Turner 1995, 35–8). The political dominance of these established elites induces a kind of institutional sclerosis (Olson 1982). The resistance to controls over greenhouse gas emissions by senators from coal-producing states in the United States exemplifies the political constraints that make it more difficult for societies to convert to new sources of energy (Fisher 2004). As the problems and expenses associated with the established fuels and technologies accumulate, small changes do occur, at the level of enterprises and households, as individuals realize that they can both save money and conserve energy through the adoption of new technologies. The remainder of this chapter outlines the conditions that shape these decisions by enterprises and households to continue using old sources of energy or become defensive environmentalists and adopt new, less polluting sources of energy.

Same Old, Same Old: Real Estate Developers, Communities of Practice, and a Continuing Reliance on Fossil Fuels

In the decades after World War II the American housing and transport industries underwent large-scale transformations that fifty years later made them the source for approximately two-thirds of the annual greenhouse gas emissions in the United States (Rome 2001; USEIA 2009). The foundations for this pattern of emissions trace back to World Wars I and II, which empowered leaders of governments and convinced them that they could and should undertake vast infrastructure projects. To this end, states built extensive networks of new roads in both developed and developing countries in the quarter century after World War II (Rudel 2009). The new roads and low fuel prices enabled automobile travel and a large-scale expansion of cities into the surrounding rural areas. Real estate developers responded to these opportunities by building large numbers of houses with virtually no change in technologies for more than fifty years, beginning in the 1950s. As outlined in the following paragraphs, builders and their subcontractors organized themselves for work in ways that impeded technological change.

Builders, manufacturers, and even households have organized their productive activities around "communities of practice" that first appeared during the 1950s and 1960s. During this period, conventions emerged among builders about what the final product should look like, who should do the work, and who should provide the financing for the new construction (Rome 2001). Guided by these rules of thumb, manufacturers built homes that bore a strong resemblance to previous homes that they had built. Previous experience guided the entrepreneur in estimating costs, deciding whom to hire, and requesting loans from banks to finance the new product. Over time, these practices acquired normative content. What had been became what should be. Loan officers in banks evaluated loan applications largely on the basis of previous successes and failures, so funded projects typically bore a strong resemblance to past projects and products that proved economically successful. This array of conventions, standard operating procedures, and personnel constituted a "community of practice" in real estate development (Beamish et al. 2000; Biggart and Beamish 2003).

Macroeconomic conditions permitting, a developer would over a twenty-year period build a series of subdivisions of single-family homes that were similar in location, design, and price; he or she hired the same subcontractors to do work on the houses and the same plumbers to work on the bathrooms. The developer went to the same bank for financing for the project where a record of success in building similar projects made it much easier to secure financing for the next project. The successes of some developers spurred "me too" projects by other developers in nearby communities. In all of these instances, producers reduced the uncertainty surrounding their projects by imitating other producers (DiMaggio and Powell 1983). They all became part of a "treadmill of production" (Gould, Pellow, and Schnaiberg 2008). The evocative power of the "treadmill" metaphor in characterizing the political economy of the environment stems in part from the way that it captures the iterative processes that characterize communities of practice among producers.

The appeal of familiar practices has several sources. People can project their costs with more precision and certainty if their next project resembles a newly completed project. The default option, doing what has been done most recently, is also attractive because it removes the burden of choice, the sometimes agonizing process of choosing between several competing tools or courses of action (Ariely 2008). When organizations and entrepreneurs rely repeatedly on the same subcontractors or suppliers for important tasks or parts, transaction costs decline. Over time, trust emerges between the parties to transactions to the point where agreements between them become noncontractual and easy to negotiate (Macauley 1963). These cost-saving shortcuts are only possible if builders and businessmen use familiar technologies and energy sources that do not involve innovations with their attendant uncertainties.

To overcome the inertia inherent in these "established ways of doing things," innovators frequently establish new businesses to disseminate new production processes with new sources of energy. These innovators face the "liability of newness," the tendency for recently established businesses to fail at higher rates than older enterprises (Stinchcombe 1965). The failures of these new businesses further entrench the preexisting communities of practice that have slowed or prevented ecological modernization. These practitioners conserved already established energy regimes and, through a process of structuration, even passed them on to new generations of producers (Giddens 1984).

Builders inscribed these energy-intensive practices into landscapes when they built low-density suburban neighborhoods with large homes and spacious lawns during the post-war era of cheap energy. To reduce greenhouse gas emissions under these circumstances, innovators would have to retrofit buildings, rebuild communities, and reform commuting patterns developed during an earlier era when no one thought about greenhouse gas emissions. Many homeowners could not afford to retrofit old houses in order to reduce the heating or cooling costs from the burning of fossil fuels. Planners found it difficult to devise mass transit systems for low-density suburban communities planned around the automobile. "Lash-ups" added to the difficulties of reforming established routines and communities of practice. Parents wanted good public schools for their children, and if these schools were located in the outer suburbs far from work, then in effect long commutes and good schools were lashed together. To get the one, parents would tolerate the other, even if it contravened their environmental values. The lash-ups extend even to food choices. Time pressures in daily routines make processed "fast" foods more appealing. These foods contain appreciable amounts of "embodied energy," the energy used to produce a "ready-to-use" product, that we consume every time that we eat fast food (Ehrhardt-Martinez 2008).

Conservative communities of practice only persist in relatively unchanging macrosocietal conditions. In this instance, an abundance of buildable land and inexpensive gasoline undergirded the building boom around which developers constructed their communities of practice. As long as these "business as usual" conditions prevail in the larger economy, developers will continue to draw upon the existing communities of practice and show little or no desire to incorporate new, energy-saving technologies into their building plans. When large-scale contextual changes, such as dramatic increases in gasoline prices, disrupt "business as usual" conditions, the probability of energy-saving innovations increases.

These patterns provide an answer to one of the most frequently articulated questions about the American environmental movement: "If American environmental values are so pervasive and strong, why is there not more environmental action?" (Kempton, Boster, and Hartley 1995, 220). In response, observers could point to the prevalence of "business as usual" conditions for long periods of time in post-war America. The resulting stasis in energy expenditures and greenhouse gas emissions has frustrated advocates for change. An article in *Orion*, a magazine aimed at environmentalists, captures these frustrations. Below the title "How to Be a Climate Hero" in the table of contents, a summary of the article exhorts us to take action: "Don't just stand there. Do something. Do anything!" (Schulman 2008).

These conservative social forces explain some apparent anomalies in efforts to discover and implement cleaner energy sources. Oil companies like British Petroleum (BP) that advertised themselves as being "green" enterprises (Beyond Petroleum?) continued to spend appreciably more money in trying to discover new deposits of oil than they did in researching cleaner alternative fuels (Mouawad 2009). BP's massive Deep Water Horizon oil spill in 2010 underscored the continuing commitment of an ostensibly innovative company to conventional fossil fuel extraction. By continuing to explore for and develop established offshore energy sources, the oil company executives tapped into established communities of practice for developing offshore oil fields, even though the special challenges of drilling at ever deeper depths made this activity anything but routine (Freudenburg and Gramling 2010). The appeal of this strategy lay in the assured flow of near-term revenue to the company from motorists who continued conventional driving practices. Once again, the familiar and the certain trumped the innovative.

Demonstration projects facilitate shifts in energy sources by providing interested parties with real-world examples of the new technologies in operation, but the history of these projects, given their innovative nature, illustrates how difficult it is for entrepreneurs to operate beyond the bounds of the existing communities of practice. The effort during the 1990s to build a large-scale paper mill in New York City to recycle some of the immense stream of waste paper generated by the city's population illustrates the difficulties of carrying out demonstration projects. Conceived and spearheaded by a staffer at the Natural Resources Defense Council, the recycling mill exhibited many of the characteristic weaknesses of pioneering projects. The sponsors had little experience in shepherding projects like this one through to completion. The project had an unusual, inner-city location for a paper mill, a foreign paper company as an operator, and financing from banks with many other, more conventional loans in their portfolios (Hershkowitz 2002). Without guidelines about how to build a paper mill in an urban context, the parties to this collective effort found it difficult to work together. One by one, organizations withdrew from the project, and it eventually collapsed after eight years of efforts to build the mill.

A somewhat similar dynamic has developed around the attempt during the past several years to build the first coal-fired power plant to sequester carbon dioxide. None of the American utilities wants to be the first company to construct a "clean" coal power plant because the costs of sequestering coal-generated carbon remain largely unknown, so the communities of practice for this endeavor do not exist. Given these unknowns, the first builders of capture-and-storage plants will inevitably make expensive mistakes, so most executives would prefer to be in a position to learn from the pioneer's mistakes. In other words, they want to be the second, third, or fourth company to build a clean coal plant, not the first (Wald 2008).

As the quote from McLuhan at the opening of this chapter suggests, technologies can trap people. In many instances, the interested parties in an industry are "trapped" in their use of old technologies by the high infrastructure costs associated with new technologies. Demonstration projects financed by a government, consortium, or encompassing organization can eliminate these "social traps." States typically have taken the lead in financing large-scale, infrastructure-related projects with costs that are difficult to estimate (Evans 1979), but sometimes even governments with their less restrictive budgetary constraints hesitate to undertake innovative, but highly uncertain, projects. For example, the decision by the Department of Energy (DOE) of the U.S. government to postpone the construction of a prototype clean coal plant in Illinois in 2008 stemmed from the difficulties that DOE officials had in estimating costs (Johnson 2009). When demonstration projects succeed, the likelihood that a new technology will diffuse to other industrial organizations rises at the same time that the novel circumstances surrounding the demonstration project slow the creation of a "community of practice" around the new technology.

Globalization, Moments of Ecological Modernization, and Defensive Environmental Practices

Despite the widespread reluctance of people and organizations to alter routines that rely on dirty fuels, they have in numerous, historically documented cases made the shift from dirtier to cleaner fuels. Repeatedly, companies have shifted to cleaner forms of energy in response to market pressures from globalization. Some analysts see these instances of ecological modernization as part of a broader pattern, referred to as the environmental Kuznets curve (EKC), in which industrialization first worsens environmental conditions and then improves them as societies become wealthier and ecological modernization efforts become more prevalent (Grossman and Krueger 1995). The following pages outline in more detail the circumstances that have accompanied and, to some extent, facilitated these defensive shifts by enterprises and households to cleaner technologies and more efficient fuels.

Recent work on corporate environmentalism in developing countries shows seemingly anomalous patterns that, upon closer examination, underscore the importance of social contacts in the adoption of cleaner technologies.[2] Just as fertility declines have occurred at lower levels of GDP per capita than demographic transition theory would have led us to expect, so the adoption of clean energy technologies has occurred at lower levels of income than expected in EKC theory. Manufacturers in many sectors of the Indian economy did not innovate until faced with foreign competition. For example, the fuel efficiency of automobiles manufactured in India did not begin to increase until the early 1980s, when Suzuki, a Japanese auto manufacturer, began selling fuel-efficient autos in a joint venture with the government. At that point, most domestic manufacturers in India began to make more fuel-efficient cars (Perkins 2007). Other foreign-influenced paths to environmental reform also ran through government agencies. When Indian officials decided to impose new emissions standards on Indian auto manufacturers in the 1990s, they adopted standards already in place in the European Community (Perkins

---

[2] Communications from acquaintances and confidants in the social networks of business executives often prove to be decisive in persuading them to adopt cleaner technologies. Work by Simone Pulver (2007) illustrates this pattern. She explains the varying stances that oil companies have taken during the past two decades to the challenges of global warming and the need to curtail sharply the emissions of greenhouse gases from the burning of fossil fuels. For at least two decades Exxon opposed all legislative initiatives to limit greenhouse gas emissions and worked to undermine science that linked the burning of fossil fuels to global warming. In contrast, British Petroleum (BP) and Royal Dutch Shell accepted, rather quickly, the science behind climate change and advertised new lines of research on alternative fuels. One important distinguishing characteristic between Exxon, on the one hand, and BP and Shell, on the other hand, involved the personal and professional associations of the oil company executives. The BP and Shell executives associated with European political and economic elites who, almost universally, acknowledged the dangers of climate change and its human origins, whereas the Exxon executives associated primarily with political and economic elites from oil-producing states who refused to accept the science of climate change and the role of fossil fuels in accelerating global warming (Pulver 2007). British Petroleum appears to have suspended its "beyond petroleum" advertising campaign after the massive Deepwater Horizon oil spill in 2010, perhaps out of embarrassment.

2007, 294). The earlier adoption of greener technologies in latecomer industrializers such as India seems attributable, at least in part, to the closer, sometimes competitive, sometimes collaborative contacts between local and global companies.

Re-engineering production processes to reduce energy expenditures or to produce more fuel-efficient products has often entailed linked innovations that require large amounts of capital and employees with diverse specialties. The highly capitalized enterprises with these attributes also receive more exposure to new technologies through international trade shows and workshops. Finally, because larger businesses, particularly if they are foreign-owned, have had a higher profile in the local media than smaller, locally owned enterprises, they frequently become the target for civil society activists seeking environmental reforms. To preempt their critics, these companies have often adopted cleaner technologies when they become available.

Brazilian and Indian cement manufacturers and sugar refineries that have participated in Clean Development Mechanism (CDM) cap-and-trade carbon markets have had attributes that, with several additional nuances, are consistent with this line of reasoning. The larger, more highly capitalized, and more internationally oriented cement and sugar enterprises were more likely to participate in CDM markets. Consultants made the CEOs of these companies aware of the new financial opportunities in the global carbon cap-and-trade markets. CEOs who saw their companies as leaders in their industries often wanted to participate in the CDM, perhaps out of a concern for the companies' image in civil society (Pulver, Hultman, and Guimaraes 2010).

A similar pattern has characterized the organic banana business. Dole, a large presence in the international banana trade for more than 100 years, has taken a leading role in promoting the cultivation and sale of organic bananas. The company subsidized the conversion of small banana plantations to organic cultivation in the coastal deserts of northern Peru, and now it sells the organic bananas internationally (Plasencia 2011).[3] Once a large firm like Dole commits to change, then structurally equivalent enterprises in the same and adjacent industrial sectors feel pressure to innovate as well (Wejnert 2003).

---

[3] Desert locations make sense for organic growers because the dry conditions limit pest populations, but desert agriculture also requires ample amounts of capital because farmers must irrigate all of the fields in production.

Having invested in the cleaner technologies, the innovating enterprises have sometimes exhibited a 'California effect" in which their executives, having complied with strict requirements for clean production in one jurisdiction, become advocates for requirements that mandate cleaner technologies or fuels in other jurisdictions (Cashore 2009). Through this kind of lobbying, the larger firms exert competitive pressure on the technological laggards like the smaller, family-owned sugar mills that participate in Brazilian CDM markets infrequently. Without exposure to international communities of practice or capital to institute new practices, smaller enterprises continue to emit copious amounts of greenhouse gases per unit of production. Living in a society without a history of effective environmental regulation, the heads of these smaller enterprises may choose to deny the existence of the problem or they may adopt an environmental fatalism in which they do not believe that they have the capacity to restrain greenhouse gas emissions through ecological modernization, so they do not try. In contrast, the heads of the larger firms, with access to more capital, would exhibit more of a "can do" attitude toward the adoption of cleaner energy sources (Haller and Hadler 2008).

They might espouse a "natural capitalism" (Hawken, Lovins, and Lovins 1999) that sees opportunities for profits in the adoption of new technologies that make more efficient use of energy and natural resources. When environmentalists argue with their friends and acquaintances that the adoption of green technologies will save the adopters money compared with the continued use of conventional technologies, they are appropriating the language and the logic of the natural capitalists.

So, when do real improvements in energy efficiency occur? Very visible and sudden changes in the prices of commodities, such as the increase in gasoline prices in the United States during 2008, have spurred increases in fuel efficiency. Political forces, such as charismatic leaders, galvanized social movements, or state agencies with mandates have induced real improvements in the energy efficiency of the built environment. "Highly visible, signature building projects" have provided a more diffuse, but still important, impetus behind improvements in energy efficiency (Biggart and Lutzenhiser 2007).

In all of these instances the increased efficiencies occur in spurts. In other words, there are moments of ecological modernization. Short-term political considerations often determine the timing of particular decisions to adopt a new technology. For example, companies building new paper and pulp mills in Southeast Asia only decided to install new chlorine-free pulping and bleaching technologies after Greenpeace disseminated information about the new technologies to local NGOs opposed to the construction of the polluting facilities (Sonnenfeld 2000, 248).

These moments of environmental reform differ from other historical periods in that they usually see associated surges in all kinds of economic innovation. Companies adopt new energy-efficient technologies when they are in the midst of adopting a host of other new technologies (Florida 1996). By embedding the additional costs of cleaner technologies within the costs of a larger overhaul of a plant, the additional costs of solar panels, for example, become less visible and onerous. By committing to the expense and trouble of replacing old technologies, managers have in effect abandoned prior "communities of practice" and opened themselves up to reformulated practices that include new, more energy-efficient technologies and routines. Companies that are more likely to innovate are therefore more likely to adopt more energy-efficient technologies, and they are more likely to undertake these green reforms when they have healthy balance sheets. The same association between the restructuring of production processes and green innovations suggests that when reforms occur, they will not always be "end of pipe" reforms that companies "patch" onto older, pollution-intensive productive processes. Instead, a re-engineering of basic production processes may occur. These tasks take considerable amounts of money, so low interest rates, which facilitate borrowing, indirectly facilitate ecological modernization. Because economic expansion typically occurs during periods of easy credit, the ties between economic expansion and increases in energy efficiency (Jevons paradox) once again become apparent.

The challenges of achieving more energy-efficient production processes vary from the old, affluent, industrial North to the industrializing, but impoverished, Global South. In the North, deteriorating air and water quality around centers of intense industrial production sparked defensive efforts after World War II to clean up places like the old, industrial belt cities in the northern United States and Western Europe (Crenson 1971). In these older, industrial areas some manufacturers had to "retrofit" their factories to reduce the volume of pollutants omitted during production. As a result, indices of air quality have improved in the affluent, long-industrialized societies of Europe and North America during the past fifty years.

While some observers have cited this historical pattern of a decline in environmental quality followed by a cleanup as support for the EKC hypothesis, more recent work attributes much of the recent improvement in local air and water quality in the affluent societies to deindustrialization and the relocation of most industrial production to developing countries (Bailey 2007). In the newly industrializing countries such as Indonesia and India where companies have recently expanded their industrial facilities, each new plant provides, potentially, a moment for ecological modernization because the builders can install new, reduced emissions technologies. This dynamic explains why technological laggards frequently "leapfrog" older manufacturing centers and adopt new technologies more rapidly than enterprises in long-established industrial centers (Grubler 1998; Perkins and Neumayer 2005).

Although the entrance of consumers in the industrializing societies into global markets for large material goods adds to the growing volume of greenhouse gas emissions, defensive environmentalist sentiments have sometimes limited the environmental damage done by additional consumers. Automobile choices illustrate this dynamic. Anxious about driving and parking cars on the narrow streets of preindustrial cities and sensitive to increases in the cost of gasoline, consumers in developing countries have followed European consumers in their automobile preferences and, in so doing, they have reinvigorated the global market for small cars such as the German-made Smart Car (Ward 2011).

The newly prosperous consumers also illustrate the limits of ecological modernization as a strategy for limiting emissions. While consumers and governments have begun to push manufacturers in the direction of more energy-efficient cars, large populations of people still rely on individual vehicles for mobility. Wholesale changes in the ways humans travel must come from encompassing organizations that can initiate systemic transformations that move humans away from resource-intensive forms of travel like automobiles and airplanes.

The association of waves of manufacturing innovation with the adoption of new, more energy-efficient technologies explains the historical prevalence of the Jevons paradox. If the adoption of the new technologies depends on an abundance of capital, then it is most likely to occur during periods when an abundance of capital also makes possible the overall expansion of economic enterprises. In this sense, increases in energy efficiency per unit of GDP come with growth in overall human impact on the biosphere. Following this logic, business cycles should produce fluctuations in greenhouse gas emissions and ecological modernization. During economic booms, many firms would undertake ecological modernization, and the overall volume of greenhouse gas emissions would grow rapidly. During busts, capital-starved enterprises would postpone efforts at ecological modernization, and greenhouse gas emissions, following trends in economic activities, would decline. During the dramatic economic downturn of 2008–9, greenhouse gas emissions in the United States declined by 2.2 percent (USEIA 2009). Given this pattern, the 2008 financial crisis was not, as some have contended (Peters et al. 2012), "an opportunity to move the global economy away from a high emissions trajectory." For this reason, the sharp rebound in global emissions during 2010 is not surprising. It follows the general pattern outlined here.

Although the long-term historical emissions data necessary to confirm these suppositions do not exist, historical fluctuations in technological innovations during the last two centuries do follow this pattern. The adoption of innovations declined markedly in the United States during the 1870s, the 1930s, and the 1970s, periods of economic depression or recession (Grubler 1998, 125). Subsequent economic recoveries have often featured leading sectors that took advantage of a new cluster of innovations that spread rapidly across the sector: railroads and steelmaking during the 1880s, personal transportation in the 1950s, and information technologies during the 1980s and 1990s. Periods of stasis dominated by established communities of practice give way during periods of prosperity to moments of ecological modernization when businesses reform or reorganize.

The same line of analysis about communities of practice and moments of ecological modernization applies to households as well as enterprises (Erickson 1997). The opportunities for significant changes in the emissions profiles of households occur early and late in household life cycles. When people form households and make decisions about where to live and what kind of housing to purchase, they make wholesale changes in their lives that have large implications for subsequent household emissions. A decision to purchase a large home in a distant suburb, far from a workplace, commits a household to emitting large volumes of greenhouse gases for years. A decision to purchase a smaller home in a community closer to the workplace contributes to a lower level of emissions.[4] Similarly, when children depart, a couple with an "empty nest" may decide to sell the now spacious house and move into a smaller unit in a more densely populated community, thereby reducing their greenhouse gas emissions. In these instances, as with enterprises, moments of ecological

---

[4] Moments of change in households can produce negative as well as positive impacts on greenhouse gas emissions. A decision to divorce raises per capita greenhouse gas emissions because per capita consumption of housing typically increases after a divorce (Liu et al. 2003).

modernization occur when social units restructure. Here, too, economic resources probably make a difference; wealthier household heads, more than poorer household heads, become convinced they can make a difference through the ecological modernization of their households (Haller and Hadler 2008).

Conclusion: Production, Pollution, and Defensive Environmentalist Practices in China

The circumstances surrounding ecological modernization in Brazil and India suggest that the globalization of markets has played an integral role in inducing enterprises to adopt environmentally less damaging technologies when they reorganize their processes of production. Nonprofit organizations have expedited ecological modernization by certifying new production processes as "sustainable." Does this dynamic of defensive environmental sentiments and ecological modernization characterize China? The immense scale of China's industrial sector makes this example particularly interesting. Certainly, the emergence of global markets has had a profound impact on Chinese producers, at the same time that they have repeatedly expressed a desire to increase energy efficiency and reduce levels of industrial pollution. Some observers have argued that defensive environmentalist sentiments, in the form of a desire to reduce local air pollution, will eventually curb the Chinese appetite for further industrialization.[5]

The recent history of energy consumption in China exhibits the uneven pattern outlined earlier: stasis expressed in a continuing reliance on coal as a source of energy coupled with the simultaneous adoption of new, cleaner forms of production in selected locales. The Chinese example also underscores the daunting challenge described at the beginning of this chapter: how to reduce greenhouse gas emissions at the same time that billions of people, largely in Asia, adopt the energy-intensive lifestyles of Americans and Europeans. For these reasons, the Chinese case provides a particularly instructive example of the central tendencies in the human quest for cleaner forms of energy during the twentieth and twenty-first centuries.

During the 1980s and 1990s, the Chinese central government focused on creating heavy industrial facilities, while local governments

---

[5] Arnulf Grubler, personal communication.

concentrated on creating small and medium-sized industrial enterprises. The rapid expansion in China's heavy industrial sector elevated global greenhouse gas emissions to levels unforeseen in IPCC projections from the mid-1990s. It also generated severe air pollution that has taken a toll on the health of the Chinese people. In 2000, China contained sixteen of the world's twenty most polluted cities (Fincher 2006). The high levels of emissions stem in large part from a concentration of polluting facilities like steel mills in cities and a reliance on inefficient, coal-fired power plants that emit large volumes of particulates, sulfur dioxide, and carbon dioxide in generating electricity (Liu and Diamond 2008). Despite the human costs of these pollutants, the first priority of local officials for the past three decades has been to alleviate poverty through industrialization (Zhang 2003). Local officials got promotions for stimulating economic development, not for curbing industrial pollution. At the same time, anxiety grew about the effects of the severe air pollution on public health. Mortality rates rose in cities on bad pollution days. In one small but symbolic response to these concerns, the U.S. embassy in Beijing had by early 2012 established a twitter feed, updated hourly, with readings on the concentrations of particulates in Beijing's air (Houser 2012).

Beginning in the mid-1990s, the central government, out of a concern with levels of pollution, began shutting down the most inefficient of the smaller industrial enterprises at the same time that it increased the rate at which it constructed larger, more efficient coal-fired power plants. The shift toward more efficient power plants in the mid-1990s and the simultaneous closure of more than 15,000 inefficient plants actually caused a decline in greenhouse gas emissions in China during the late 1990s (Streets et al. 2001). Defensive environmentalist practices seemed to have taken hold in policymaking circles. The tangible benefits of clean air in their communities had persuaded people to take actions that in an unanticipated way had benefited the global environment.

This policymaking dynamic shifted after 2000 to one exemplified by the recent experience of China Light and Power (CLP), a large utility in the Far East. The company struggled to build a biomass plant in rural eastern China that would generate 6 megawatts of power. The difficulties stemmed in part from parts suppliers who could not deliver the specialized boilers for the power plant. A community of practice for generating electricity from biomass did not exist. At the same time, CLP built a coal-fired power plant in southern China that would generate 1,200 megawatts of power. CLP completed the coal-fired plant on schedule and did so for half of the cost that a similar plant would have cost in Europe or the United States (Bradsher 2007). The comparative ease with which CLP could build the conventional coal-fired plant reflected the existence of a community of practice surrounding the construction of conventional power plants in China.

The construction of new power-generating facilities should provide a moment for ecological modernization, and so it did in the late 1990s when the larger, more efficient coal-fired plants replaced the smaller, more antiquated coal-fired plants. A community of practice quickly developed around the new coal-fired plants. When robust economic growth began to cause power shortages after 2000, Chinese officials turned to the larger, conventional coal-fired plants to expand their power supply, and what had been a force for ecological modernization ten years earlier now exacerbated problems of global warming. In 2007 the Chinese pledged to increase energy efficiency by 20 percent by 2010. To do so, they continued their past practice of shutting down inefficient industrial plants. In 2007 they closed 1,000 antiquated cement plants, but the rate at which they continued to build the coal-fired power plants overwhelmed the reductions in emissions from closing old facilities (World Resources Institute 2009). In 2006 alone, China added 92 gigawatts of coal-fired generating capacity, more than the entire generating capacity in the United Kingdom (Logan 2007). The absence of any global gains in energy efficiency from 2001 to 2006, visible in Figure 8.1, stems in large part from the tremendous increase in coal-fired power plants in China since the late 1990s.

This depiction of energy expenditures in the midst of industrial transformation in China paints a bleak environmental picture, but it misses an essential historical dynamic. Three times between 1997 and 2007 catastrophic environmental events, sometimes referred to as "shocks," mobilized the Chinese state to undertake, with popular approval, major environmental protection initiatives. The 1998 floods in the Yangtze River basin focused attention on the widespread deforestation in the upper reaches of the watershed that exacerbated the floods. In the aftermath of the floods, state officials expanded the "grain for green" program in which the state subsidized farmers who reforested a portion of their lands. A 2005 chemical spill in northeastern China prompted the adoption of new guidelines about the location of chemical plants in populous areas. In 2007 extensive algae blooms in well-known Chinese lakes convinced government officials that they had to close dozens of polluting factories on the shores of these lakes (Liu and Diamond 2008). In each of these instances, focusing events led to political mobilization and the imposition of new regulations by extra-local authorities. The following chapter describes this historical dynamic in more detail.

9

Focusing Events, Altruistic Environmentalists, and the Environmental Movement

> In that moment, our country was on her knees; we were on our knees. It felt as if we had lost a mother. And when we looked one another in the eyes, we all felt the same thing – we were struck by the same calamity. We were people lost in a tremor but united by a common fate.
>
> Kettly Mars (2011), on the first few days after the 2010 earthquake in Port au Prince, Haiti

Introduction: What Are Focusing Events?

Large-scale, globally connected societies coupled tightly to the natural world experience a recurring pattern of events, described by Homer-Dixon (1999, 24) a decade ago in a discussion of China:

> Resource and environmental stresses increase the susceptibility of the Chinese economy and society to sudden shocks like droughts, floods, and sharp changes in the international economy.... A slight shortfall in grain production in 1994 pushed up inflation sharply;... each June the whole country seems to breathe a sigh of relief if a good wheat harvest is announced. Serious environmental scarcities and population pressure mean there is little slack in the system to keep the effects of sudden, unanticipated shocks from propagating through the economy and society.

What Homer-Dixon calls shocks others might describe as focusing events, because they focus public attention on a particular issue. This chapter investigates these disruptive, potentially transformative moments that convert people into altruistic environmentalists and galvanize social movements. It begins with a description of focusing events and traces their effects on people who experience the events, on social movements that find political opportunities in the events, and on the subsequent politics of environmental reform. The political analysis examines the interactions between defensive and altruistic environmentalists during the moments of reform. The chapter concludes with a case study of an organizational conversion experience at Wal-Mart in the months after a focusing event, Hurricane Katrina, devastated New Orleans.

Except in rare instances, sudden, unanticipated turns of events ("avalanches" in Bak's terminology) do not precipitate thoroughgoing transformations of societies. They have unclear origins and few observable social effects. Observers, with good reason, are often reluctant to attribute single events like an intense hurricane to a systemic change like global warming. Extraordinary clusters of events that depart from historical norms stem more clearly from macroscopic changes like global warming. When an event or a cluster of events stimulates efforts to reduce vulnerabilities, the reforms may leave large-scale systems changed only in some incremental way. Human-induced, threshold-crossing events, like the sudden melting of Arctic sea ice during the summer of 2007, have recently occurred in regional ecologies, but only the scientific community noted the change. The collapse of the Grand Banks cod fishery during the 1990s represented a threshold-crossing event, but in this instance the global scale of the fish market dampened the effect of the collapse in a single, albeit very important, fishery.

In recognition of this larger societal inertia, critics have sounded notes of desperation in their assessments of environmental problems. When James Gustave Speth (2008) asked "Do societies have conversion experiences?," he implied that only a thoroughgoing transformation in the ways in which we think and act will save us from disruptive and even life-threatening climate changes. Societies do have "conversion experiences." Probably the most dramatic, large-scale conversion experiences occur at the beginning of wars. The Japanese attack on Pearl Harbor on December 7, 1941, converted the American public, almost overnight, into a population of people committed to winning a war with Japan, whatever the cost. The surprise attack refocused people's attention on a single, large-scale problem. Typically, it takes a dramatic, large-scale event like a disaster, a catastrophe, or an attack to redirect the public's attention toward a particular issue and provide the impetus for thoroughgoing political reforms that address the event's causes. Even then, a random element characterizes all of these events. While they may be more common in large, tightly coupled systems, their origins often lie beyond human control.

Focusing events vary in their geographic reach. An event with a transformative impact at a local scale may be an insignificant event at a more global scale. For example, the very small numbers of salmon returning to the Columbia River during the mid-1990s alarmed the Columbia River fisheries community, got the attention of the state legislators, and produced a significant change in the regulation of the river's salmon runs, but it did not transform fisheries regulation beyond the Columbia River basin. Usually, the political effects of focusing events vary with the magnitude of the event and the size of the political arena. Events like the Exxon Valdez oil spill, the death of Chico Mendes, and a surge in tropical deforestation rates in Brazil had appreciable effects in particular environmental arenas, but they did not transform environment–society relationships globally. In this sense, focusing events are scale-specific in their effects.

Hurricane Katrina, for example, did tremendous damage to one city and transformed several important organizations, but it would be hard to categorize the storm as a "transformative or catalytic event" for the larger society. Indeed, the most salient effects after the hurricane involved efforts by the larger society in the form of volunteers, NGOs, state, and federal aid workers to restore New Orleans to its pre-flood state. This effort most closely resembles the "restoration" path in Figure 2.2 where agents for the larger system work to restore an injured subunit to its pre-disaster state. In this sense, Katrina does not seem like a "transformative event" that might precipitate a societal collapse or a fundamental reorganization of society. It did, however, have a transforming effect on one large American organization, Wal-Mart. Among recent events, only the attacks of 9/11/2001 seem to have been a focusing event with a transformative global impact.

Sometimes events occur in such a rapid sequence that they have a combined effect in the minds of consumers. In February 1989, Americans became aware that many of the apples that they had been packing in their children's lunch boxes contained residues of Alar, a potent pesticide that growers had sprayed on their orchards. One month later, another scare, involving cyanide-laced grapes imported from Chile, received wide coverage in the national media. Later that month, the Exxon Valdez oil spill occurred, and, although it involved a different commodity, it reinforced in many people's minds the vulnerabilities associated with a global agricultural economy. In subsequent months, local and organic food advocates in California reported sharp increases in the public's interest in their campaigns to relocalize the American agricultural economy (Friedland 2011).

Charles Perrow (1999, 123–69) has noted that manufacturers and regulators of new technologies make them safer when the technologies, aircraft for example, regularly expose elites to risks, in this instance because influential people fly so frequently. Following this line of thinking, focusing events should be especially effective in promoting policy changes when policy elites either experience the events directly or feel threatened by them. Perhaps the attacks of 9/11/2001 on New York and Washington, DC, produced so many policy changes in part because the attacks targeted elites. A similar dynamic may occur when focusing events call attention to environmental problems.

The circumstances surrounding the passage of a law establishing the Soil Conservation Service in 1935 in the United States illustrate how exposure of elites to focusing events can expedite environmental policy changes. The Great Plains experienced probably the most severe drought of the twentieth century during the depression years of the 1930s. The drought followed forty years of agricultural expansion in which smallholders' plows converted large areas of the southern plains into wheat fields. The recently turned earth dried out with the drought and much of it became wind-borne dust that periodically swirled into massive dust storms. Twice during 1934 these storms, called "dusters," carried dust from the plains as far as the eastern seaboard of the United States. In the spring of 1935, the winds whipped up another storm just as the United States Senate began to hold hearings about the creation of a Soil Conservation Service to combat problems of wind- and water-driven soil erosion. With the new storm approaching from the west, Hugh Hammond Bennett, a strong advocate of the legislation, delayed his testimony until the day when the storm hit Washington, DC, the site of the hearings. The dust cast a copper-colored pall over the Washington landscape and became grit in the mouths of senators and citizens while Bennett made his case for the new agency (Brink 1951; Worster 1979). Direct experience with the drought-driven dust storms probably focused the senators' attention on the soil erosion problem in ways that testimony in hearings could not. The senators may have felt a sense of defensive environmentalism, a new appreciation for the storms' destructive impacts, and a sharpened desire to save themselves, their families, and their constituents from further exposure to the storms. The storm and Bennett's testimony contributed to the passage several weeks later of the legislation that established the Soil Conservation Service.

The dynamic of elite exposure and subsequent environmental reform now shapes activists' discursive strategies. For example, in an effort to get the attention of federal legislators, activists concerned with retaining coastal lands in Louisiana recently predicted that between 2010 and 2050 Louisiana would lose to the sea an area of land equivalent to the entire Washington and Baltimore metropolitan area – the region, not coincidentally, where many federal legislators have homes (Petrolia and Kim 2011).

Focusing Events, Common Fate, and Altruistic Environmentalists

Focusing events mobilize people because the visceral experience of the event, its magnitude, and its destructive impact shake their confidence in the system. What was a risk has become in some instances a terrifying reality. Sentiments of a common fate, a sense that "we are all in this together," grow in a population. The epigram from Kettly Mars describes how the devastating 2010 earthquake in Port au Prince united Haitians in a common fate, a collective experience of devastation and death (Sell and Love 2009). By destroying expensive homes and ramshackle huts, the earthquake had a literal leveling effect, eliminating some barriers to cross-class fraternization, and, at least initially, focusing everyone on the search for survivors. These situations often stir sentiments of altruistic environmentalism in people. The sense of a common fate inspires selfless devotion to a cause and undergirds the selfless activities that Rebecca Solnit (2009) has observed in the immediate aftermath of disasters. First responders, for example, seek to save lives whatever the cost. Ordinary motorists direct traffic at intersections without traffic lights. If the focusing event is environmental in its dimensions, a selfless devotion to environmental causes, an altruistic environmentalism, can emerge among victims and bystanders.

With the evocative phrase "a paradise built in hell," Solnit (2009) captures the extraordinary political circumstances that follow catastrophic focusing events. She writes, "[I]n disaster people seem to come together... where the old divides between people seem to have fallen away... where much once considered impossible, good and bad, is now possible and present" (301–6). In the aftermath of these events people feel a "purposeful energy, like soldiering" that Solnit likened to "the Moral Equivalent of War" (James 1906). Like wars, catastrophic events destroy wealth as well as people's lives. As Solnit, quoting historian Mark Healey, writes (2009, 2,648–55), "insurrections by a nature that had seemed subdued... unsettle, disrupt, and potentially overthrow apparently 'natural' structures of social power." The unanticipated reshaping of these "natural" social orders raises questions about their legitimacy and, in so doing, loosens the elite's grip on the reins of power.

The altered circumstances impress people with the need for systemic change to counter the devastating effects of the focusing event. The disaster fuels an altruistic environmentalism expressed in a desire to repair and reform the larger system. The unexpected events unleash a social energy in which people show a new enthusiasm for "getting ahead collectively" (Hirschman 1984; Uphoff 1992). Social relations become more transparent because people do less scheming for narrow or sectarian purposes. Social relations also become more visibly caring because people want to promote the public good. People listen to their altruistic impulses and undertake overtly political activities that support environmental reform and offer them no immediate personal return. The lofty expressions of altruistic environmentalism on the Web sites of environmental NGOs inspire people, so they join, contribute to, or volunteer their time to the NGOs. Young adults, having fewer material obligations and social constraints than their elders, may be particularly drawn to expressing and embodying altruistic environmentalism in their choices about personal practices, volunteer activities, and political views.

By intensifying concern for the common good, focusing events provide social movements with political opportunities (MacAdam 1988). Activists can sometimes "frame" the interpretation of the event in a way that advances reform efforts (Snow et al. 1986). The first pieces of information that people receive about a traumatizing event after having experienced it can be extraordinarily influential in helping them interpret the event (Sell and Love 2009). The new information about environmental destruction combines with the events to draw attention to issues and bolster the prospects for significant policy changes. Activists are well aware of this connection, referring to it as "information politics." In the words of one activist, "we promote change by reporting facts" (Keck and Sikkink 1998, 19). Concern about the environment and information about it often generate a mutually reinforcing dynamic in which an event-driven concern about the environment prompts efforts to collect more information about it. Once the information becomes available, frequently in the form of ominous trend lines that imply environmental destruction, concern about the environment rises to still higher levels. Efforts at environmental reform both rely on information about the environment and intensify efforts to gather it (Mol 2008). Focusing events frequently set this dynamic of information and political mobilization in motion.

Mobilizing popular support for policy change becomes much easier if a powerful image comes to symbolize the issue for the public (Szasz 1994). A brief history of the Cuyahoga River fire in Cleveland illustrates this process. When a short stretch of the Cuyahoga River caught on fire during June 1969, it was only the most recent fire on the river. It had caught on fire at least ten times during the preceding fifty years. Two weeks after the 1969 fire, *Time* magazine ran a picture of "the river on fire" on the front cover of its weekly edition, and the "river on fire" came to symbolize the dire environmental conditions prevailing on the nation's waterways. Given that we use water to douse flames, only an extremely polluted waterway could actually burn. The powerful symbolism encouraged a wide range of politicians to join Carl Stokes, then mayor of Cleveland, and his brother, Louis Stokes, a congressman from Cleveland, in working for the passage of the Clean Water Act by the federal government in 1972. This legislation provided the statutory basis for subsequent efforts that cleaned up the Cuyahoga River (Scott 2009).

Sometimes people become the symbols of an issue. In 1988, when ranchers in the Brazilian Amazon murdered Chico Mendes, the rubber-tappers leader, they put "a human face" on the deforestation issue (Hochstetler and Keck 2007, 165). The 2005 murder of Dorothy Stang by two gunmen brought further attention to the depredations of loggers and large landowners in the eastern Amazon. Not only was Stang a nun, but she was born in the United States, so her story resonated beyond the borders of Brazil. Mendes and Stang became both martyrs and environmental icons[1] for the cause of sustainable development in the tropics. When icons come to symbolize an issue in media with global reach, it becomes more likely that high-level government officials will make significant changes in policy.

When focusing events do occur, they reset political agendas. The surge in attention to an issue thrust into prominence by a focusing event usually takes the form of an issue-attention cycle (Downs 1972). Figure 9.1 outlines the phases in the cycle. The focusing event triggers a first phase of "alarmed discovery." Newly concerned people, some of them altruistic environmentalists, working with organized environmental groups, then try during a second phase to "strike when the iron is hot" and get legislative reform. Usually during a third phase, politicians, NGO

---

[1] Environmental icons symbolize in one image the essentials of an environmental problem. Baby harp seals, 55-gallon drums, and conning towers at nuclear plants have all become environmental icons. See Szasz (1994).

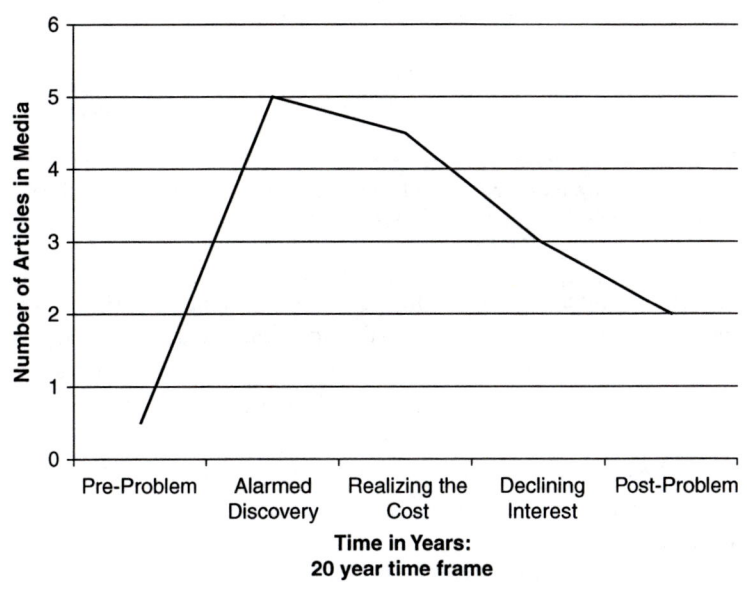

FIGURE 9.1. The Issue Attention Cycle

representatives, and engaged portions of the public grapple with the costs of a remedy at the same time that they underwrite relief and restoration efforts. In the post-problem phase, attention to the issue declines. Although attention levels to the issue during the post-problem phase begin to approximate attention levels during the pre-problem phase, the political circumstances during the two phases are quite different. The political attention and policy changes during the second and third phases of an issue attention cycle have created an infrastructure, a series of laws, experts, agencies, and NGOs concerned with the issue, that can become active when another focusing event occurs.

The issue attention cycle has characterized a wide array of issues in American political life during the past three decades (Wrobel and Connelly 2002), but on occasions events have not precipitated issue attention cycles because other pressing issues have made it more difficult to get the public's attention (Hilgartner and Bosk 1988). For example, despite mounting signs of globally significant climate change during the past decade, the onset of the great recession in 2008 reduced the public's interest in global warming (Scruggs and Benegal 2012). Alternatively, an event may not capture the attention of the public because the particular characteristics of the event, an absence of drama, for example,

168 *Defensive Environmentalists and the Dynamics of Global Reform*

↑ Scale of Event **+** ↑ Tightness of Coupling **=** ↑ Length of Chain Reaction

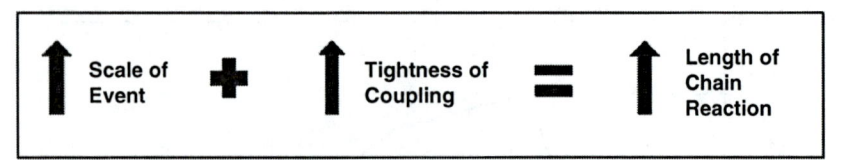

FIGURE 9.2. The Scale of a Focusing Event, Tightness of System's Coupling, and the Length of Chain Reactions: A Hypothesis

make it less compelling. For example, the Copenhagen Climate summit of late 2009 generated a surge in media attention to climate change issues (Boykoff 2011), but despite the rhetoric of many people at the meeting, there was no apparent increase in altruistic environmentalism during the meeting, and no encompassing organizations formed. In this instance, the event did not spur collective action, perhaps because, as a planned meeting, it did not set off enough alarm bells among observers or participants.

The Big Bang Theory of Environmental Reform

The idea that focusing events spur environmental reforms might be referred to as the "big bang theory" of environmental reform. The theorists (Bak, Catton) of large-scale systemic change identify sudden, large-scale events, like the avalanches in Bak's sandpile or the pulses in the press–pulse dynamics (PPD) framework (Collins et al. 2011), as triggers for significant changes. The focusing events would not have to involve large-scale disturbances to induce dramatic change (Uphoff 1992, 408). Even small-scale events could produce cascades of effects in tightly coupled systems. Effects from small events in more loosely coupled systems would be absorbed by the slack in the system, so the chain reactions would not be as long or as disruptive as they would be in tightly coupled systems. Large-scale focusing events may have such strong impacts that the slack in loosely coupled systems may not be able to absorb or dampen down the effects from the events. The conjuncture of a tightly coupled system and large-scale, destabilizing events should produce long, unpredictable chains of cascading effects that contribute to political upheavals. Figure 9.2 portrays the hypothesized relationship.

The events trigger change by indicting the existing political order for failing to prevent the disturbances or for failing to make the existing system more resilient (Birkland 2006). Political scientists and resilience theorists extend this emphasis on focusing events by stressing the historical unevenness of change. Periods of stasis alternate with abrupt episodes of change. Focusing events, coupled with other changes, would in this line of reasoning precipitate the cascades of policy changes identified by political scientists (Repetto 2006) as points of punctuation in cycles of punctuated equilibria.

Focusing events provide the points of inflection in cycles of punctuated equilibria. They end periods of business as usual and begin periods of accelerated political change. In this understanding of political processes government officials, just like citizens, have limited attention spans. In this context agenda setting is a crucial political process. Punctuated equilibrium theorists maintain that slow incremental processes can lay the foundations over time for policy punctuations, a cluster of policy changes adopted within a short time of one another (Repetto 2006). Sometimes it is the interaction of these long-established trends that makes it possible for an issue to "catch fire" (True, Jones, and Baumgartner 2006, 160–2; Gladwell 2000). In other instances a single, large-scale event like a tsunami, a terrorist attack, or a severe drought causes politicians and citizens to refocus their political agendas on issues raised by the catastrophe. In many instances politicians try to remedy, to the extent possible, the structural problems revealed by the catastrophes, and, in so doing, significant political changes occur.

While punctuated equilibrium theorists emphasize that rapid political change can occur at both local and global scales of governance, their language suggests that political turmoil pushes governance issues into larger-scale arenas. In periods of political quiescence, "political activity clusters in small venues." In the words of several punctuated equilibrium theorists,

Subsystem politics is the politics of equilibrium – the politics of policy monopoly, incrementalism, a widely accepted (policy) image, and negative feedback (True, Jones, and Baumgartner 2006, 162).

These policy monopolies collapse when events or trends lead other people to demand a seat at the negotiating table. In the words of the same theorists,

Macropolitics is the politics of punctuation – the politics of large-scale change, competing policy images... and positive feedback (True et al. 2006, 162).[2]

---

[2] A policy image conveys a widespread understanding about how causes produce effects within a particular policy domain (Repetto 2006, 81–2).

To accommodate the growing number of interested parties and the wider interest in policies during crises, higher-level officials take a more active interest in policies, and deliberations over policies move to larger arenas where the interested parties can create encompassing organizations. The political process begins in the aftermath of a focusing event when people perceive a threat to the larger society or environment and they act to preserve it, with little expectation of personal gain except in the general sense that everyone's fortunes will improve if the society is saved. Altruistic environmentalists emerge and contribute to social movements that press for new policies and sometimes an entirely new level of governance. In the latter instance, policymakers create an encompassing institution with a mandate to curtail particular activities in order to restore a natural resource or the environment (Olson 1982). The United Nations, the European Community, the International Monetary Fund, and the World Bank represent the world's best-known cluster of encompassing organizations. World leaders created them in the immediate aftermath of a devastating event, World War II.

Social cascades and positive feedback processes characterize politics during periods of punctuation. With cascades "innovations that might be impossible to accomplish if considered separately are swept along as other critical decisions fall into place" (Ingram and Fraser, 2006, 95). These are the moments of ecological modernization described in the previous chapter. Through positive feedbacks, bandwagons emerge; energized activists create new public interest groups, and parallel institutions appear in different jurisdictions as politicians mimic one another in their legislative actions (DiMaggio and Powell 1983; Dunn 2006, 205).

Focusing events have their most pronounced effects in already organized political arenas where individual NGOs and advocacy coalitions of NGOs already have policy proposals on the table (Boudet 2011). Focusing events do not produce new ideas so much as they redirect attention toward already existing policy ideas (Birkland 2006, 165). With the "pressures of the moment" to do something in the immediate aftermath of an event, preexisting proposals get enacted. For example, the Brazilian rubber tappers union had succeeded in getting an extractive reserve established on an experimental basis prior to Chico Mendes's assassination. After his death extractive reserves became a common approach to rain forest preservation in other areas of the Amazon. In the aftermath of Dorothy Stang's assassination in the eastern Amazon, the federal government in Brazil went ahead and demarcated already outlined protected areas. It also outlawed legal strategies that land grabbers had repeatedly used to substantiate their claims to land. Both of these actions by the federal government ratified proposals that the "social greens" had introduced before Stang's death (Hochstetler and Keck 2007, 160–85).[3]

The episodic patterns of punctuated equilibria have characterized a large range of environmental policy arenas. Three examples illustrate different aspects of these patterns. The Exxon Valdez oil spill in Alaska's Prince William Sound represented a large-scale focusing event compared with earlier, smaller oil spills. In the two years following the Exxon Valdez disaster the U.S. federal government enacted a new, stricter statute regulating oil spills, and more than thirty American states passed laws to regulate oil transport within their boundaries (Faass 2009).

Following a drought in the Sahel during the 1980s, international environmental NGOs increased their activities in the region and countries adopted "forest reforms" that gave villages or smallholders living on the land more secure tenure over their land and the trees on their land (see Chapter 4). This wave of forest reforms reflected in part the decisions of politicians to enact reforms that had been adopted in neighboring states and in part the work of staff members from international NGOs who spread the word about forest reforms from nation to nation (Benjamin 2004).

A third example involves the CAFE (Corporate Average Fuel Economy) regulations that govern gasoline mileage required of American automakers. The initial regulations were adopted during the early 1970s after consumer advocate Ralph Nader (1965) reframed the debate about auto safety with a highly publicized expose of the design dangers built into American automobiles (*Unsafe at Any Speed*). The simultaneous adoption by American legislatures of new environmental policies in other domains (a social cascade) may have facilitated the passage of the first set of mileage regulations. A period of relative stasis ensued during the 1980s and 1990s as automobile makers, in regular negotiations with government officials and NGO staff, became entrenched opponents of increases in required gasoline mileage for their fleets. In addition, they used a loophole through which they were able to reduce the mileage requirements for their fleets by having gas-guzzling automobiles reclassified as "light trucks" (Dunn 2006). The stasis ended in 2008 when a sharp recession forced two of the three American automakers to seek financial assistance from the federal government and restructure their operations.

---

[3] "Social greens" express simultaneous concerns with conservation and with equity.

In these tumultuous times the automakers accepted significant increases in automobile mileage requirements.

The first two examples outlined in the preceding discussion, an oil spill and a drought, altered political agendas and precipitated clusters of policy changes. In the third example, the CAFE negotiations, a confluence of factors, rather than a single focusing event, spurred the first cluster of policy changes during the 1970s. The second wave of change in CAFE undoubtedly had its origins in the 2008–9 economic turmoil. These examples suggest an affinity between focusing events and subsequent periods of accelerated changes in policy that could in some instances lead to scaled-up governance systems.

The likelihood of this kind of dynamic characterizing a particular environmental problem depends in part on the particular ways that the problem manifests itself: in dramatic, large-magnitude events, like a massive dust storm, or in small increments, like a slow rise in air temperatures over the years. If the latter, the problem takes a "crecive" form, appearing little by little over a long time period (Beamish 2002). Global warming has many manifestations, but in at least one influential understanding it takes a predominantly crecive form, especially in the mid latitudes of the earth where most people live. Winters warm and become shorter and the frequency of heat waves rises, but these long-term changes in climate occur in the midst of daily fluctuations that mask the long-term trends. Collective sentiments about the need for policy changes often do not crystallize around these smaller events because they are so easy to overlook.

Severe economic inequalities could prevent the crystallization of collective sentiments around the need for thoroughgoing policy reform, especially in those instances where the disturbances are relatively small in magnitude. People in egalitarian societies would probably have a more widespread and persistent sensation of a "common fate" after a focusing event than would people in highly stratified societies. In the latter context, a "disaster capitalist" scenario could unfold in which companies with connections to political leaders take advantage of the political turmoil in the aftermath of a focusing event to secure lucrative contracts to provide services or to repair damaged structures (Klein 2007). This prospect is more likely with smaller-scale events that do not overturn the status quo. In these instances, events are not dramatic enough to refocus popular attention on the longer-term problem, so well-financed coalitions that defend industries that emit greenhouse gases or pollute would win most political battles (Lane 2006).

The Local (Defensive) and Global (Altruistic) Environmental Dynamic

People do, in some instances, protect the environment because it pays off for them locally, but in virtually all of these instances "larger than local" structures, which have grown rapidly in number and influence since World War II (Tarrow 2000), facilitate environmental conservation. National governments provide enabling legislation to make it easier for fishing cooperatives to organize; international family planning programs research and distribute contraceptives; networks of farmers and NGOs provide support for individual farmers who practice alternative agriculture; some state and national governments make recycling mandatory; and central governments provide financial subsidies to enterprises that use renewable energy. Do the environmentally defensive efforts of individuals and communities have a reciprocal effect, enabling the creation of these larger-scale political structures, or are they just "a drop in the bucket," of little significance in the larger polity? Michael Pollan (2004, 20) addresses this question in an essay entitled "Why Bother?":

> For us to wait for legislation or technology to solve the [environmental] problem of how we're living our lives suggests we're not really serious about changing – something that our politicians cannot fail to notice. They will not move until we do.

Learning from efforts to reform irrigation systems in Sri Lanka, Norman Uphoff comes to a similar conclusion (Uphoff 1992, 273):

> [P]aradoxical though it may seem, "top down" efforts are usually needed to introduce, sustain, and institutionalize "bottom up" development. We are commonly constrained to think in either or terms – the more of one, the less of the other – when both are needed to achieve our purposes.

People with defensive environmentalist persuasions would presumably play more prominent roles in bottom-up efforts, whereas people with more altruistic perspectives might be more salient among the agents of top-down efforts. Several examples should clarify how defensive and altruistic environmentalists interact in these political processes.

One example concerns the passage of the Superfund legislation in 1984 in the midst of a conservative Republican administration. This unlikely event began with the discovery of toxins buried beneath a school at Love Canal in western New York state. In a classic example of defensive environmentalism, local residents organized to have the site cleaned up. The quintessentially suburban setting of the contamination, coupled with an articulate spokesperson, Lois Gibbs, attracted a great deal of interest from the media (Szasz 1994). In response to the heightened awareness, reporters and citizens began to look for similar instances of illegal dumping and contaminated water in other locales. Not surprisingly, they found other sites, many of them in poor, rural, and politically Republican communities in the United States. By this time, Lois Gibbs and others like her had moved beyond defensive environmentalism. She began to press for more general legislation to prevent episodes like Love Canal. Beginning as a defensive environmentalist, she became over the course of several years an altruistic environmentalist. Gibbs set up an NGO, Citizens' Clearinghouse for Hazardous Waste, and began to assist newly formed neighborhood groups in their campaigns to have nearby toxic waste sites cleaned up. Greenpeace and the National Toxics Campaign also assisted local groups. The discovery of the contaminated sites and the accumulation of defensive environmentalist groups in their political districts caused a number of conservative Republican representatives to vote in 1984 for the creation of a Superfund to clean up these sites. An issue that began with small meetings of defensive environmentalists in a neighborhood outside of Buffalo metamorphosed over a five-year period into an altruistic environmental struggle that eventually imposed a higher degree of public control over toxic wastes in the United States and, not coincidentally, improved the ability of defensive environmentalists to pursue cleanups of toxic waste sites near their homes (Szasz 1994).

The other example involves the renovation of the dilapidated Gal Oyo irrigation system in a rice-cultivating region of southeastern Sri Lanka during the 1980s. After thirty years of use and little repair, the water flowing through the Gal Oya canals resembled a degraded common pool resource, delivering benefits to some users and not to others. The system fell into disrepair because neither the engineers from the government irrigation agency nor the small farmers served by the system worked steadily to repair and refurbish it. By the late 1970s, seepage of water from the damaged canals had increased to the point where many downstream farmers in the system did not receive any water. Frequent droughts plagued the region, and farmers began to try to steal water from one another. It was a situation of "steal water or have your water stolen."[4]

In this wearying situation foreign development assistance officials, in partnership with the government irrigation agency, launched a five-year project to repair the system. The aid organizations hired and trained

---

[4] Personal communication, Norman T. Uphoff, Cornell University, July 2011.

the community organizers who organized the farmers to clean up the canals. The setting was not promising for collective action. Although some of the oldest farmers may have cooperated extensively in the initial settlement of the area and construction of the irrigation works, they did not have a recent history of working together on the canals despite chronic difficulties obtaining water for their crops. Nonetheless, the Gal Oya smallholders responded to the proposed program enthusiastically. When farmers showed enthusiasm for collective efforts to refurbish the canals, the government's irrigation engineers felt social pressures to increase their efforts to repair the damaged irrigation works. Through their combined efforts, project organizers, the farmers, and the engineers made the system effective again. The small farmers participated in this effort as defensive environmentalists whose farms benefited from the rehabilitated system. The community organizers, the sponsoring government officials, and the outside experts earned lower-than-market salaries and framed their work as an altruistic endeavor.[5]

The altruistically inclined outsiders served as "catalysts" who mobilized the small farmers. The farmers' visible commitment to cleaning out the clogged irrigation canals, in turn, created the social energy among other participants that led to more effective and timely repair work by the engineers (Uphoff 1992). In this instance there was no large-scale focusing event; instead, a small-scale event in the form of a project initiated by outsiders initiated a cascade of events that resembled a virtuous circle. The project tapped into the widespread dissatisfaction of farmers with the dilapidated condition of the canals and created political opportunities for farmers and outsiders, working in tandem, to reform the system. The catalyzing event did not achieve change by disrupting the existing socio-ecological order. It spurred change by tapping into a widespread discontent with the deteriorating irrigation system and drawing upon an unrecognized willingness among small farmers to work to restore important public works.

Both the Gal Oyo and Love Canal episodes of environmental reform demonstrate that the activities of defensive and altruistic environmentalists often have synergistic effects. During "business as usual" periods defensive environmentalists persist and can even grow in number while the numbers of altruistic environmentalists decline. The activities

---

[5] The lower salaries did generate high rates of turnover in the project's personnel, especially among the community organizers (Uphoff 1992).

of defensive environmentalists have two types of residual effects that can become important during later, more politically opportune, periods.

First, by bringing people together in pursuit of a common cause such as restoring a degraded community forest, defensive environmentalists increase the social capital in communities (Klyza, Isham, and Savage 2006). The capital comes in the form of social networks that prove useful in mobilizing people in later years to press for other policy changes. These networks are the "silent partners" of social movements. Relative to the general public, network participants trust one another. They reaffirm their collective identities when they communicate about emerging political opportunities (Tarrow 2000). The immediate cause around which activists in local networks first mobilized may have disappeared, but the organizations and networks constructed around these controversies persist. When a new environmental issue arises, these organizations and the earlier networks provide the social foundations for later lobbying efforts, sometimes in larger political arenas (MacAdam 1988).

Second, defensive efforts in particular locales become in some instances "demonstration projects" that, in the unusual political circumstances following a focusing event, can be implemented in larger political arenas. For example, the farm reforestation efforts in Niger that followed the drought during the 1980s and the subsequent clarification of tree tenure (see Chapter 4) served as a demonstration project for the Great Green Wall initiative in the Sahara and the Sahel, a multi-country effort being undertaken under the auspices of the United Nations (SSO 2008). Of course, demonstration projects sometimes serve more nefarious purposes, allowing organizations with uncertain environmental commitments to appear otherwise (greenwashing). Even these defensive environmental efforts can create a population of projects that politicians in larger political arenas can draw upon in fashioning new political orders after focusing events. They also provide, as Pollan suggests, visible evidence to political leaders that rank-and-file organizations and citizens care about environmental issues. This diffuse sense of environmental concern may play an important but difficult-to-discern role in promoting change in large-scale organizations.

The following short history of the circumstances in which Wal-Mart launched its green campaign in 2005 provides another, more detailed example of the ways in which already initiated defensive environmentalist activities can, together with a focusing event, generate the political impetus for change in larger social and economic arenas.

Hurricane Katrina and the Wal-Mart Sustainability Initiative

In the early years of the twenty-first century Wal-Mart, the world's largest retailer, became embroiled in a series of controversies involving alleged sex discrimination, union busting, and sweatshop working conditions overseas, all of which cast the retailer in a negative light in the eyes of many American consumers. Surveys suggested that these negative images of Wal-Mart had begun to persuade some consumers to shop elsewhere, so Wal-Mart executives began to look for ways to redeem themselves in the eyes of American consumers. In this context, Wal-Mart hired some environmental consultants who argued, using the rhetoric of natural capitalism, that, if Wal-Mart eliminated waste in their supply chains, sold goods produced through sustainable practices, and focused on energy efficiency in the delivery and display of goods, they could honestly portray themselves as a "green" company and thereby win the acclaim of environmentally concerned consumers. Several of these goals, efficiency in energy use and the elimination of waste, fit well with Wal-Mart's core cultural emphasis on EDLP, "everyday low prices." In 2004 and early 2005 a small group of Wal-Mart executives began to look at the company's operations for examples of what a "green" approach would mean in financial terms for Wal-Mart. To this point, the interests of Wal-Mart executives in sustainability represented a defensive environmentalism, focused on the near-term benefits of green activities for the company.

Then Hurricane Katrina hit the Gulf Coast. The storm flooded 80 percent of the city of New Orleans, killed more than 1,800 people, and did more damage to coastal property than any previous hurricane in the United States (Knabb, Rhome, and Brown 2006). A slow and inept government response to the devastation, coupled with real-time media reports of the predicament of people in the hurricane zone, underscored the gravity of the situation and made the case for offering to help, in whatever way possible. With a number of their stores flooded, some of their employees without homes, and thousands of customers in distress, Wal-Mart officials wanted to help. They could help almost immediately, in part because Wal-Mart had its headquarters in Bentonville, Arkansas, some 650 miles by car from New Orleans, Louisiana.

They did help. In the weeks following the disaster the company donated $26 million to relief funds, hauled more than 2,100 truckloads of free merchandise to the victims, prepared 100,000 free meals for displaced people, dispensed free prescription medicines to evacuated people, and donated 150 computers to Red Cross emergency shelters in the disaster zones. Individual Wal-Mart workers also came to the rescue of afflicted people, converting a store into a shelter, commandeering bottled water for the residents of a retirement home, and giving away supplies in parking lots outside of the stores (Humes 2011, 98). For the first time in years, a spate of news stories praised the company for showing leadership and compassion for people in a difficult situation.

Inside the company, Katrina became the catalyzing event that launched Wal-Mart's sustainability initiative. Six weeks after the storm hit Louisiana and Mississippi, Wal-Mart CEO Lee Scott (2005), in a speech to all Wal-Mart employees, described the company's new sustainability initiative and explained its origins. In his words,

> there was one event that pushed us from a learning process into taking more aggressive action. I am sure many of you saw and remember the desperate images of Hurricane Katrina: entire neighborhoods under water, families waving for rescue from their rooftops, elderly men and women dying in the open from sickness and exposure. Katrina was one of the worst disasters in the history of the United States. But it also brought out the best in our company.... [O]ur entire company rallied and responded quickly and decisively. We responded by doing what we do best: We empowered our people and leveraged our presence and logistics to deliver the supplies that hurricane victims so desperately needed. Hurricane Katrina changed Wal-Mart forever. And it changed us for the better.

The response of Wal-Mart's workers to the storm catalyzed the company's decision to go green, but without the work before the storm with the environmental consultants it is hard to see how company officials could have made such a dramatic, large-scale commitment. While scientists at the time had not achieved consensus about the connection between intensified hurricanes during the last three decades of the twentieth century and global warming, many scientists and insurance company officials saw storms like Katrina as a harbinger of things to come with additional global warming. In this respect, Katrina symbolized what could happen to people if environmental problems like global warming went unattended. This diffuse understanding shared by both the consultants and company executives pre-dated Katrina and prompted the pre-Katrina discussions between company officials and consultants about how the company should respond to environmental questions. Katrina prompted a surge of attention to these issues, as focusing events do. It reshaped the agenda of the company's executives and, in so doing, provided the impetus to get Wal-Mart's Sustainability Initiative launched.

Even then, the Wal-Mart initiative still had a defensive environmentalist quality, with a focus on the company's public image and the tangible, near-term savings achieved through more efficient transportation and less packaging. In the following five years the initiative began to transform Wal-Mart's suppliers. When Wal-Mart officials insisted on greener products, the subsequent overhaul in the suppliers' production processes led to other, unrelated product innovations. For example, efforts to increase sustainable practices at the dairies that sold milk to Wal-Mart led to efforts to convert the waste on the farms into biofuels through the use of methane digesters (Humes 2011). In another effort, Wal-Mart began to work on the creation of a carbon index that would measure the ecological footprint (impact) of each product that it sold. These efforts reached beyond the organization and, over time, made Wal-Mart's initiative less defensive and more encompassing in its effects.

Wal-Mart may find it difficult to live up to some of the promises of its sustainability initiative. The large size of their stores requires locations outside of city centers that can be reached only by people in automobiles, and their long supply chains reach across the globe to unfamiliar suppliers who then send the products on long, energy-consuming trips to Wal-Mart distribution centers. These questions notwithstanding, the Wal-Mart initiative is instructive and significant in part because it demonstrates how historical events, in this case a single, cataclysmic event, can spur an institution with global reach to undertake important environmental reforms.

Conclusion: Focusing Events and the Historical Accumulation of Defensive Environmentalist Practices

It is important to recall that focusing events occur in a context marked by the historical accumulation of defensive environmentalist activities described earlier in this book. In each case these practices spread over time, spawned social movements devoted to their further spread, and raised questions about the global extent of their effects. Resource partitioning proceeded in suburbs, in the rain forests, out on coastal waters, in degraded dry forests, and along the semi-arid fringes of deserts. The conservation effects of partitioning could sometimes be seen in the surrounding region, extending even to the national scale, but at the global scale the effects of the increased conservation associated with the partitioning were difficult to see. The population losses occasioned by prolonged periods of below-replacement fertility are perhaps the most visible consequence of a more pervasive defensive environmentalist orientation.

A historically effective family planning movement has certainly spurred the declines in fertility, but the global population of humans continues to increase, so the eventual scale of the trend toward below-replacement fertility remains open to question. Organic agriculture and conservation agriculture have spread rapidly during the past thirty years, and both practices have given rise to social movements dedicated to their further spread. Nonetheless, organic agriculture remains a niche agricultural practice, and only most recently has conservation agriculture, a more limited set of practices, begun to gain acceptance among large farmers in diverse locales. Recycling has followed a similar trajectory of steady increases in frequency, but, for example, only recently has it begun, in combination with paperless technologies, to reduce the overall volume of paper use. Finally, while some of the advanced industrial societies have begun to show slowing rates or small absolute declines in energy use, the overall global pattern remains best summarized by Jevons paradox: increased efficiency of use coupled with an overall expansion in the volume of energy consumed.

Were these localized environmental practices the only dynamic at play in environmental reform efforts, the prognosis for making significant strides toward more sustainable societies would be poor. There is, however, another dynamic that, working in concert with defensive environmental practices, could at least theoretically produce moments of effective overall environmental reform. This chapter and the next chapter outline in largely theoretical terms how this second, more globalized dynamic might work.

While the affinity between focusing events and periods of accelerated, scaled-up political change is real, it can be overstated. Do the effects of focusing events in different parts of the world aggregate in the global media in a way that reorders political agendas and spurs change? In other words, do droughts in Australia and the American Southwest, coupled with intensified hurricanes and observations of sea ice loss in the Arctic Ocean, aggregate to have an effect that refocuses the global political agenda? The likelihood that these localized events will have an aggregated effect probably depends, as Pollan recognized, on the degree to which individuals and groups in the affected localities connect their suffering to a larger global cause like global warming. Government representatives are then more likely to take the event-initiated concerns to higher levels of governance. Recent historical trends and modeled projections both suggest that humans will experience more extreme weather events in the coming decades as the earth's atmosphere warms, so the effects of these events on politics at all scales of human life will probably increase (USEPA 2010; IPCC 2011; Coumou and Rahmstorf 2012).

The randomness inherent in coupled human and natural systems makes it particularly difficult to outline strong paths of cause and effect in these instances. For example, had Hurricane Katrina taken a path slightly farther to the east in late August of 2005, the storm surge from Katrina might not have topped New Orleans' levees; the hurricane would have caused less damage, and the refocusing moment might not have occurred at Wal-Mart. This scenario only underscores the point that, while there is an affinity between focusing events, altruistic environmentalism, and scaled-up efforts at environmental reform, the association could be stronger. Its strength depends in part on sweeping, but contingent, transformations in governance that sometimes follow from destabilizing events and could, at least theoretically, produce a sustainable development state. The next chapter addresses this link between focusing events and governance.

10

A Sustainable Development State?

> As usual in the history of the human relation to the natural environment, effective countermeasures began to be taken only after an immense, undeniable disaster had occurred.
>
> Warren Dean (1995, 347)

Introduction

Spokespeople for the worldwide environment movement have begun in recent years to speak in more apocalyptic, militarized terms about global warming. Their language has turned apocalyptic because they see so little progress toward a sustainable society. Increasingly, environmentalists talk about a "war on emissions" or a "war on climate change" (Cohen 2011). Some call for converting to emissions-free technologies with "wartime speed" (Brown 2006, 143). Others cite the mobilization of the United States in the year after the Pearl Harbor attack as a relevant example for combating greenhouse gas emissions (Baer 2008). Another called for a "Manhattan Project for the environment" (Kammen 2006). Still others investigate the "environmental politics of sacrifice" (Maniates and Meyer 2010) and imagine an "environmental war economy," observing that "the sacrifices made by ordinary people during wartime are the beginnings of a framework and a plan to meet the challenges of global warming" (Simms 2001).

Environmentalists use military terms because they seem to think that states, with their capacity to make war, are the only organizations capable of carrying out the massive social transformations necessary to make societies sustainable. Only states, or perhaps churches in centuries past, have had the potential for becoming legitimate encompassing organizations with the power to make societies sustainable (Chang 1999). States can impose politically difficult tax increases and commandeer large areas from resistant landowners for the production of renewable energy because catastrophic events, such as wars, strengthen states politically. The large magnitude of the disaster, as Warren Dean observed, makes a case for concerted corrective action, usually by the state. The late Charles Tilly argued that "war makes the state and the state makes war" (Tilly 1975, 42). States grow stronger when faced with external threats because "under conditions of systemic vulnerability, only coherent bureaucracies and broad public-private linkages could produce the revenues to ... secure state survival" (Doner et al. 2005, 356).

Faced with disasters that represent tangible and imminent threats to human society, people acknowledge the need for transformative changes (Klein 2007), which in turn creates political opportunities for fundamental change (Meyer 2004).[1] To this end, political leaders commit the state to a "hegemonic project" involving a single-minded commitment to achieve a particular end (Gramsci 1971; Pempel 1999). To address the challenges of global warming, the heads of states would commit the states' resources to sustainable development, making them "sustainable development states." Their mission would be to "meet the needs of the present without compromising the ability of future generations to meet their own needs" (WCED 1987). These needs would include economic growth, environmental preservation, and equitable socio-economic outcomes (Barbier 1987). A sustainable development state would, presumably, promote these three goals within the context of a hegemonic project organized around sustainability. The hegemonic project, coupled with political changes, would spur changes in cultural toolkits and make climate denialism more difficult to practice. At the same time, this

---

[1] This argument shares, with Klein's work (2007), an appreciation of the authoritarian moments that disasters create, but it dissents from her view of political elites as instruments of economic elites who want to practice disaster capitalism. The argument made here presumes that states and political leaders have more political autonomy and more variable economic relations with elites. This argument also dissents from the view that environmental "shocks" provide a political opening for free-market capitalism. It is certainly true that focusing events unsettle the existing order, which facilitates political change, but environmental challenges, with their focuses on the deterioration of common goods, call attention to the need for a stronger central authority, not free-market liberalism. In that sense, Klein's hypothesized sequence of disaster followed by exploitative disaster capitalism would not seem likely to characterize system-shaking environmental crises.

overarching goal could increase the tendency of officials in sustainable development states to "see like a state" (Scott 1998) and push for a uniform set of reforms across a wide range of local communities. Indeed, one could argue that an insistence on this kind of uniformity might be necessary to make substantial strides toward sustainability. If so, the human costs of implementing a sustainable development state could be high.

As noted earlier in this chapter, the same focusing events that strengthen the state often weaken other centers of power in society by destroying wealth or discrediting political strategies. By weakening potential loci of resistance, disasters create political opportunities that make it easier for the state or associated elites to accomplish their own ends (Grabowski 1994). Larger-scale focusing events do have the potential to overturn or radically rearrange unequal social orders. If a focusing event does not, by itself, destroy concentrations of wealth, then states, in order to finance responses to the disaster, may tax concentrated wealth and, in so doing, reduce economic and political inequalities. Focusing events and the political reaction to them may in this sense represent a process of creative destruction (Schumpeter 1942) that clears out a sclerotic institutional order of special interests and allows for the creation of an encompassing coalition that would support a sustainable development state (Olson 1982). The atmosphere of crisis surrounding these political changes makes it easier for former antagonists to form encompassing coalitions and agree upon a common course of action (Lee 1993).

Where do focusing events come from? After a class discussion about East Asian developmental states as models for sustainable development states and the role of war in creating developmental states, one Rutgers University undergraduate remarked that the earth would have to be invaded by aliens before we would see the widespread creation of sustainable development states! The focusing events that would mobilize people around a hegemonic project devoted to sustainability would most likely take the form of multiple disasters with socially constructed components, events such as droughts or storms related to climate change that affect large numbers of people in cities. Certainly the ecological and social dimensions of globalization could affect the severity of focusing events by increasing the scale of climatic disturbances and the size of the affected human settlements (Perrow 2007). These large-scale events would spur a mobilization to combat climate change through an encompassing organization such as a national government. The commitment by activists and officials to this hegemonic project, at least initially, would represent "altruistic environmentalism," a dedication to environmentally friendly actions with little expectation of personal gain.

The joint commitments to collective action by leaders and local residents also emerge in the absence of large-scale focusing events, but they do so in more circuitous and surprising ways. The history of the Gal Oya irrigation project in Sri Lanka, recounted in Chapter 9, illustrates this alternative dynamic. Government and foreign aid officials provided the initial impetus for change with their proposal to renovate the irrigation system. The proposal called for the assistance of smallholders in repairing and cleaning the canals. The Gal Oya smallholders responded enthusiastically. Chronic difficulties with obtaining water for their crops had made them willing to work on the canals, even though they did not have a history of working together. The emergence and promotion of effective leaders by the project's community organizers and other farmers played an important role in the success of the program and its expansion from a pilot project to a large-scale renovation effort covering 25,000 hectares (Uphoff 1992).

While the social logic for post-disaster mobilizations should be clear, historical examples of these kinds of mobilizations should exist if they represent real possibilities for addressing environmental challenges. The Maldives, a small, low-lying island state threatened with inundation from rising sea levels, offered the only existing example of a sustainable development state (Hadhazy 2009) until February 2012, when a coup ousted the democratically elected president of the country. The Maldives government had adopted the hegemonic project of becoming carbon-neutral by 2020 after a series of models projected the complete inundation of the islands through warming-induced sea level rises during the twenty-first century. For descriptions about how larger-scale sustainable development states might operate, there are two imperfect historical examples, one from the East Asian developmental states and the other from the Brazilian state's recent experience curbing deforestation in the Amazon basin. They provide glimpses of the ways in which sustainable development states would govern environmentally stressed societies and negotiate with one another about international environmental treaties.

The East Asian Developmental State: A Model for the Sustainable Development State?

During the period immediately following World War II, a distinctive political economic dynamic began to characterize Japan. The practices integral to this dynamic constituted the first historical instance of what Chalmers Johnson (1982) and others came to call the "developmental state." One analyst (Kohli 1999, 134) described it in the following terms:

> A bureaucratized and penetrating authoritarian state with clear, growth oriented goals, armed with a panoply of economic instruments and allied with propertied but against laboring social classes, is the stuff of which transformative power in the hands of the state is made.

Developmental states, more than any other democratic political regime since World War II, demonstrated an ability to achieve radical transformations in the societies that they governed. Policymakers in developmental states, working in concert with economic elites and less closely with workers, managed to build urban and industrial economies within a single generation during the second half of the twentieth century. These concentrated increases in economic production vaulted all of the developmental states into the ranks of the world's most affluent nations. To be sure, the East Asian elites who directed these collective efforts varied in their immediate circumstances and benefited from extraordinary levels of external political support. As frontline states in the Cold War, these governments received large amounts of military assistance. As industrial latecomers that essentially copied technologies developed in the West, their economies were able to industrialize at a rapid pace (Wong 2011). These facilitating conditions notwithstanding, the magnitude and the rapidity of the East Asian societal transformations still seem startling.

Why did the laboring classes submit to this kind of political order? Woo-Cumings (1999, 20) offers two reasons for popular acceptance of the developmental state. In her words, "the power of the developmental state grows both out of the barrel of a gun and its ability to convince the population of its political, economic, and moral mandate." The legitimacy of the state's mandate, in turn, had several sources. First, external threats, embodied in cataclysmic wartime events, played an important role in the political formation of developmental states. The Japanese developmental state emerged out of a population that never fully demobilized following defeat during World War II. In Taiwan, the Kuomintang refugees from the Chinese civil war considered themselves to be at war with the Communist regime on the mainland during the 1950s and the 1960s, so their regime called for wartime discipline from rank-and-file Taiwanese. The South Koreans faced a continuing threat from North Korea after the Korean War. All of these states received military assistance from the

United States. The other societies that have been characterized as "developmental states," Austria in the 1960s, Finland in the 1950s and 1960s, and Israel during the second half of the twentieth century, also occupied precarious geopolitical positions during the periods in which the developmental state model seems most applicable to them (Levi-Faur 1998; Doner et al. 2005).

Political elites addressed the widespread apprehension among their citizens by articulating a hegemonic project designed to reduce the geopolitical threats faced by their societies. The elites argued that their societies, as "late developers" in difficult geopolitical circumstances, had an urgent need to "catch up" with the more affluent, economically powerful nations of the West. A country's position as a "late developer" justified intervention by the state to expedite economic development (Gerschenkron 1962; Woo-Cumings 1999). State officials committed resources to fostering economic development on the premise that rapid economic development would in turn strengthen their nation's geopolitical position. Once accepted by businessmen, workers, and politicians, this shared commitment to economic development served as a "binding agent," bringing people together in a collective effort to increase their productive capacity in a short period of time (Hirschman 1958, 8).

Developmental states have compiled their most impressive records of achievement when they have tapped into and given expression to widely shared sentiments among their citizens. The seemingly pivotal role of wars in fostering developmental states underscores this point. For the hegemonic projects of developmental states to produce results, norms about collective action in the national interest have to be very salient in the larger population. Otherwise, citizens will not support the sacrificial actions (such as paying taxes at high rates) necessary to achieve the goals of the hegemonic project. Because success in wars demands these self-sacrificing actions, clothing a hegemonic project in wartime rhetoric prepares the ground for the sacrifices required by the state's project. The association between the experience of war and the strength of these norms of collective sacrifice was underscored during the Asian economic crisis of the late 1990s when some South Korean citizens offered to give their personal reserves of gold and foreign currency to the national government to shore up its finances (Polidano 2001). The wartime experiences, coupled with post-war land reforms, destroyed the wealth of Korea's rural elites, one potential source of resistance to the state's hegemonic project. In this way, the egalitarian effects of wartime devastation probably strengthened the "common fate" response among Koreans.

A similar dynamic occurred in the other Asian developmental states. The destruction of wealth caused by wars (World War II, the Chinese Civil War, and the Korean War), coupled with post-war land reforms, eliminated the landlord class and won the allegiance of peasants, creating an egalitarian social context within which the East Asian states could more easily pursue their hegemonic projects. In this sense, focusing events contributed to the creation of strong states in weak societies, a setting that maximized the states' efficacy. Politicians maximized these probabilities through discursive strategies. The nationalist rhetoric used to present a hegemonic project makes it difficult for potential opponents of the state's project to resist it openly (Woo-Cumings 1999).

Strong state–society links have made developmental states more efficacious in a quite different way. Peter Evans (1995) has argued that regulatory regimes are most effective when officials exhibit a kind of "embedded autonomy" in their decision making about economic policies. State officials have to exhibit autonomy from organized interest groups, something that officials, selected through meritocratic processes and empowered by a strong moral mandate such as their nation's survival, can do. Otherwise, officials will have a difficult time rewarding enterprises that make the most progress as opposed to those that exercise the most political influence. To do an effective job of implementing regulations, officials must also be embedded in the industry, so they can see the impacts of programs on productive activities and make the necessary adjustments. The most common program undertaken by the developmental state involves subsidies from the state to enterprises that agree to meet certain production criteria (Onis 1991). Embedded officials are most likely to give accurate assessments of the subsidies' effects at the same time that their embeddedness increases the chances that they will be captured by the regulated. Embeddedness also increases the chances that the reformers' proposals for transformations will acknowledge local social conditions. These regulatory regimes do not promise social equality. Although the strongest developmental states have emerged in relatively egalitarian societies (South Korea, Japan), government interventions in industrial activities have tended to favor some groups over other groups (Pempel 1999).

The efficacy of a developmental state still depends in large part on its ability to reach ordinary citizens and enlist them in the larger cause. In this regard, it is worth remembering that the defensive environmentalist behaviors generated by modular succession stem from the same scaling-up of human societies that produces more tightly coupled societies and an increased incidence of focusing events. The efficacy of a sustainable development state could therefore depend to a considerable degree on its ability to enlist defensive environmentalists in the state's hegemonic project of sustainability. This conclusion raises questions about the ways in which interactions between leaders and citizens advance or retard the state's hegemonic project.

Many of these interactions occur in the context of campaigns launched by government officials to achieve subsidiary goals. During the 1970s and 1980s the South Korean government launched campaigns to revitalize rural areas, save energy, and solicit blood donations. The campaigns have often unfolded in a corporatist way.[2] The New Villages campaign, designed to revitalize rural areas, involved cooperative endeavors between federal and local officials. When developmental states have operated in a corporatist mold, their efficacy has increased (Vartiainen 1999), presumably because the state-sanctioned sectoral associations both convey popular sentiments to the central state and oversee the implementation of state policies in localities (Wiarda 1996). Autonomy at the local level, subject to monitoring by the sectoral associations, would, at least in theory, promote efficacious implementation of sustainability initiatives, including the spread of innovations from government-supported research and development efforts (Vartiainen 1999). To implement state policies, activists might build on local initiatives, perhaps first created to advance a defensive environmentalist agenda that emerged in response to globalization (Hess 2009). If local groups achieve this kind of "accountable autonomy" in a corporatist structure (Fung 2004), then a kind of political remodularization or decoupling will have occurred (Perrow 2008). This kind of local autonomy might prevent sustainable development states from trying to push for local uniformity in ways that would raise the human costs of sustainability initiatives.

All three of these links between governors and the governed – the widely shared norms about the importance of collective action, the embedded and yet autonomous social positions of state officials in industries, and the corporatist arrangements founded on the accountable autonomy of local activists – serve the self-interests of political elites in developmental states. These institutional arrangements increase the likelihood that the state will work for rather than against its popular base, so these links should prolong the elites' tenure in office (Polidano

---

[2] Some of the best known corporatist arrangements in the twentieth century, in Franco's Spain for example, had a "top down" emphasis, with the sectoral associations serving largely as one-way conduits for information and enforcement of the central state's policies. In theory, there is no reason why a corporatist structure could not serve as a two-way conduit for information and policymaking, as, for example, in Fung's (2004) work.

2001; Doner et al. 2005). At the same time, sustainable developmental states would most likely exhibit to some extent the common tendency to "see like a state" (Scott 1998) and in this way try to implement programs that ignore local histories and, in so doing, alienate and oppress local populations.

Historically, developmental states have waxed and waned in their ability to get things done (Minns 2001). In South Korea, the simultaneous organization of both large-scale industrial enterprises and economic policymaking apparatuses in the 1960s made possible the accelerated rates of investment and economic growth between 1965 and 1980. During the 1960s and the 1970s, the developmental states in Japan, South Korea, and Taiwan poured funds into selected industries and achieved very high rates of economic growth. All three countries achieved annual rates of growth in GDP per capita of between 8 and 10 percent for a substantial number of years between 1960 and 1980, when the rest of the world was averaging 2 to 3 percent growth in GDP per year (Heston, Summers, and Aten 2011). By the 1990s, growth rates had slowed in the three countries and the apparatuses of the developmental states had lost some of their effectiveness.

In the words of Peter Evans, echoing Marx, "when developmental states succeed, they call forth their own grave diggers" (Evans 1995, 229). For example, during the initial phase of the Japanese development state, export-oriented manufacturing enterprises depended on state subsidies to finance research and development programs. This dependence allowed state bureaucrats to reward firms for superior performance relative to other firms. Over time, as the export-oriented enterprises grew in size, they became more capable of financing their own research and development programs, and the state lost one of its most effective tools for influencing the direction of technological development in industrial enterprises (Polidano 2001). Similarly, as the catastrophic focusing events of World War II and the Korean War receded over time in the memories of citizens, the hegemonic project slowly lost its grip on the popular imagination in ways consistent with issue attention cycles. As the hegemonic project fades, the state loses its ability to persuade people to contribute to the common good. Still, the experience with the developmental state can leave a powerful legacy. Think of the patriotic response, mentioned earlier, of Korean citizens to the currency crisis in the late 1990s. This outpouring of concern for the common good seems intelligible in a post-developmental state society like South Korea, but it is difficult to imagine this level of concern in societies that do not have the legacy of successful collective efforts orchestrated by a developmental state.

The preceding discussion of the developmental state presumes that, at least in its essentials, this model of rapid economic development can be generalized to other places and, for our purposes, to other issues. Woo-Cumings (1999, 41) thinks that the historical experience of the developmental state is generalizable, provided that a nation shows a high level of commitment to transforming its economy. Several analysts have recently argued that the trajectory and tools of economic development in China over the past two decades bear some resemblance to the political economic dynamics that accompanied the emergence of developmental states in other East Asian societies (Baek 2005). The range of societies described as developmental states indicates that it has not been an exclusively East Asian phenomenon. In addition to Japan, South Korea, and Taiwan, regimes as diverse as Singapore (Pereira 2008), Israel (Levi-Faur 1998), Austria (Vartiainen 1999), Finland (Vartiainen 1999), France after World War II (Loriaux 1999), and nineteenth-century Prussia (Chang 1999) have all been described as developmental states. Certainly, the idea seems generalizable in its essentials. People band together to deal with a common threat, and the state, the focal point for most previous efforts at collective action, becomes the "catalytic agent" for organizing new efforts (Woo-Cumings 1999).

Portions of this system are already in place. Through targeted subsidies a wide range of governments in the affluent countries now try to stimulate research, outreach, and innovation around renewable fuels (MacNeil and Paterson 2012). Many of the new programs in sustainable development states would build off of earlier successful efforts at political mobilization. States, for example, could create "energy-grant universities" modeled after the land-grant universities created almost 150 years ago during the American Civil War. The land-grant universities did research on a wide range of issues of concern to the predominantly agricultural population of the United States, with the intention of extending these findings to the nation's farmers. Like the land-grant universities, energy-grant universities would serve as a conduit from laboratories to end users for new sources of energy (Falkowski and Goodman 2009).

The Link between Brazil's Domestic and International Environmental Politics: Deforestation and a Global Forest Compact

Does a new emphasis on sustainability in domestic politics have implications for international environmental compacts? A comparison of domestic and international climate change policies in Japan, the Netherlands, and the United States underscores the close link between the two (Fisher 2004), so, theoretically, a shift in domestic environmental politics in particularly influential nations could alter the probability of reaching international environmental accords. The recent history of Brazilian forest policy offers a suggestive example about the repercussions of sustainable domestic policies on international environmental negotiations.

The Brazilian state cannot be considered a developmental state, and it is certainly not a sustainable development state, but Brazilian politicians engage in several political practices that are also common in developmental states. Like developmental states, the Brazilian regime has demonstrated authoritarian tendencies, especially during periods of military rule in the twentieth century. Like the leaders of other large developing countries, Brazilian political figures have long had aspirations that their country would "catch up" economically with the wealthier countries (Fajnzylber 1990) and become a major force in institutions of international governance such as the United Nations, the IMF, and the World Bank. Like the developmental states, the Brazilian government has long pursued interventionist policies in more concerted and systematic ways than the governments of its Latin American neighbors, but the state's effectiveness as an instrument of policymaking has been hampered by patrimonial tendencies in staffing decisions (Evans 1995; Roett 1999). These attributes of state policymaking have all influenced the course of forest policymaking in Brazil during the past quarter century.

The rates of deforestation in the Brazilian Amazon have varied dramatically over the past twenty-five years (see Figure 10.1). They increased throughout the 1980s, driven in part by large-scale government colonization programs. After a decline during the early 1990s, the pace of deforestation rose in 1995, followed by another decline and a rise to another peak in 2004. Since 2005, the rates of deforestation have dropped sharply. The fluctuations in rates of deforestation during the past two decades reflect variations in the magnitude of two familiar, but opposed, forces: the globalization of markets for agricultural commodities and the attempts by states, indigenous peoples, and environmentalists to prevent the destruction of old-growth forests by people who profit from the global flows of commodities.

The circumstances surrounding the 1995 increase in deforestation rates indicated a change in the forces driving Brazilian deforestation. Uncertainties generated by cloud cover in the remote-sensed images used to calculate the 1995 rise in deforestation rates have raised questions about the magnitude of the increase. It seems to have stemmed in part from the

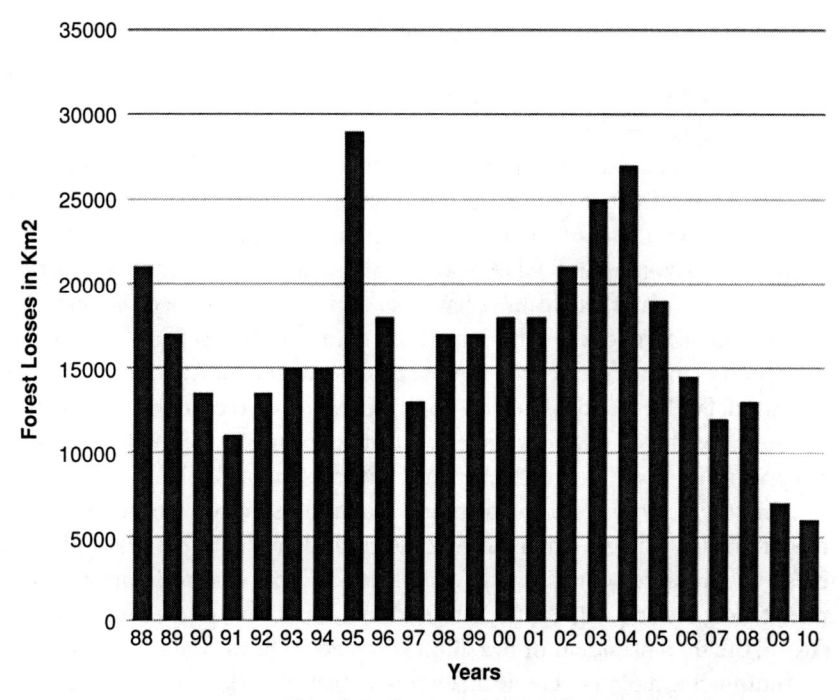

FIGURE 10.1. Trends in Forest Loss, Brazil, 1988–2010

government's *Plano Real* economic overhaul that reformed its finances and changed currencies, replacing the *cruzeiro* with the *real*. In 1994–5, the value of the *real* increased against the dollar and interest rates in Brazil plummeted. The low interest rates, in turn, sparked a surge in applications for loans from Brazilian farmers, some of which went for land clearing and the purchase of cattle (Laurance et al. 2001). The historical coincidence of changes in interest rates and changes in deforestation rates suggests that the chief drivers of Amazonian deforestation had shifted by the mid-1990s from government-sponsored colonization programs to large-scale commercial enterprises that produced for global markets and financed their land clearing with loans.

The same period saw a shift in the parties responsible for most road building in the Brazilian Amazon. During the 1980s, the federal and state governments constructed most of the roads. Beginning in the 1990s, loggers, ranchers, and other groups of investors built most of the roads, in almost all instances as parts of plans to log or farm lands covered with old-growth forests (Arima et al. 2005). With the mid-1990s surge in deforestation, international criticism of the forest destruction swelled, and

Fernando Enrique Cardoso, then president of Brazil, pledged in response to preserve more of the rain forest as parks (Manning 1998).

Brazilian deforestation rates then declined for several years before rising, aided this time by a now devalued *real*, to a new high in 2004 (see Figure 10.1). This second surge seems connected to globalization-induced market pressures to expand the production of beef and soybeans. In 2000, Brazil finally eradicated hoof and mouth disease in its herds in the southern Amazon basin (USDA 2000). This achievement opened up European consumer markets to Brazilian beef at a time when the discovery of bovine spongiform encephalopathy (BSE, mad cow disease) had increased European demand for the free-range cattle produced on Amazon ranches (Nepstad, Stickler, and Almeida 2006b). Growers also cleared large areas of forest for the cultivation and export of soybeans to feed Chinese and European livestock. At the same time, middle-class Brazilians increased in number. They wanted to eat more beef and use more wood to build bigger houses. The growth in both domestic and international demand for these commodities contributed to substantial increases in deforestation rates through 2004. Again, the international criticism of Brazil increased. Again, the then president of Brazil, Luiz Inacio da Silva (Lula), responded by announcing a plan to create an extensive belt of parks across the northern Amazon (Environment News Service 2005). By 2009, between 44 and 51 percent of the lands in the Brazilian Amazon had a protected status (Nepstad et al. 2009; Mongabay 2011a), a very high proportion of protected lands in comparison with other countries. While park boundaries have not prevented the selective logging of some park lands, they have largely prevented the deforestation of lands for agricultural expansion (Asner et al. 2009).

In both 1995 and 2005 the release of new information on deforestation rates became focusing events that spurred changes in rain forest preservation policy. In addition to park expansion, the Brazilian government had attempted to restrain deforestation by establishing laws stipulating the proportion of their land that farmers could clear. In 1965, after an international outcry about the loss of tropical forests, the military government decreed that farmers could not deforest more than 50 percent of the lands on their properties. In 1996, after the rates of deforestation had again risen to high levels, the president increased the requirement for farm forests to 80 percent of the land area on farms (Alston and Mueller 2007).

In 2004, when the deforestation rates again approached alarming levels, the federal government changed the way it implemented regulations about forests on farms. Government officials began examining satellite imagery every two weeks in order to detect illegal burning or clearing in plots larger than 25 hectares. When state officials discovered clusters of illegal clearing and burning, they imprisoned some operators, banned agricultural loans to others, and pressured merchants to stop purchasing illegally harvested timber (Nepstad et al. 2009). By 2011, the federal government had imposed credit restrictions on farmers in fifty Brazilian municipalities (MMA 2011). A large majority of the Brazilian public (79 percent in 2011) supported the government's policy (Mongabay 2011b).

The specter of losing access to credit proved to be an effective deterrent to further clearing of old-growth rain forest (Camara 2010). In this context, feedlot operations for Brazilian cattle grew rapidly (Macedo et al. 2012). International pressure on Brazilian soybean growers through Greenpeace, leading to a two-year moratorium on the clearing of rainforest lands for soybean cultivation, also proved to be effective (Greenpeace 2011). The economic context for the new policies included an appreciating *real* coupled with, after a short crash in global soy prices in 2005–6, increases in the prices of agricultural products in global markets. These two trends had offsetting effects on Brazilian farmers. Rising agricultural prices encouraged agricultural expansion, whereas the appreciating *real* discouraged it (Richards et al. 2012). By 2010, forest losses were only 25 percent of the losses in 2004 (see Figure 10.1).[3,4]

Given that tropical forests sequester carbon at much higher rates than temperate forests and that Brazil contains the world's largest expanse of tropical forest, its representatives occupied a very influential position in the global climate negotiations in Copenhagen and Cancún in 2009 and 2010, particularly with respect to agreements about payments for carbon sequestration in forests. Unlike the Copenhagen negotiations over limiting industrial greenhouse gas emissions that descended into acrimony and produced no more than platitudes in the final communiqué, the REDD+ (Reducing Deforestation and Degradation) negotiations about sequestering carbon in forests produced a global agreement. The accord, later confirmed at the 2010 Cancún meeting, established a system of payments to tropical countries, and through them to landowners, for sequestering carbon in the forests on their lands.

---

[3] Giovana Espindola and Douglas Morton, personal communications.
[4] The variations in the proportion of protected lands in the Amazon forest stem from different definitions about what constitutes a "protected forest."

The Brazilian delegates had some reservations about the initial form of the REDD+ proposal because they preferred a single government-controlled REDD+ fund rather than a market-based cap-and-trade mechanism for REDD+ payments. They also knew that, given their position as the preeminent tropical forest nation, they could block any global REDD+ agreement if they chose to do so (Martinent and Christovam 2009). They also probably felt a desire to exert leadership on this issue, in part out of a desire to project Brazilian power on a global stage and in part out of pride at their recent record of success in controlling deforestation. In addition, several state governments in the Amazon region, such as Acre, wanted to implement agreements similar to REDD+ with regional governments outside of Brazil. With this mixture of motives, the Brazilian delegation went ahead and supported REDD+ at Copenhagen and Cancún (Mongabay 2009). Other developing countries followed their lead, and negotiators reached agreement on a global forest compact. This historical episode suggests that the adoption of sustainable development policies in federal and provincial governments at home, as might be expected from a sustainable development state, also increases the likelihood that the national state will support the adoption of substantively similar environmental compacts abroad.

11

Conclusion

Defensive Environmentalists, Sustainable Development States, and Global Environmental Reform

> The Johannesburg [meeting] was about rural Africa and the people that globalization left behind. For... [them] "environment" means the food they eat, the water they drink, the medicines they take, and the houses they live in.
>
> David Kaimowitz (2002)

The Argument

Figure 11.1 situates the sustainable development state in an overall model of environmental reform. The figure summarizes in a visual way the argument developed in this book. Historically, the argument begins with the tremendous growth in the volume and scope of human activity during the past two centuries. In response to the adverse, long-term environmental trends generated by the scaling up of human activities, people have adopted defensive environmental practices in an attempt to exert control over their immediate environments. They have partitioned natural resources, limited their fertility, eaten contaminant-free (organic) foods, recycled waste, and made personal efforts to increase energy efficiency. Slogans capture the common element in these activities. Organic consumers endorse a "not in my body ethic," and suburban homeowners support "not in my backyard" groups. People undertake these activities because, in industrialized societies, defensive environmental practices produce tangible, short-term benefits for individuals and households.

Defensive environmental practices accumulate independently of the large-scale, crisis-driven environmental initiatives undertaken by nation-states. At this writing, new clusters of defensive environmentalist activity

198 *Defensive Environmentalists and the Dynamics of Global Reform*

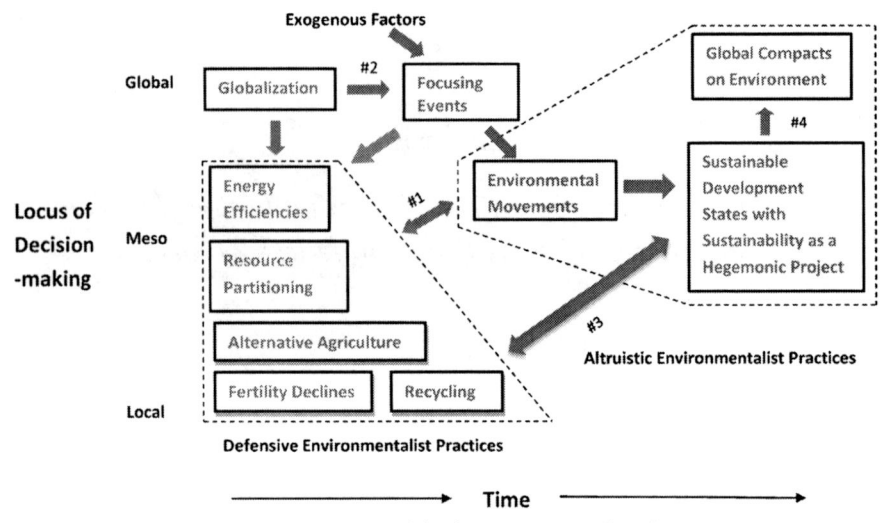

FIGURE 11.1. A Model of Environmental Reform

have emerged among South African farmers and the residents of rural communities in the northeastern United States. They have mobilized to resist drilling companies that want to extract natural gas from underground shale by fracking (a form of drilling that chews up rock formations below ground) without regard for the effects of fracking on the quality of ground water. At the same time, farmers in the American Great Plains have organized to stop the construction of a large pipeline (the Keystone Pipeline) across their lands out of a concern that oil spills from the pipeline could contaminate their ground water. These expressions of defensive environmentalist sentiments have occurred at the same time that altruistic environmentalist concerns about climate change have declined among the American public.

Focusing events should, in theory, disrupt this "business as usual" dynamic. These events originate in a globalized, ever more tightly coupled natural and human system (path #2 in Figure 11.1), and their appearance persuades significant numbers of people of the grave systemic consequences that humans face if they do not curb their unsustainable practices. On a personal level, people take action, presumably intensifying defensive environmental actions, such as recycling and preserving local forests, at the same time that they renew their support for large-scale environmental initiatives. With these shifts, the political climate for initiating a hegemonic project surrounding sustainability improves, and politicians create a sustainable development state. It becomes a vehicle for pursuing environmental reforms by extracting sacrifices from enterprises and individuals in pursuit of a common good. Officials of the sustainable development state work with industrialists, perhaps in a corporatist framework, to reduce greenhouse gas emissions and energy consumption. Other government programs provide subsidies and guidance for defensive environmental initiatives such as recycling, energy conservation, and organic agriculture. Overall, a pattern of interactive governance (Kooiman 2008) prevails in which people at all scales of society in a defensive and sometimes more altruistic capacity interact with one another in governing the use of natural resources and in creating higher, global-scale systems of governance (path #4 in Figure 11.1).

Under "business as usual" conditions, defensive environmentalists may help to perpetuate environmental movement organizations through continued membership (path #1 in Figure 11.1). The presence of these organizations and associated activists can, after a focusing event, be pivotal in exploiting the political moment to set in motion a hegemonic "sustainability" project. While the activists in these efforts may exhibit an altruistic orientation, the political bases for their hegemonic project are often among citizens with predominantly local involvements. The commitment to collective action among ordinary citizens must be clear to politicians at the apex of the political pyramid (path #3 in Figure 11.1) if they are to advocate for large-scale societal transformations (Pollan 2008). Similarly, implementation of new policies by locals may not occur if national leaders do not demonstrate a commitment to change (Uphoff 1992). These dual commitments could occur under a wide range of conditions, but they are most likely to emerge in the immediate aftermath of an environmental catastrophe that demonstrates the unsustainable and destabilizing bases of the global economy.

Viewed from this perspective, questions about the relative efficacy of local environmental actions compared to national policies present us with a false choice. We need both. Local actions, especially in the aftermath of some catastrophic events, send a message to politicians that they need to commit to hegemonic projects of sustainable development. Large-scale reforms from a sustainable development state send a return message to local residents and contribute to a virtual environmentalism, where governments create situations in which people choose the sustainable course of action, whether conscious of it or not (Bell 2009). In the terms of a frequently heard phrase, defensive environmental actions do represent "drops in a bucket," but political elites recognize, especially in the aftermath of destabilizing events, that the drops will eventually fill the bucket, so they push for environmental reforms.

Given the political difficulties surrounding attempts to enact comprehensive government programs to reduce greenhouse gas emissions, it is only reasonable to ask how focusing events might produce the cultural changes that would provide a mandate for a hegemonic project surrounding sustainability. One can foresee this kind of shift in popular sentiment in circumstances that recall "Romer's rule." A. S. Romer, a twentieth-century ecologist, argued that many of the most important evolutionary changes had the effect of allowing the adapting organism to continue to pursue a previous way of life. So, fish first developed bony limbs when they had to travel more frequently in a drying climate between ponds of water where they could continue to swim (Allaby 2004). The analogous pattern with humans would have people mobilizing for change when they see a previously prized way of life under threat. This line of reasoning would explain the actions of the *campesinos* in southern Mexico referred to in the quote that prefaces this book (Womack 1969). It would also accord with defensive environmental practices detailed in the preceding pages. Finally, this understanding of human responses would be consistent with prospect theory, in which humans show more concern with prospective losses than with prospective gains (Kahneman and Tversky 1979). In this instance, people would mobilize to combat climate change when it threatens to destroy the affluence achieved through industrialization during the past two centuries.

Taken together, these dynamics recall Kingsley Davis's description of the causes for the dramatic declines in Japanese fertility during the 1950s. Rich and poor Japanese "responded in every manner then known to some powerful stimulus" (Davis 1963, 349). The citizens in a sustainable development state would do the same thing, so a polycentric approach to reducing emissions, both in neighborhoods and in national capitals, would emerge (Ostrom 2010). Implementation of this approach would certainly be easier if a corporatist structure facilitated communications between high-level policymakers and local decision makers. In effect, a corporatist structure would unite defensive environmentalists in communities with altruistic environmentalists at the political apex of a sustainable development state. Accountable autonomy and a selective remodularization or decoupling of CNH systems would then allow for the full exploration of the many avenues for change described by Davis.

The reflexive quality of CNHs, run by leaders who amend their policies, may incline them to partial collapses, not the wholesale collapses envisaged in models of the adaptive cycle constructed by resilience theorists (Holling, Gunderson, and Ludwig 2002). Nodes of defensive environmental activity such as farmers' markets might provide the institutional infrastructure for subsequent decoupling efforts, but, as the preceding case studies of defensive environmentalists make clear, these activities are unlikely to grow in the absence of initial support from social movements and sympathetic government authorities. For this reason, selective decoupling is most likely to occur in a context marked by a strong sustainable development state with a clearly articulated hegemonic project of sustainability. Otherwise, people might frame the focusing events and global warming in quite different terms, perhaps in fatalistic "will of God" terms, and decline to join efforts at environmental reform.[1] Still others, with preferential access to decision makers and economic interests in the status quo, could halt the reforms, as occurred in the summer of 2011 in Indonesia with Rimba Raya, the country's first REDD+ project (Fogarty 2011).

If citizens mobilize similarly across societies in response to the same focusing events, then their representatives in international organizations may be able to move collectively toward sustainable development. These moments of reform are most likely to occur if international environmental organizations are poised to push for reform in the immediate aftermath of focusing events. Timely political pressure by inclusive coalitions of environmentalists could culminate in legislation that resets international economic incentives in a more sustainable direction.

While the creation of the new rules and institutions may occur precipitously in the aftermath of focusing events, the implementation of reforms in subsequent years could represent more of a "hard slog" than a "leapfrog" (Rock et al. 2009). Consistent with issue attention cycles (Downs 1972; Jones and Baumgartner 2005) and the historical patterns with developmental states (Minns 2001), the salience of the mandate for sustainable development states would wax and wane historically, as anticipated in the political scientists' model of punctuated equilibria (Repetto 2006). This perspective on the coupled natural and human conditions that generate moments of environmental reform has an open-ended quality to it. Because inherently unpredictable historical events play an important role in creating moments of reform, the timing of reforms remains uncertain (Sewell 2005).

Sustainable developmental states are also likely to compile an uneven record in achieving the three goals of sustainable development efforts. In particular, it seems unlikely that they will achieve the equitable dimension in the manner anticipated by theorists. Given the preferential access to state subsidies enjoyed by high-performing industrial groups and the political priority that officials placed on suppressing restive workers, developmental states have often had unequal effects across economic sectors and classes (Pempel 1999). The larger set of historical events involving focusing events and developmental states did have unanticipated equity-inducing effects. The wars destroyed wealth, and the developmental states used the dire circumstances to justify levying high taxes on the remaining concentrations of wealth. In this manner, the catalytic events and subsequent state actions produced more equitable societies by destroying wealth among the rich rather than creating wealth among the poor.

The heads of long-established development assistance agencies and prominent environmental NGOs have come in recent years to recognize the defensive–altruistic distinction in environmental practices, and they have tried to build it into their efforts to mitigate greenhouse gas emissions. Their new emphasis on programs to eliminate black carbon and ozone has both a defensive, close to home, appeal and a global, altruistic appeal. Black carbon is a primary component in particulates that cause serious health problems for residents living near polluting manufacturing plants and for cooks tending fires in the kitchens of poor rural households. These substances also contribute to global warming, so campaigns to reduce black carbon and ozone benefit impoverished peoples in their homes and help to stabilize the global climate (UNEP 2011).

National environmental NGOs such as the Sierra Club, imbued with altruistic environmentalism, have begun to craft strategies that appeal to both defensive and altruistic environmentalists. During a recent "business as usual" period, the staff of the national organization began to work with local chapters of the club to pressure for the retirement of old, polluting coal-fired power plants in the regions covered by each chapter (Kaufman 2011). In this way, the national organization pursued a goal with both defensive and altruistic environmental appeal.

Recent shifts in communication strategies by climate scientists reflect a similar appreciation of the potential gains to be had from tapping into people's defensive environmentalist sentiments. Scientists who try to project the impacts of climate on humans through computer modeling increasingly use "nested scenarios" in which they try to bring the anticipated changes down to the level of local communities, with the hope that these projections will provoke defensive environmentalist reactions among citizens and, in so doing, spur them to support both grassroots and global mitigation efforts (Moss et al. 2010).

The use of binary categories such as "defensive–altruistic" can sometimes suppress important distinctions within categories, in this instance between different types of defensive environmental practices. These practices will probably not rise and fall together in their frequency. Contextual changes could suppress one kind of defensive environmentalism at the same time that it promotes another kind of defensive environmentalism. For example, the sharp recession of 2008–9 may have slowed down efforts at ecological modernization, but at the same time it reduced crude birth rates and encouraged people to reuse more materials (Richtel 2011), so diminished expectations in this historical moment about the potential of ecological modernization should be accompanied by an appreciation of the growing conservation potential of reused materials and below-replacement fertility.

Questions for Further Research

The descriptions of defensive environmentalists earlier in this book may have led some readers to the mistaken conclusion that only wealthy and powerful people become defensive environmentalists. As David Kaimowitz (2002) suggests in the epigram to this chapter, poor and disadvantaged people engage with the environment primarily as defensive environmentalists. The success of the burgeoning, transnational environmental justice movement testifies to the concern about local environmental issues among poor peoples (Carmin and Agyeman 2011). The preceding discussion of defensive environmentalists has focused on the behavior of affluent households only because their efforts have been more evident, most likely because, with additional financial resources, they have had more success in safeguarding their immediate environments.

An association between socio-economic status, defensive environmentalist practices, and altruistic environmental practices would appear to follow from differences in individual loci of control across the classes. Defensive environmentalist practices should be evident among all people, but altruistic environmentalist practices would appear more frequently among people with internal loci of control who tend, more than other people, to think that they can control larger situations. Not surprisingly, internal loci of control appear more frequently among people with higher social status (Schultz and Schultz 2008). These arguments are of course only hypotheses. Research on class differences in defensive environmentalist practices has not been done.

Although the theoretical logic of the larger, focusing event driven argument seems clear, empirical studies to confirm it have not been done. Event-triggered environmental and political processes have received some attention from researchers (Walters and Vayda 2009), but studies of generalized historical sequences stemming from large-scale focusing events, while recommended (Abbott 1995), have not been carried out. The historical record contains few examples of focusing events dramatic enough and large enough in scale to reshape the political agendas of a large polity like the United States. Pearl Harbor and 9/11/2001 refocused the American political agenda, but even as salient an event as Hurricane Katrina, with its connection to global warming, did not systemically reorder political agendas in the United States. The storm's most enduring effect may have been the rise of sustainability initiatives in Wal-Mart's corporate agenda. As Warren Dean (1995) would have recognized, focusing events sometimes have to have cataclysmic effects before they decisively reorder political agendas.

Furthermore, there are no large-scale examples of the link between a focusing event and a sustainable development state. There are, however, examples of links between defensive environmentalists, smaller focusing events, and policy reactions that would typify the politics of sustainable development states. The rubber tappers' resistance to ranchers intent on destroying the forests containing their rubber trees, a clear instance of defensive environmentalism, coupled with the 1988 assassination of the rubber tappers' leader, Chico Mendes, triggered the preservation of large tracts of endangered rain forests by the Brazilian government. The creation of the Superfund program in 1984, after widespread agitation by defensive environmentalists concerned about toxic waste sites near their homes, involved a slightly different sequence: first the small-scale focusing events, then a more pervasive defensive environmental activism, and finally a large-scale policy change.

These sequences of events, new information, more defensive environmentalist practices, and policy changes argue against a fatalistic interpretation of global warming. Certainly, the indeterminate contingencies surrounding the occurrence of focusing events and their seeming necessity to generate the political will to curtail damaging environmental practices suggest that the political struggle depends to some important extent on uncontrollable circumstances. These contingencies are not, however, so all-determining as to justify a fatalistic attitude toward climate change. As Richerson and Boyd (2005) have argued, culture may have emerged among early humans largely as a way of accelerating human responses to changes in climate. In this sense, humans already have the cultural tools necessary to meet the challenges of a changing climate.

In both the rubber tappers' campaign and the Love Canal conflict, events, information, and defensive environmental reactions in small places expedited national policy responses in a significant way. In these episodes the building blocks for at least segments of a sustainable development state had local origins. In tumultuous times, discordant events and new information propel cultural change as people discard old schemata and adopt new ones with more altruistic environmentalist ideologies (Swidler 1986). In this sense, science, by identifying important feedback effects such as increased methane emissions from melting permafrost, matters. Both science and defensive environmentalism make altruistic environmentalism and sustainable development states more likely, although in very different ways.

References

Abbott, Andrew. 1995. "Sequence Analysis: New Methods for Old Ideas." *Annual Review of Sociology* 21:93–113.

Ackerman, Frank. 1997. *Why Do We Recycle?: Markets, Values, and Public Policy.* Washington, DC: Island Press.

Agin, Daniel. 2009. *More Than Genes: What Science Can Tell Us About Toxic Chemicals, Development, and the Risk to Our Children.* New York: Oxford.

Agrawal, Arun. 2000. "Small Is Beautiful, But Is Larger Better? Forest Management Institutions in the Kumaon Himalaya, India." In *People and Forests: Communities, Institutions, and Governance.* Edited by C. Gibson, M. McKean, and E. Ostrom, 57–86. Cambridge, Mass.: MIT Press.

Aguirre, Juan A. 2007. "The Farmer's Market Organic Consumer of Costa Rica." *British Food Journal* 109:145–54.

Allaby, Michael. 2004. Romer's Rule. *A Dictionary of Ecology.* New York: Oxford University Press. Available at: www.encyclopedia.com/doc/1O8-Romersrule.html.

Allen, Patricia. 2004. *Together at the Table: Sustainability and Sustenance in the American Agrifood System.* University Park, Penn.: Pennsylvania State University Press.

Alston, Lee and B. Mueller. 2007. "Legal Reserve Requirements in Brazilian Forests: Path Dependent Evolution of De Facto Legislation." *EconomiA, Selecta, Brasília* 8:25–53.

Alter, Bonnie. 2006. Billion Tree Campaign. Available at: www.treehugger.com/files/2006/11/billion_tree_ca.php.

Altieri, Miguel A. 1995. *Agroecology: The Science of Sustainable Agriculture.* Boulder, Colo.: Westview Press.

Anderson, Sarah, editor. 2007. *Wal-Mart's Sustainability Initiative: A Civil Society Critique.* Washington, DC: Institute for Policy Studies.

Ariely, Dan. 2008. Predictably Irrational. Presentation in the Climate Change and Social Policy Series, November 6, 2008.

Arima, Eugenio, P. Richards, R. Walker, and M. M. Caldas. 2011. "Statistical Confirmation of Indirect Land Use Change in the Brazilian Amazon." *Environmental Research Letters* 6(2). DOI:10.1088/1748-9326/6/2/024010.

Arima, Eugenio, R. T. Walker, S. G. Perz, and M. Caldas. 2005. "Loggers and Forest Fragmentation: Behavioral Models of Road Building in the Amazon Basin." *Annals of the Association of American Geographers* 95:525–41.

Arnalot, Jose. 1977. *Lo Que los Achuar Me Han Enseñado*. Quito, Ecuador: Ediciones Abya-Yala.

Asner, Gregory P., T. K. Rudel, T. M. Aide, R. DeFries, and R. Emerson. 2009. "A Contemporary Assessment of Change in Humid Tropical Forests." *Conservation Biology*. DOI: 10.1111/j.1523-1739.2009.01333.x.

Autotropolis. 2011. Japan Earthquake Pushes Used Car Prices Higher. Available at: www.autotropolis.com/usedcar-buyingguide/japan-earthquake-pushes-used-car-prices-higher.html.

Ayres, Robert U. and L. Ayres, editors. 2002. *A Handbook of Industrial Ecology*. Northampton, Mass.: Edward Elgar Publishing.

Azarnert, Leonid V. 2010. "Free Education, Fertility, and Human Capital Accumulation." *Journal of Population Economics*. 23:449–68.

Badgley Catherine, J. K. Moghtader, E. Quintero, E. Zakem, M. J. Chappell, K. R. Avilés Vázquez, A. Samulon, and I. Perfecto. 2007. "Organic Agriculture and the Global Food Supply." *Renewable Agriculture and Food Systems* 22:86–108.

Baek, Seung-Wook. 2005. "Does China Follow the East Asian Development Model?" *Journal of Contemporary Asia* 35:485–98.

Baer, Paul. 2008. Greenhouse Gases: The Urgent Need to Reduce Emissions. Presentation in Seminar, Department of Human Ecology, Rutgers University, New Brunswick, NJ, January 2008.

Bailey, Ian. 2007. "Market Environmentalism, New Environmental Policy Instruments, and Climate Policy in the United Kingdom and Germany." *Annals of the Association of American Geographers* 97:530–50.

Bailey, Jeff. 2005. "Rumors of a Shortage of Dump Space Were Greatly Exaggerated." *New York Times*. August 12. Available at: www.nytimes.com/2005/08/12/business/12trash.html?_r=1&pagewanted=all.

Bak, Per. 1996. *How Nature Works: The Science of Self-Organized Criticality*. New York: Springer-Verlag.

Bak, Per and K. Chen. 1991. "Self-Organized Criticality." *Scientific American*. 264:46–53.

Baker B., C. Benbrook, E. Groth, and K. Benbrook. 2002. "Pesticide Residues in Conventional, IPM Grown, and Organic Foods: Insights from Three Data Sets." *Food Additives and Contaminants* 19:427–46.

Baptista, Sandra R. 2008. "Forest Recovery and Just Sustainability in the Florianópolis City-region. PhD diss., Rutgers University.

Barbier, Edward. 1987. "The Concept of Sustainable Development." *Environmental Conservation* 14:101–10.

Barraclough, Solon and K. Ghimire. 1996. "Deforestation in Tanzania: Beyond Simplistic Generalizations." *The Ecologist* 26:104–9.

Barrow Edmund, B. Kaale, and W. Mlenge. 2003. Forest Landscape Restoration in Shinyanga, The United Republic of Tanzania. Proceedings of the 12th World Forestry Congress, Food and Agricultural Organization of the United Nations (FAO), Québec, Canada.

Barry, Deborah and R. Meinzen-Dick. In press. "The Invisible Map: Community Tenure Rights in the Forest." In *The Social Life of Forests*. Edited by K. Morrison, C. Padoch, and S. Hecht. Chicago: University of Chicago Press.

British Broadcasting Corporation (BBC). 2005. Recycling Around the World. June 25. Available at: news.bbc.co.uk/1/hi/world/europe/4620041.stm.

British Broadcasting Company (BBC). 2011. Brazil: Amazon Deforestation Rises Sharply. May 19. Available at: www.bbc.co.uk/news/world-latin-america-13449792.

Beamish, Thomas D. 2002. *Silent Spill: The Organization of an Industrial Crisis*. Cambridge, Mass.: MIT Press.

Beamish, Thomas D., R. Kunkle, L. Lutzenhiser, and N. W. Biggart. 2000. *Why Innovations Happen: Structural Actors and Emergent Outcomes in the Commercial Building Sector*. Washington, DC: American Council for an Energy-Efficient Economy.

Beck, Ulrich. 1999. *World Risk Society*. Cambridge, UK: Polity Press.

Beck, Ulrich, A. Giddens, and S. Lash. 1994. *Reflexive Modernization: Politics, Tradition, and Aesthetics in the Modern Social Order*. Cambridge, UK: Polity Press.

Becker, Gary. 1991. *A Treatise on the Family*. Enlarged edition. Cambridge, Mass.: Harvard University Press.

Bell, Michael Mayerfield. *An Invitation to Environmental Sociology*. 2009. 3rd edition. Thousand Oaks, Calif.: Pine Forge Press.

Bell, Michael Mayerfield with S. Jarnagan, G. Peter, and D. Bauer. 2004. *Farming for Us All: Practical Agriculture and the Culture of Sustainability*. University Park, Penn.: Pennsylvania State University Press.

Benjamin, Charles. 2004. "Livelihoods and Institutional Development in the Malian Sahel: A Political Economy of Decentralized Natural Resource Management." PhD diss., University of Michigan.

Berglund, Christen, P. Soderholm, and M. Nilsson. 2002. "A Note on Inter-Country Differences in Waste Paper Recovery and Utilization." *Resources, Conservation, and Recycling* 34:175–91.

Berkes, Fikret. 2007. "Community Based Conservation in a Globalized Age." *Proceedings of the National Academy of Sciences* 104:15,188–193.

Berkes, Fikret, J. Colding, and C. Folke, editors. 2004. *Navigating Social-Ecological Systems: Building Resilience for Complexity and Change*. Cambridge, UK: Cambridge University Press.

Berkes, Fikret, T. Hughes, R. Steneck, J. Wilson. D. Bellwood, B. Crona, C. Folke, L. Gunderson, H. Leslie, J. Norberg, M. Nystrom, P. Olsson, H. Osterblom, M. Scheffer, and B. Worm. 2006. "Globalization, Roving Bandits, and Marine Resources." *Science* 311:1,557–8.

Biggart, Nicole W. and T. D. Beamish. 2003. "The Economic Sociology of Conventions: Habit, Custom, Practice, and Routine in Market Order." *Annual Review of Sociology* 29:443–64.

Biggart, Nicole W. and L. Lutzenhiser. 2007. "Economic Sociology and the Social Problem of Energy Efficiency." *American Behavioral Scientist* 50:1,070–87.

Bilger, Burkhard. 2011. "The Great Oasis: A Plan to Combat Desertification." *New Yorker* December 19 & 26.

Billari, Francisco and H. P. Kohler. 2004. "Patterns of Low and Lowest Low Fertility in Europe." *Population Studies* 58:161–76.

Birkland, Thomas A. 2006. *Lessons of Disaster: Policy Change After Catastrophic Events*. Washington, DC: Georgetown University Press.

Boli, John and F. J. Lechner. 2001. "Globalization and World Culture." In *International Encyclopedia of the Social and Behavioral Sciences*. Edited by Neil Smelser and P. Baltes, 6,261–6. Amsterdam: Elsevier.

Boling, Patricia. 2008. "Demography, Culture, and Policy: Understanding Japan's Low Fertility." *Population and Development Review* 34:307–26.

Bongaarts, John and R. Bulatao, editors. 2000. *Beyond Six Billion: Forecasting the World's Population*. Washington, DC: National Academy Press.

Bongaarts, John and S. Watkins. 1996. "Social Interactions and Contemporary Fertility Transitions." *Population and Development Review* 22:639–82.

Bormann, F. Herbert and G. E. Likens. 1979. *Pattern and Process in a Forested Ecosystem: Disturbance, Development, and the Steady State Based on the Hubbard Brook Ecosystem Study*. New York: Springer-Verlag.

Botkin, Daniel. 1990. *Discordant Harmonies: A New Ecology for the Twenty-First Century*. New York: Oxford.

Botshon, Ann. 2007. *Saving Sterling Forest: The Epic Struggle to Preserve New York's Highlands*. Albany: State University of New York Press.

Bouagnimbeck, Herve. 2010. "Organic Farming in Africa." In *The World of Organic Agriculture: Statistics and Emerging Trends, 2010*. Edited by H. Willer and L. Kilcher, 104–16. Bonn, Germany: FiBL and IFOAM.

Boudet, Hilary S. 2011. "From NIMBY to NIABY: Regional Mobilization Against Liquefied Natural Gas Facility Siting in the U.S." *Environmental Politics* 20:786–806.

Boykoff, Maxwell. 2011. *Who Speaks for the Climate: Making Sense of Media Reporting on Climate Change*. Cambridge, UK: Cambridge University Press.

Bradsher, Keith. 2007. "China's Green Energy Gap." *New York Times* October 24. Available at: www.nytimes.com/2007/10/24/business/worldbusiness/24power.html?pagewanted=all.

Bradsher, Keith. 2008. "A New Oil Quandary; Costly Fuel Means Costly Calories." *New York Times* January 1. Available at: www.nytimes.com/2008/01/19/business/worldbusiness/19palmoil.html?pagewanted=all.

Brechin, Steven R. and W. Kempton. 1994. "Global Environmentalism: A Challenge to the Postmaterialism Thesis?" *Social Science Quarterly* 74:245–69.

Brink, Wellington. 1951. *Big Hugh: The Father of Soil Conservation*. New York: MacMillan.

Brown, Lester R. 2006. *Plan B, 2.0: Rescuing a Planet Under Stress and a Civilization in Trouble*. New York: W.W. Norton.

Bruce, Judith and J. Bongaarts. 2010. "The New Population Challenge." In *A Pivotal Moment: Population, Justice, and the Environmental Challenge*. Edited by L. Mazur, 260–75. Washington, DC: Island Press.

Bruegmann, Robert. 2005. *Sprawl: A Compact History*. Chicago: University of Chicago Press.
Brulle, Robert J. and L. Young. 2007. "Advertising, Individual Consumption Levels, and the Natural Environment, 1900–2000." *Sociological Inquiry* 77: 522–42.
Bruner, A. G., R. Gullison, R. Rice, and G. da Fonseca. 2001. "Effectiveness of Parks in Protecting Tropical Biodiversity." *Science* 29:125–8.
Bunker, S. G. 1996. "Raw Material and the Global Economy: Oversights and Distortions in Industrial Ecology." *Society and Natural Resources* 9:419–29.
Burras, L., H. Cheng, J. Kimble, D. Kissel, R. Lal, R. Luxmoore, M. Mausbach, C. Rice, G. Uehara, and L. Wilding. 2001. "Carbon Sequestration: Position Paper by the Soil Science Society of America." Ankeny, Iowa: Soil and Water Conservation Society of America. Available at: www.soils.org/society-info/.
Burros, Marian. 2002. "Study Finds Far Less Pesticide Residue on Organic Produce." *New York Times*, May 8. A25.
Buttel, Frederick. 2003. "Environmental Sociology and the Explanation of Environmental Reform." *Organization and Environment* 16:306–44.
Cadenasso, Mary L., Steward T. A. Pickett, K. C. Weathers, and C. Jones. 2003. "A Framework for a Theory of Ecological Boundaries." *BioScience* 53:750–8.
Caldwell, John C. 1980. "Mass Education as a Determinant of the Timing of Fertility Decline." *Population and Development Review* 6:225–56.
Caldwell, John C. 2001. "The Globalization of Fertility Behavior." *Population and Development Review* 27:93–115.
Caldwell, John C. 2006. "The Western Fertility Decline: Reflections from a Chronological Perspective." *Journal of Population Research* 23:225–42.
Caldwell, John C. and T. Schindlmayr. 2003. "Explanations of the Fertility Crisis in Modern Societies: A Search for Commonalities." *Population Studies* 57:241–63.
Caldwell, John C. and Z. Zhao. 2009. "China's Demography in Perspective." In *Transition and Challenge: China's Population at the Beginning of the 21st Century*. Edited by Z. Zhao and F. Guo, 271–85. New York: Oxford University Press.
Caltabianco, Marcantonio, M. Castiglioni, and A. Rosina. 2009. "Lowest Low Fertility: Signs of Recovery in Italy." *Demographic Research* 21:681–718.
Camara, Gilberto. 2010. Governance in Amazonia: Comparing REDD with Multi-dimensional Policies. Paper presented at the open meeting of the Global Land Project, November, Tempe, Arizona.
Canadell, J. G., C. Le Quere., M. Raupach, C. Field, E. Buitenhuis, P. Ciais, T. Conway, N. Gillett, R. Houghton, and G. Marland. 2007. "Contributions to Accelerating Atmospheric CO2 Growth from Economic Activity, Carbon Intensity, and Efficiency of Natural Sinks." *Proceedings of the National Academy of Sciences* 104:18,866–70.
Carmin, Jo Ann and J. Agyeman, editors. 2011. *Environmental Inequalities Beyond Borders: Local Perspectives on Global Injustices*. Cambridge, Mass.: MIT Press.

Carpenter, S. and W. Brock. 2002. "Toward an Integrative Synthesis." In *Panarchy: Understanding Transformations in Human and Natural Systems*. Edited by L. Gunderson and C. S. Holling, 419–38. Washington, DC: Island Press.
Carson, Rachel. 1962. *Silent Spring*. New York: Houghton-Mifflin.
Cashore, Benjamin. 2009. Conflict and Cooperation: Tools for Governing Tropical Forests: Remarks. Presentation at Yale University, International Society of Tropical Foresters, School of Forestry and Environmental Studies, March 28.
Casson, Anne. 2000. The Hesitant Boom: Indonesia's Oil Palm Sub-Sector in an Era of Economic Crisis and Political Change. CIFOR Occasional Paper No. 29. Bogor, Indonesia: Center for International Forestry Research.
Catton, William R. 1980. *Overshoot: The Ecological Basis of Revolutionary Change*. Urbana and Chicago: University of Illinois Press.
Catton, William R. and R. Dunlap. 1978. "Environmental Sociology: A New Paradigm." *The American Sociologist* 13:41–9.
Cavlovic, T., K. Baker, R. Berrens, and K. Gawande. 2000. "A Meta-analysis of Kuznets Curve Studies." *Review of Agricultural Economics*. 29:32–42.
Chang, Ha-Joon. 1999. "The Economic Theory of the Developmental State." In *The Developmental State*. Edited by M. Woo-Cumings, 182–99. Ithaca, NY: Cornell University Press.
China Shipping Lines – North America. 2008. Available at: www.chinashippingna.com/.
Clark, William. 1985. *On the Practical Implications of the Carbon Dioxide Question*. Laxenburg, Austria: International Institute of Applied Systems Analysis.
Clarke, Lee. 2006. *Worst Cases: Terror and Catastrophe in the Popular Imagination*. Chicago and London: University of Chicago Press.
Clements, Frederic. 1916. *Plant Succession: An Analysis of the Development of Vegetation*. Publication 242. Washington, DC: Carnegie Institute.
Coale, Ansley J. and S. Cotts Watkins, editors. 1986. *The Decline of Fertility in Europe*. Princeton, NJ: Princeton University Press.
Cohen, Maurie J. 2011. "Is the UK Preparing for War?: Military Metaphors, Personal Carbon Allowances, and Consumption Rationing in Historical Perspective." *Climatic Change*. 104:199–222. DOI 10.1007/s10584-009-9785-x.
Colfer, Carol J. Pierce, editor. 2005. *The Equitable Forest: Diversity and Community in Sustainable Resource Management*. Washington, DC: Resources for the Future.
Collins, Scott L., S. R. Carpenter, S. M. Swinton, D. E. Orenstein, D. L. Childers, T. L. Gragson, N. B. Grimm, J. M. Grove, S. L. Harlan, J. P. Kaye, A. K. Knapp, G. P. Kofinas, J. J. Magnuson, W. H. McDowell, J. M. Melack, L. A. Ogden, G. P. Robertson, M. D. Smith, and A. C. Whitmer. 2011. "An Integrated Conceptual Framework for Long-term Social–Ecological Research." *Frontiers in Ecology and the Environment* 9:351–7. Available at: http://dx.doi.org/10.1890/100068.
Conklin, Harold. 1957. *Hanunoo Agriculture: An Example of Shifting Cultivation in the Philippines*. Rome: FAO.
Connelly, Matthew. 2008. *Fatal Misconception: The Struggle to Control World Population*. Cambridge, Mass.: Harvard University Press.

Conservation Technology Information Center. 2011. Tillage Survey Results. Available at: www.ctic.purdue.edu/CRM/.

Corolan, Michael. 2005. "Barriers to the Adoption of Sustainable Agriculture on Rented Land: An Examination of Contesting Social Fields." *Rural Sociology* 70:387–413.

Costello, Christopher, S. Gaines, and J. Lynham. 2008. "Can Catch Shares Prevent Fisheries Collapses?" *Science* 321:1,678–81.

Cottrell, Frederick William. 1955. *Energy and Society: The Relation Between Energy, Social Change, and Economic Development*. Westport, Conn.: Greenwood.

Coughenour, C. Milton. 2003. "Innovating Conservation Agriculture: The Case of No-till Cropping." *Rural Sociology* 68:278–304.

Coughenour, C. Milton and S. Chamala. 2000. *Conservation Tillage and Cropping Innovation: Constructing the New Culture of Agriculture*. Ames, Iowa: Iowa State University Press.

Coumou, Dim and S. Rahmstorf. 2012. "A Decade of Weather Extremes." *Nature Climate Change* 2. DOI:10.1038/nclimate1452.

Craven, Avery O. 1965. *Soil Exhaustion as a Factor in the Agricultural History of Virginia and Maryland, 1606–1860*. Gloucester, Mass.: Smith.

Crenson, Matthew. 1971. *The Unpolitics of Air Pollution: A Study in Nondecisionmaking in Cities*. Baltimore, Md.: Johns Hopkins University Press.

Cronkelton, Peter, P. Taylor, D. Barry, S. Stone-Jovicich, and M. Schmink. 2008. Environmental Governance and the Emergence of Forest Based Social Movements. CIFOR Occasional Paper 49. Bogor, Indonesia: Center for International Forestry Research.

Cronon, William. 1983. *Changes in the Land: Indians, Colonists, and the Ecology of New England*. New York: Hill and Wang.

Davis, Kingsley. 1963. "The Theory of Change and Response in Modern Demographic History." *Population Index* 29:345–66.

Dean, Warren. 1995. *With Broadax and Firebrand: The Destruction of the Brazilian Atlantic Forest*. Berkeley, Calif.: University of California Press.

Demick, Barbara 2011. "In China What You Eat Tells Who You Are." *Los Angeles Times* September 9. Available at: articles.latimes.com/2011/sep/16/world/la-fg-china-elite-farm-20110917.

Dennett, Daniel. 1995. *Darwin's Dangerous Idea: Evolution and the Meaning of Life*. New York: Simon and Schuster.

Depuis, E. Melanie. 2002. *Nature's Perfect Food*. New York: New York University Press.

Desrochers, Pierre. 2002. "Industrial Ecology and the Rediscovery of Inter-firm Recycling Linkages." *Industrial and Corporate Change* 11:1,031–57.

Diamond, Adam V. 2006. "Transformation and Reproduction: Constructing the Organic Milk Commodity Chain in the Northeast United States." PhD diss., Rutgers University.

Diamond, Jared. 2005. *Collapse: How Societies Choose to Fail or Succeed*. New York: Viking.

Dietz, Thomas, A. Fitzgerald, and Rachael Shwom. 2005. "Environmental Values." *Annual Review of Environment and Resources* 30:335–72.

Dietz, Thomas, E. Rosa, and R. York. 2007. "Driving the Human Ecological Footprint." *Frontiers in Ecology and the Environment* 5:13–18.
DiMaggio, Paul. 1997. "Culture and Cognition." *Annual Review of Sociology* 23:263–87.
DiMaggio, Paul and W. W. Powell. 1983. "The Iron Cage Revisited: Institutional Isomorphism and Collective Rationality in Organizational Fields." *American Sociological Review* 48:147–60.
Dimitri, Carolyn and C. Greene. 2007. Recent Growth Patterns in the U.S. Organic Foods Market. USDA, Organic Center. Available at: www.ers.usda.gov/publications/aib777/aib777c.dbf.
Dimitri, Carolyn and L. Oberholtzer. 2007. Organic Price Premiums Remain High. USDA, Organic Center. Available at: http://www.ers.usda.gov/publications/aib777/aib777c.dbf.
Doner, Richard F., Bryan K. Ritchie, and D. Slater. 2005. "Systemic Vulnerability and the Origins of Developmental States: Northeast and Southeast Asia in Comparative Perspective." *International Organization* 59:327–61.
Donnelly, James S., Jr. 2001. *The Great Irish Potato Famine*. Stroud, UK: Sutton Publishing.
Downs, Anthony. 1972. "Up and Down with Ecology: The Issue Attention Cycle." *Public Interest* 28:38–50.
Duany, Andres, E. Plater-Zyberk, and J. Speck. 2000. *Suburban Nation: The Rise of Sprawl and the Decline of the American Dream*. New York: North Point Press.
Dunlap, Riley E. and K. D. Van Liere. 1984. "The Dominant Social Paradigm and Concern for Environmental Quality: An Empirical Analysis." *Social Science Quarterly* 65:1,013–28.
Dunlap, Riley E. and R. York. 2008. "The Globalization of Environmental Concern and the Limits of the Post-Materialist Explanation: Evidence from Four Cross-National Surveys." *Sociological Quarterly* 49:529–63.
Dunn, James A. 2006. "Automotive Fuel Efficiency Policy: Beyond the CAFE Controversy." In *Punctuated Equilibria and the Dynamics of U.S. Environmental Policy*. Edited by R. Repetto, 197–231. New Haven, Conn.: Yale University Press.
Durkheim, Emile. 1893 (1933). *The Division of Labor in Society*. New York: Free Press.
Dzioubinski, Oleg and R. Chipman. 1999. Trends in Consumption and Production: Household Energy Consumption, Department of Economic and Social Affairs, United Nations, New York. Available at: www.un.org/esa/sustdev/publications/esa99dp6.pdf. Sept 18, 2010.
Earth Policy Institute (EPI). 2009. U.S Corn Production and Use for Fuel Ethanol, 1980-2009. Available at: www.earthpolicy.org.
Ehrhardt-Martinez, Karen. 2008. Behavior, Energy and Climate Change: Policy Directions, Program Innovations and Research Paths: Ideas, Resources and Program Summaries from the Behavior, Energy and Climate Change Conference. Washington, DC: ACEEE.
Eliasoph, Nina. 2002. "The Work of Avoiding Politics." In *Cultural Sociology*. Edited by L. Spillman, 130–40. Malden, Mass.: Blackwell.

Environment News Service. 2005. Amazon Rainforest Cleared Faster than Brazil Can Protect It. May 20. Available at: www.ens-newswire.com/ens/may2005/2005-05-20-05.asp.

Erickson, Rita. 1997. *Paper or Plastic?: Energy, Environment, and Consumerism in Sweden and America*. Westport, Conn: Praeger.

European Union. 2011. Renewable Energy in the Transport Sector. Available at: http://ec.europa.eu/energy/renewables/biofuels/biofuels_en.htm.

Evans, Peter. 1979. *Dependent Development: The Alliance of Multinational, State, and Local Capital in Brazil*. Princeton, NJ: Princeton University Press.

Evans, Peter. 1995. *Embedded Autonomy: States and Industrial Transformation*. Princeton, NJ: Princeton University Press.

Evans, Peter. 2005. "The Challenges of the 'Institutional Turn': New Interdisciplinary Opportunities in Development Theory." In *The Economic Sociology of Capitalist Institutions*. Edited by V. Nee and R. Swedberg, 90–116. Princeton, NJ: Princeton University Press.

Evans, Tom. 2004. *Race to the Middle: The Homogenization of Population Density and What It Is Costing New Jersey*. Trenton, NJ: New Jersey Futures.

Faass, Josephine. 2009. "Mission Accomplished or Mission Impossible: Current Practices, Common Challenges, and Innovative Solutions in State-Level Oil Pollution Regulation." Ph.D. diss., Rutgers University.

Facelli, Jose M. and S. T. A. Pickett. 1991. "Plant Litter: Its Dynamics and Effects on Community Structure." *Botanical Review* 57:1–32.

Fajnzylber, Fernando. 1990. "The United States and Japan as Models of Industrialization." In *Manufacturing Miracles: Paths of Industrialization in Latin America and East Asia*. Edited by G. Gereffi and D. L. Wyman, 323–52. Princeton, NJ: Princeton University Press.

Falkowski, Paul G. and R. M. Goodman. 2009. "Future Energy Institutes." *Science* 325:655.

Faminow, Merle and K. Klein. 2000. "Adoption of Agro-forestry in Nagaland, India Using Farmer Led Technology Development and Dissemination." *Canadian Journal of Agricultural Economics* 48:585–95.

Faye, Djidiack. 2003. Organic Fruit and Vegetables from the Tropics. United Nations Conference on Trade and Development. New York and Geneva: United Nations.

Feyisetan, Bamikale and J. B. Casterline. 2002. "Socioeconomic Status, Fertility Preferences, and Contraceptive Change in sub-Saharan Africa." *African Journal of Population* 15:1–24.

Fincher, Leta Hong. 2006. In 2000 China Contained Sixteen of the World's Twenty Most Polluted Cities. Worldwatch Institute. VOA News. Available at: www.voanews.com/english/archive/2006-06/20060628voa36.cfm?CFID=36234535&CFTOKEN=81782323.

Firey, Walter. 1960. *Man, Mind, and Land: A Theory of Resource Use*. Glencoe, Ill.: the Free Press.

Fisher, Dana R. 2004. *National Governance and the Global Climate Change Regime*. Lanham, Md.: Rowman and Littlefield.

Fisher, Ian. 2008. "European Commission Sues to Force Italy to Take Out the Garbage." *New York Times* May 7. Available at:www.nytimes.com/2008/05/07/world/europe/07italy.html?ref=ianfisher.

Florida, Richard. 1996. "Lean and Green: The Move to Environmentally Conscious Manufacturing." *California Management Review* 39:80–105.

Fogarty, David. 2011. How Indonesia Crippled Its Own Climate Change Project. August 16. Available at: www.trust.org/alertnet/news/how-indonesia-crippled-its-own-climate-change-project/.

Food and Agricultural Organization of the United Nations (FAO). 1999. Agroforestry Parklands in Sub-Saharan Africa. Rome: Forestry Division. Available at: www.fao.org/DOCREP/005/X3940E/X3940E08.htm.

Food and Agricultural Organization of the United Nations (FAO). 2006. Forest Resource Assessment. 2005. Rome: Forestry Division. Available at: www.fao.org/forestry/site/fra2005.

Food and Agricultural Organization of the United Nations (FAO). 2012. FAOSTAT. Rome: FAO.

Foresta, Ronald A. 1991. *Amazon Conservation in the Age of Development*. Gainesville, Fla.: University of Florida Press.

Forsyth, Adrian and K. Miyata. 1984. *Tropical Nature: Life and Death in the Rain Forests of Central and South America*. New York: Simon and Schuster.

Foster, John B., B. Clark, and R. York. 2010. *The Ecological Rift: Capitalism's War on the Earth*. New York: Monthly Review Press.

Frank, Robert H. 2000. *Luxury Fever: Why Money Fails to Satisfy in an Era of Excess*. Princeton, NJ: Princeton University Press.

Frejka, Tomas. 2004. *Childbearing Trends and Prospects in Low Fertility Countries: A Cohort Analysis*. Dordrecht, Netherlands: Kluwer Academic Publishers.

Freudenburg, William and R. Gramling. 2010. *Blowout in the Gulf: The BP Oil Disaster and the Future of Energy in America*. Cambridge, Mass.: MIT Press.

Friedland, William H. 2011. Changing Socio-Economic Structures and Globalization: Driving Forces for Social Change and Agrifood Social Movements. Paper presented at the Rural Sociological Society meetings, July 30–August 2, Boise, Idaho.

Fung, Archon. 2004. *Empowered Participation: Reinventing Urban Democracy*. Princeton, NJ: Princeton University Press.

Fung, Archon and C. Sabel. 2000. *Beyond Backyard Environmentalism*. Boston, Mass.: Beacon Press.

Garibay, Salvador and R. Ugas. 2010. "Organic Farming in Latin America and the Caribbean." In *The World of Organic Agriculture: Statistics and Emerging Trends, 2010*. Edited by H. Willer and L. Kilcher, 160–72. Bonn, Germany: FiBL and IFOAM.

Gelbspan, Ross. 1997. *The Heat Is On: The Climate Crisis, the Cover-up, and the Prescription*. Cambridge, Mass.: Perseus Books.

Gerschenkron, Alexander. 1962. *Economic Backwardness in Historical Perspective: A Book of Essays*. Cambridge, Mass.: Harvard University Press.

Gibbs, Holly. 2011. The Land Reserve in Indonesia: A Country Case Study. Presentation at a Workshop on the Global Land Reserve: Where Is It? What are the Constraints. Academica Belgica. Rome, Italy, October 23–26.

Giddens, Anthony. 1984. *The Constitution of Society: Outline of the Theory of Structuration*. Berkeley, Calif.: University of California Press.

Gillis, Justin and C. Dugger. 2011. "U.N. Forecasts 10.1 Billion People by Century's End." *New York Times* May 3. Available at: www.nytimes.com/2011/05/04/world/04population.html.

Gitlitz, Jennifer. 2006. Aluminum Cans: Production and Consumption. Available at: http://goliath.ecnext.com/coms2/gi_0199-5516709/Aluminum-cans-production-and-consumption.html.

Gladwell, Malcolm. 2000. *The Tipping Point: How Little Things Can Make a Big Difference*. Boston, Mass.: Little Brown.

Goldstein, Joshua. 2003. "The Emergence of Sub-replacement Family Size Ideals in Europe." *Population Research and Policy Review* 22:479–96.

Goldstein, Joshua, T. Sobotka, and A. Jasilioniene. 2009. "The End of Lowest, Low Fertility." *Population and Development Review* 35:663–92.

Gould, Kenneth A., D. Pellow, and A. Schnaiberg. 2008. *The Treadmill of Production: Injustice and Unsustainability in the Global Economy*. Boulder, Colo.: Paradigm Publishers.

Gould, Stephen J. and N. Eldredge. 1977. "Punctuated Equilibrium: The Tempo and Mode of Evolution Reconsidered." *Paleobiology* 3:115–51.

Grabowski, Richard. 1994. "The Successful Developmental State: Where Does It Come From?" *World Development* 22:413–22.

Graedel, Thomas. 1994. "Industrial Ecology: Definition and Implementation." In *Industrial Ecology and Global Change*. Edited by R. Socolow, C. Andrews, F. Berkhout, and V. Thomas, 23–41. Cambridge, UK: Cambridge University Press.

Grafton, R. Quentin, D. Squires, and K. Fox. 2000. "Private Property and Economic Efficiency: A Study of a Common Pool Resource." *Journal of Law and Economics* 43:679–713.

Gramsci, Antonio. 1971. *Selections from the Prison Notebooks*. Edited and translated by Q. Hoare and G. Nowell-Smith. London: Lawrence and Wishart.

Grant, Peter R. and B. R. Grant. 2006. "Evolution of Character Displacement in Darwin's Finches." *Science* 313:224–6.

Greenberg, Michael. 2009. "NIMBY, CLAMP, and the Location of New Nuclear-related Facilities: U.S. National and 11 Site Specific Surveys." *Risk Analysis* 29:1,242–54.

Greenpeace. 2011. Amazon Soya Moratorium Renewed for Another Year. Available at: www.greenpeace.org.uk/.../amazon-soya-moratorium-renewed-another-year-20100709.

Griffin, J. N. and B. R. Silliman. 2011. "Resource Partitioning and Why It Matters." *Nature, Education, Knowledge* 2:8.

Grossman, Elizabeth. 2006. *High Tech Trash: Digital Devices, Hidden Toxics, and Human Health*. Washington, DC: Island Press.

Grossman, Gene M. and A. B. Kreuger. 1995. "Economic Growth and the Environment." *Quarterly Journal of Economics* 110:353–77.

Grubler, Arnulf. 1994. "Industrialization as a Historical Phenomenon." In *Industrial Ecology and Global Change*. Edited by R. Socolow, C. Andrews, F. Berkhout, and V. Thomas, 43–68. Cambridge, UK: Cambridge University Press.

Grubler, Arnulf. 1998. *Technology and Global Change*. Cambridge, UK: Cambridge University Press.

Gu, Baochang. 2009. "The Arrival of Low Fertility in China." In *Ultra-low Fertility in Pacific Asia: Trends, Causes, and Policy Issues*. Edited by P. Straughan, V. Chan, and G. Jones, 73–95. London: Taylor and Francis.

Gunderson, Lance H. and C. S. Holling, editors. 2002. *Panarchy: Understanding Transformations in Human and Natural Systems*. Washington, DC: Island Press.

Guthman, Julie. 2004. *Agrarian Dreams: The Paradox of Organic Farming in California*. Berkeley, Calif.: University of California Press.

Hadhazy, Adam. 2009. "The Maldives, Threatened by Drowning due to Climate Change, Set to Go Carbon Neutral." *Scientific American* May 16. Available at: www.scientificamerican.com/blog/post.cfm?id=maldives-drowning-carbon-neutral-by-2009-03-16.

Hagen, Joel B. 1992. *An Entangled Bank: The Origins of Ecosystem Ecology*. New Brunswick, NJ: Rutgers University Press.

Halberg, Niels, H. Alroe, and E. Kristensen. 2005. "Synthesis: Perspectives for Organic Agriculture in a Global Context." In *Global Development of Organic Agriculture*. Edited by N. Halberg, M. Knudsen, H. Alroe, and E. Kristensen, 343–68. London: CABI Publishers.

Hallam, David. 2002. "The Organic Market in the OECD Countries: Past Growth, Current Status, and Future Potential." In *Organic Agriculture: Sustainability, Markets, and Policies*. Proceedings from an OECD Workshop, Washington DC, September, 179–86. Wallingford, UK: CABI Publishing.

Haller, Max and M. Hadler. 2008. "Dispositions to Act in Favor of the Environment: Fatalism and Readiness to Make Sacrifices in a Cross-National Perspective." *Sociological Forum* 23:281–311.

Hanisch, Carola. 2000. "Is Extended Producer Responsibility Effective?" *Environmental Science and Technology* 34:170–5.

Hardin, Garrett. 1968. "The Tragedy of the Commons." *Science* 162:1,243–8.

Hart, John Fraser. 2003. *The Changing Scale of American Agriculture*. Charlottesville, Va.: University of Virginia Press.

Hawken, Paul. 2007. "To Remake the World: Something Earth Changing is Afoot among Civil Society." *Orion* May–June. Available at: www.orionmagazine.org/index.php/articles/article/265/.

Hawken, Paul, A. Lovins, and H. Lovins. 1999. *Natural Capitalism: Creating the Next Industrial Revolution*. Boston, Mass.: Little Brown.

Hays, Sharon. 1996. *The Cultural Contradictions of Motherhood*. New Haven, Conn.: Yale University Press.

Hershkovitz, Allen. 2002. *Bronx Ecology: Blueprint for a New Environmentalism*. Washington, DC: Island Press.

Hess, David J. 2009. *Localist Movements in a Global Economy*. Cambridge, Mass.: MIT Press.

Heston, Alan, R. Summers, and B. Aten. 2011. Penn World Table Version 7.0. Center for International Comparisons of Production, Income and Prices at the University of Pennsylvania, May 2011. Available at: http://pwt.econ.upenn.edu/.

Hilgartner, Steven and C. Bosk. 1988. "The Rise and Fall of Social Problems: A Social Arenas Model." *American Journal of Sociology* 94:53–78.
Hinrichs, C. Clare and E. Barham. 2007. "A Full Plate: Challenges and Opportunities in Remaking the Food System." In *Remaking the North American Food System: Strategies for Sustainability*. Edited by C. C. Hinrichs and T. Lyson, 345–56. Lincoln and London: University of Nebraska Press.
Hirao, Keiko. 2007. "The Privatized Education Market and Maternal Employment in Japan." In *The Political Economy of Japan's Low Fertility*. Edited by F. Rosenbluth, 170–97. Stanford, Calif.: Stanford University Press.
Hirsch, Frederick. 1978. *The Social Limits to Growth*. London: Routledge.
Hirschman, A. O. 1958. *The Strategy of Economic Development*. New Haven, Conn.: Yale University Press.
Hirschman, A. O. 1984. *Getting Ahead Collectively: Grassroots Experiences in Latin America*. New York: Pergamon Press.
Hobbs, P. R. 2007. "Conservation Agriculture: What Is It and Why Is It Important for Future Sustainable Food Production?" *Journal of Agricultural Science* 145:127–37.
Hochstetler, Kathryn and M. E. Keck. 2007. *Greening Brazil: Environmental Activism in State and Society*. Durham, NC: Duke University Press.
Hofstadter, Richard. 1944. *Social Darwinism in American Thought*. Philadelphia: University of Pennsylvania Press.
Holdren, John P. 2007. "Energy and Sustainability." *Science* 315:737.
Holland, J. M. 2004. "The Environmental Consequences of Adopting Conservation Tillage in Europe: Reviewing the Evidence." *Agriculture, Ecosystems, and Environment* 103:1–25.
Holland, Margaret, F. de Koning, M. Morales, and L. Naughton-Treves. In press. "Complex Tenure and Deforestation: Implications for Conservation Incentives in the Ecuadorian Amazon." *World Development*.
Holling, C. S., L. Gunderson, and D. Ludwig. 2002. "In Quest of a Theory of Adaptive Change." In *Panarchy: Understanding Transformations in Human and Natural Systems*. Edited by L. Gunderson and C. S. Holling, 3–22. Washington, DC: Island Press.
Holmgren, Peter, E. Masakha, and H. Sjoholm. 1994. "Not All African Land Is Being Degraded: A Recent Survey of Trees on Farms in Kenya Reveals Rapidly Increasing Forest Resources." *Ambio* 23:390–5.
Homer-Dixon, Thomas K. 1999. *Environment, Scarcity, and Violence*. Princeton, NJ: Princeton University Press.
Houser, Trevor. 2012. China's Energy Emergence. Presentation, Rutgers Energy Institute, New Brunswick, NJ, March 22, 2012.
Howlett, Michael. 1997. "Issue-Attention and Punctuated Equilibria Models Reconsidered: An Empirical Examination of the Dynamics of Agenda-Setting in Canada." *Canadian Journal of Political Science / Revue Canadienne de Science Politique* 30:3–29.
Humes, Edward. 2011. *Force of Nature: The Unlikely Story of Wal-Mart's Green Revolution*. New York: Harper-Collins.

Hurley, Andrew. 1995. *Environmental Inequalities: Class, Race, and Industrial Pollution in Gary, Indiana, 1945–1980*. Chapel Hill: University of North Carolina Press.

Hvistendahl, Mara. 2011. "China's Population Growing Slowly, Changing Fast." *Science* 332:650–1.

Ingram, Helen and L. Fraser. 2006. "Path Dependency and Adroit Innovation: The Case of California Water." In *Punctuated Equilibria and the Dynamics of U.S. Environmental Policy*. Edited by R. Repetto, 78–109. New Haven, Conn.: Yale University Press.

Intergovernmental Panel on Climate Change (IPCC). 2011. *Summary for Policymakers. Special Report on Managing the Risks of Extreme Events and Disasters to Advance Climate Change Adaptation*. Edited by C. B. Field, V. Barros, T. F. Stocker, D. Qin, D. J. Dokken, K. L. Ebi, M. D. Mastrandrea, K. J. Mach, G. K. Plattner, S. K. Allen, M. Tignor, M. and P. M. Midgley. Cambridge, UK: Cambridge University Press.

International Aluminum Institute. 2008. Statistics. Available at: www.world-aluminium.org/Statistics.

International Fertilizer Industry Association. 2012. Statistics. Available at: www.fertilizer.org/HomePage/STATISTICS.

Jackson, Kenneth T. 1987. *Crabgrass Frontier: The Suburbanization of the United States*. New York: Oxford University Press.

Jacob, Jeffrey. 1998. *New Pioneers: The Back to the Land Movement and the Search for a Sustainable Future*. University Park, Penn.: Pennsylvania State University Press.

James, William. 1906 (1971). "The Moral Equivalent of War." In *The Moral Equivalent of War and Other Essays*. Edited by J. Roth, 3–16. New York: Harper Torch Books.

Jensen, Derrick and A. McBay. 2009. *What We Leave Behind*. New York: Seven Stories.

Jervis, Robert. 1997. *System Effects: Complexity in Political and Social Life*. Princeton, NJ: Princeton University Press.

Johns, Timothy. 2007. "Agrobiodiversity, Diet and Human Health." In *Managing Biodiversity in Agricultural Ecosystems*. Edited by D. I. Jarvis, C. Padoch, and D. Cooper, 382–406. New York: Columbia University Press.

Johnson, Chalmers. 1982. *MITI and the Japanese Miracle: The Growth of Industrial Policy, 1925–1975*. Stanford, Calif.: Stanford University Press.

Johnson, Josee and Shyon Baumann. 2010. *Foodies: Culture and Status in the American Foodscape*. New York: Routledge.

Johnson, Keith. 2009. "Future Gen Fiasco: Killing Illinois Plant Set Clean Coal Back 10 Years, Congress Says." *Wall Street Journal* blog. March 11. Available at: http://blogs.wsj.com/environmentalcapital/2009/03/11/futuregen-fiasco-killing-illinois-plant-set-clean-coal-back-10-years-congress-says/.

Johnson, Steven. 2006. *The Ghost Map: The Story of London's Most Terrifying Epidemic and How It Changed Science, Cities, and the Modern World*. New York: Penguin.

Jones, Bryan D. and F. Baumgartner. 2005. *The Politics of Attention: How Government Prioritizes Problems*. Chicago: University of Chicago Press.

Jones, Bryan D., T. Sulkin, and H. Larsen. 2003. "Policy Punctuations in American Politics." *American Political Science Review* 97:151–69.
Jones, Gavin W. 2007. "Delayed Marriage and Very Low Fertility in Pacific Asia." *Population and Development Review* 33:453–78.
Jones, Gavin, P. Straughan, and A. Chan. 2009. "Fertility in Pacific Asia: Looking to the Future." In *Ultra-low fertility in Pacific Asia: Trends, Causes, and Policy Issues*. Edited by P. Straughan, A. V. Chan, and G. Jones, 204–14. London: Taylor and Francis.
Jones, Robert Emmet and R. E. Dunlap. 1992. "The Social Bases of Environmental Concern: Have They Changed Over Time?" *Rural Sociology* 57:28–47.
Joppa, Lucas N. and A. Pfaff. 2011. "Global Protected Area Impacts." *Proceedings of the Royal Society B: Biological Sciences* 278:1633–8.
Kahn, Joseph and Mark Landler. 2007. "China Grabs the West's Smoke Spewing Factories." *New York Times*. December 21. Available at: www.nytimes.com/2007/12/21/world/asia/21transfer.html?_r=1&oref=slogin
Kahneman, Daniel and A. Tversky. 1979. "Prospect Theory: An Analysis of Decision Under Risk." *Econometrica* 47:263–91.
Kaimowitz, David. 2002. The Meaning of Johannesburg. Polex – CIFOR. September 26. Available at: www.cifor.org/online-library/polex-cifors-blog-for-and-by-forest-policy-experts/english/detail/article/1222/the-meaning-of-johannesburg-1/browse/9.html.
Kaimowitz, David and J. Smith. 2001. "Soybean Technology and the Loss of Natural Vegetation in Brazil and Bolivia." In *Agricultural Technologies and Tropical Deforestation*. Edited by A. Angelsen and D. Kaimowitz, 195–212. Wallingford, UK: CABI Press.
Kammen, Daniel. 2006. Do We Need a Manhattan Project for the Environment? Testimony before the Committee on Government Reform. U.S. House of Representatives. September 21. Available at: http://rael.berkeley.edu/Kammen-HouseGovernmentReformCommittee- Testimony.
Kampayana, Theobald. 1992. Rareté des Terres et Strategies d'Utilisation du Bois: Resultats d'une Enquête Pontuelle dans les Ménages Agricoles Ruraux au Rwanda. Kigali, Rwanda: Ministère de l'Agriculture et de l'Elevage.
Kane, S., P. Dieble, J. D. Wulfhorst, B. Foltz, and D. Young. 2011. Socio-economic Factors Affecting Tillage Practices in Northwest Dryland Agriculture. Proceedings of the Rural Sociological Society Meetings, July 30–August 2, Boise, Idaho.
Kasperczyk, Nadja and K. Knickel. 2006. "Environmental Impacts of Organic Farming." In *Organic Agriculture: A Global Perspective*. Edited by P. Kristiansen, A. Taji, and J. Reganold, 259–94. Ithaca, NY: Cornell University Press.
Kassam, A., T. Friedrich, F. Shaxson, and J. Pretty. 2009. "Economic and Social Impacts of Organic Agriculture." *International Journal of Agricultural Sustainability* 7:292–320.
Kasterline, Alexander. 2010. "Organic Agriculture and Carbon Markets." In *The World of Organic Agriculture: Statistics and Emerging Trends, 2010*. Edited by H. Willer and L. Kilcher, 86–90. Bonn, Germany: FiBL and IFOAM.
Katz, Jane. 2002. "What a Waste." *Regional Review – Federal Reserve Bank of Boston* 12:22–30.

Kaufman, Leslie. 2011. "Environmentalists Get Down to Earth." *New York Times* December 17. Available at: www.nytimes.com/2011/12/18/sunday-review/environmentalists-get-down-to-earth.html?pagewanted=all.

Keck, Margaret and K. Sikkink. 1998. *Activists Without Borders: Advocacy Networks in International Politics*. Ithaca, NY: Cornell University Press.

Keene, New Hampshire, Department of Public Works. 2007. A Tour Around the World. Available at: www.ci.keene.nh.us/publicworks/recycle/around-theworld.htm.

Keilman, Nico. 2003. "The Threat of Small Households." *Nature* 421:489–90.

Kelleher, Maria. 2007. "Anaerobic Digestion Outlook for MSW Streams." *Biocycle*. 48:51.

Kempton, Willett, J. S. Boster, and J. A. Hartley. 1995. *Environmental Values in American Culture*. Cambridge, Mass.: MIT Press.

Kerr, Richard A. 2012. "A Quick, (Partial) Fix for an Ailing Atmosphere." *Science* 335:156.

Kim, Doo-Sub. 2009. "The 1997 Asian Economic Crisis and Changes in the Pattern of Socioeconomic Differentials in Korean Fertility." In *Ultra-low fertility in Pacific Asia: Trends, Causes, and Policy Issues*. Edited by P. Straughan, A. V. Chan, and G. Jones, 110–31. London: Taylor and Francis.

Kimerling, Judith. 1991. *Amazon Crude*. New York: Natural Resources Defense Council.

Kingsland, Sharon. 2005. *The Evolution of American Ecology, 1890–2000*. Baltimore, MD: Johns Hopkins University Press.

Kingsolver, Barbara, C. Kingsolver, and S. Hopp. 2007. *Animal, Vegetable, Miracle: A Year of Food Life*. New York: Harper Collins.

Kissling, Frances. 2010. "Reconciling Differences: Population, Reproductive Rights, and the Environment." In *A Pivotal Moment: Population, Justice, and the Environmental Challenge*. Edited by L. Mazur, 383–91. Washington, DC: Island Press.

Klein, Naomi. 2007. *The Shock Doctrine: The Rise of Disaster Capitalism*. New York: Henry Holt.

Klyza, Christian M., J. Isham, and A. Savage. 2006. "Local Environmental Groups and the Creation of Social Capital: Evidence from Vermont." *Society and Natural Resources* 19:905–19.

Knabb, Richard D., J. Rhome, and D. Brown. 2006. Katrina: 23–30 August 2005. Miami, Fla.: National Hurricane Center.

Koh, Lian Pin and D. Wilcove. 2008. "Is Oil Palm Agriculture Really Destroying Tropical Biodiversity?" *Conservation Letters* 1:1–5.

Kohli, Atul. 1999. "Where Do High Growth Political Economies Come From?: The Japanese Lineage of Korea's Developmental State." In *The Developmental State*. Edited by M. Woo-Cumings, 93–126. Ithaca, NY: Cornell University Press.

Kooiman, Jan. 2008. "Interactive Governance and Governability: An Introduction." *Journal of Transdisciplinary Environmental Studies* 7:1–11.

Kornrich, Sabino and F. Furstenberg. In press. "Investing in Children: Changes in Parental Spending from 1972 to 2007." *Demography* 49.

Kristiansen, Paul and C. Merfield. 2006. "Overview of Organic Farming." In *Organic Agriculture: A Global Perspective*. Edited by P. Kristiansen, A. Taji, and J. Reganold, 1–23. Ithaca, NY: Cornell University Press.

Kroodsma, David A. and C. Field. 2006. "Carbon Sequestration in California Agriculture." *Ecological Applications* 16:1,975–85.

LaFraniere, Sharon. 2008. "Empty Seas: Europe Takes Africa's Fish, and Boatloads of Migrants Follow." *New York Times* January 14. Available at: www.nytimes.com/2008/01/14/world/africa/14fishing.html.

Lane, Lee. 2006. "The Political Economy of Greenhouse Gas Controls." In *Punctuated Equilibria and the Dynamics of U.S. Environmental Policy*. Edited by R. Repetto, 162–96. New Haven, Conn.: Yale University Press.

Larson, A. M., P. Cronkleton, D. Barry, and P. Pacheco. 2008. Tenure Rights and Beyond: Community Access to Forest Resources in Latin America. Occasional Paper 50. Bogor, Indonesia: Center for International Forestry Research.

Laurance, William F., M. A. Cochrane, S. Bergen, P. M. Fearnside, P. Delamônica, C. Barber, S. D'Angelo, and T. Fernandes. 2001. "The Future of the Brazilian Amazon." *Science* 291:438–9. DOI: 10.1126/science.291.5503.438.

Lawson, David W. and R. Mace. 2010. "Optimizing Modern Family Size: Trade-offs Between Fertility and the Economic Costs of Reproduction." *Human Nature* 21:39–61.

Lea, E. and T. Worsley. 2005. "Australians' Organic Food Beliefs, Demographics and Values." *British Food Journal* 107:855–69.

Lee, Barrett A. 2007. "Invasion-Succession." In *Blackwell Encyclopedia of Sociology*. Edited by George Ritzer 5:2,418–20.

Lee, Kai. 1993. *Compass and Gyroscope: Integrating Science and Politics for the Environment*. Washington, DC: Island Press.

Lee, Ronald. 2011. "The Outlook for Population Growth." *Science* 333:569–73. DOI: 10.1126/science.1208859.

Lerner, Amy, D. Burbano, T. Katan, C. Mena, L. Schneider, M. McGroddy, and T. K. Rudel. 2012. The Spontaneous Emergence of Silvopastoral Landscapes in the Ecuadorian Amazon: Patterns and Processes. Paper presented at the meetings of the Association of American Geographers, February 23–26, New York.

Lesthaeghe, Ron and L. Niedert. 2006. "The Second Demographic Transition in the United States: Exception or Textbook Example?" *Population and Development Review* 32:669–91.

Levi-Faur, David. 1998. "The Developmental State: Israel, South Korea, and Taiwan Compared." *Studies in Comparative International Development* 33:65–93.

Levin, Simon. 1999. *Fragile Dominion: Complexity and the Commons*. Cambridge, Mass.: Perseus Publishing.

Levin, S. A., S. Barrett, S. Aniyar, W. Baumol, C. Bliss, B. Bolin, P. Dasgupta, P. Ehrlich, C. Folke, I. Gren, C. Holling, A. Jansson, B. Jansson, K. Maler, D. Martin, C. Perrings,, and C. Sheshinski. 2001. "Resilience in Natural and Socioeconomic Systems." *Environment and Development Economics* 3:221–62.

Likaka, Osumaka. 1997. *Rural Society and Cotton in Colonial Zaire*. Madison, Wisc.: University of Wisconsin Press.

Lindeman, Raymond L. 1942. "The Trophic-Dynamic Aspect of Ecology. "*Ecology* 23:399–417.

Linh, Nguyen Si. 2010. "Vietnam: Organic Development." In *The World of Organic Agriculture: Statistics and Emerging Trends, 2010*. Edited by H. Willer and L. Kilcher, 128–130. Bonn, Germany: FiBL and IFOAM.

Liu, J., G. Daily, P. Ehrlich, and G. Luck. 2003. "Effects of Household Dynamics on Resource Consumption and Biodiversity." *Nature* 421:530–3.

Liu, J. and J. Diamond. 2005. "China's Environment in a Globalizing World." *Nature* 435:1,179–83.

Liu, J. and J. Diamond. 2008. "Revolutionizing China's Environmental Protection." *Science* 319:37–8.

Liu, Jianguo, T. Dietz, S. R. Carpenter, M. Alberti, C. Folke, E. Moran, A. N. Pell, P. Deadman, T. Kratz, J. Lubchenco, E. Ostrom, Z. Ouyang, W. Provencher, C. L. Redman, S. H. Schneider, and W. W. Taylor. 2007a. "Complexity of Coupled Human and Natural Systems." *Science* 317:1,513–16.

Liu, Jianguo, T. Dietz, S. Carpenter, C. Folke, M. Alberti, C. Redman, S. Schneider, E. Ostrom, A. Pell, J. Lubchenco. W. Taylor, Z. Ouyang, P. Deadman, T. Kratz, and W. Provencher. 2007b. "Coupled Human and Natural Systems." *Ambio* 36:639–49.

Logan, Jeffrey. 2007. China's Emissions Conundrum. Washington, DC: World Resources Institute. Available at: www.wri.org/stories/2007/03/chinas-emissions-conundrum.

Logan, John and H. Molotch. 2007. *Urban Fortunes: The Political Economy of Place*. 2nd edition. Berkeley: University of California Press.

Loriaux, Michael. 1999. "The French Developmental State as Myth and Moral Ambition." In *The Developmental State*. Edited by M. Woo-Cumings, 235–75. Ithaca, NY: Cornell University Press.

Lu, Chensheng, K. Toepel, R. Irish, R. Fenske, D. Barr, and R. Bravo. 2006. "Organic Diets Significantly Lower Children's Dietary Exposure to Organophosphorus Pesticides." *Environmental Health Perspectives* 114:260–63.

Lutz, Wolfgang, B. O'Neill, and S. Scherbov. 2003. "European Population at a Turning Point." *Science* 299:1,991–2.

Lynn, Barry. 2005. *End of the Line: The Rise and Coming Fall of the Global Corporation*. New York: Doubleday.

Lyson, Thomas A. 2004. *Civic Agriculture: Reconnecting Farm, Food, and Community*. Medford, Mass.: Tufts University Press.

MacAdam, Douglas. 1988. *Freedom Summer*. New York: Oxford University Press.

MacArthur, Robert H. and E. O. Wilson. 1967. *The Theory of Island Biogeography*. Princeton, NJ: Princeton University Press.

Macauley, Stewart. 1963. "Non-Contractual Relations in Business: A Preliminary Study." *American Sociological Review* 28:55–67.

MacBride, Samantha. 2011. *Recycling Reconsidered: The Present Failure and Future Promise of Environmental Action in the United States*. Cambridge, Mass.: MIT Press.

MacDonald, Garry W., Vickie E. Forgie, and C. MacGregor. 2006. "Treading Lightly: Ecofootprints of New Zealand's Aging Population." *Ecological Economics* 56:424–39.

MacDonald, Peter. 2006. "Low Fertility and the State." *Population and Development Review* 32:485–510.

MacDonald, Peter. 2009. "Explanations of Low Fertility in East Asia: A Comparative Perspective." In *Ultra-low fertility in Pacific Asia: Trends, Causes, and Policy Issues*. Edited by P. Straughan, A. V. Chan, and G. Jones, 23–39. London: Taylor and Francis.

Mace, Ruth. 2008. "Reproducing in Cities." *Science* 319:764–6.

Macedo, Marcia, R. S. DeFries, D. C. Morton, C. M. Stickler, G. L. Galford, and Y. E. Shimabukuroe. 2012. "Decoupling of Deforestation and Soy Production in the Southern Amazon during the late 2000s." *Proceedings of the National Academy of Sciences* 109:1,341–6. Available at: www.pnas.org/cgi/doi/10.1073/pnas.1111374109.

MacKay, David J.C. 2008. *Sustainable Energy: Without the Hot Air*. Cambridge, UK: UIT Cambridge.

MacNeil, Robert and M. Paterson. 2012. "Neoliberal Climate Policy: From Market Fetishism to the Developmental State." *Environmental Politics* 21:230–47.

Macura, Miroslav. 2004. "The Reasons for Eastern Europe's Low Fertility." *Population Studies* 57:86–9.

Makower, Joel. 2009. Calculating the Gross National Trash. Available at: http://www.greenbiz.com.

Maniates, Michael and J. Meyer, editors. 2010. *The Environmental Politics of Sacrifice*. Cambridge, Mass.: MIT Press.

Mann, Michael. 1986. *The Sources of Social Power, Volume I: A History of Power from the Beginning to A.D. 1760*. Cambridge, UK: Cambridge University Press.

Manning, E. 1998. Skeptics Wary of Amazon Initiative. United Press International Science News, April 29. Available at: http://forests.org/forests/brazil.html.

Marchak, Patricia. 1995. *Logging the Globe*. Montreal: McGill-Queens University Press.

Margalef, Ramon. 1968. *Perspectives in Ecological Theory*. Chicago, Ill.: University of Chicago Press.

Margolis, Maxine. 1973. *The Moving Frontier. Social and Economic Change in a Southern Brazilian Community*. Gainesville: University of Florida Press.

Mars, Kettly. 2011. "Haiti Without Walls" *New York Times* January 2. p. WK8.

Martinet, Anne and M. Christovam. 2009. The Countries' Positions on REDD Mechanism and the Determinants of These. Paris, France: Office National des Forêts – ONF Internacional, Agence Francaise de Developpement.

Mather, Alexander. 1992. "The Forest Transition." *Area* 24:367–79.

Mather, Alexander. 2007. "Recent Asian Forest Transitions in Relation to Forest Transition Theory." *International Forestry Review* 9:491–502.

Mathews, Emily and A. Grainger. 2001. User Perspectives on the FRA 2000. Background Paper. Washington, DC: World Resources Institute. Available at: www.fao.org/forestry/site/2429/en/page.jsp#user_perspectives.

Mayr, Ernst 1959. "Typological versus Population Thinking." In *Evolution and Anthropology*. Edited by B. J. Meggers, 1–10. Washington, DC: The Anthropological Society of Washington.

McCay, Bonnie J. 2010. Enclosing the Fishery Commons: From Individuals to Communities. Presentation at Workshop on the Evolution of Property Rights Related to Land and Natural Resources. Lincoln Institute of Land Policy, September 20, Cambridge, Mass.

McCright, Aaron M., and R. E. Dunlap. 2003. "Defeating Kyoto: The Conservative Movement's Impact on U.S. Climate Change Policy." *Social Problems* 50:348–73.

McKibben, William. 1998. *Maybe One: A Personal and Environmental Argument for Single Child Families*. New York: Simon & Schuster.

McLaughlin, Paul. 2012. "The Second Darwinian Revolution: Steps Toward a New Evolutionary Environmental Sociology." *Nature and Culture* 7(3): 231–258.

McLuhan, Marshall. 1964. *Understanding Media: The Extensions of Man*. New York: McGraw-Hill.

Meiners, S. J. and S. T. A. Pickett. 2011. "Succession." In *Encyclopedia of Biological Invasions*. Edited by D. Simberloff and M. Rejmanek, 651–7. Berkeley, Calif.: University of California Press.

Meyer, David S. 2004. "Protest and Political Opportunities." *Annual Review of Sociology* 30:125–45.

Meyfroidt, Patrick and E. Lambin. 2008. "The Causes of the Reforestation in Vietnam." *Land Use Policy* 25:182–97.

Meyfroidt, Patrick, T. K. Rudel, and E. Lambin. 2010. "Forest Transitions, Trade, and the Displacement of Land Use." *Proceedings of the National Academy of Sciences* 107:20,917–22. DOI:10.1073/pnas.1014773107.

Millenium Ecosystem Assessment. 2005. *Ecosystems and Human Well-being: Synthesis*. Washington, DC: Island Press.

Miller, Jordana. 2007. "Tests Reveal High Chemical Levels in Kids' Bodies." CNN, Planet in Peril Series. October 22. Available at: http://edition.cnn.com/2007/TECH/science/10/22/body.burden/index.html.

Mills, C. Wright. 1956. *The Power Elite*. New York: Oxford University Press.

Ministerio do Meio Ambiente (MMA), Brasil. 2011. Portaria de N° 175, de 24 de Maio de 2011. Available at: www.biomassabr.com/bio/resultadonoticias.asp?id=365.

Minns, John. 2001. "Of Miracles and Models: The Rise and Decline of the Developmental State in South Korea." *Third World Quarterly* 22:1,025–43.

Mol, Arthur P. J. 2008. *Environmental Modernization in the Information Age*. Cambridge, UK: Cambridge University Press.

Mol, Arthur P. J. and D. A. Sonnenfeld, editors. 2000. *Ecological Modernization Around the World: Perspectives and Critical Debates*. London and Portland: Frank Cass/ Routledge.

Mol, Arthur P. J., G. Spaargaren, and D. Sonnenfeld. 2009. *The Ecological Modernization Reader*. London, UK: Routledge.

Molotch, Harvey. 2003. *Where Stuff Comes From: How Toasters, Toilets, Cars, Computers and Many Other Things Come to Be as They Are.* New York and London: Routledge.
Mongabay. 2007. Biofuels, Logging May Spur Deforestation in Guyana. Available at: www.Mongabay.com.
Mongabay. 2009. Brazil to Support REDD in Copenhagen. October 28. Available at: http://news.mongabay.com/2009/1028-brazil.html.
Mongabay. 2011a. Protected Areas Cover 44% of the Brazilian Amazon. Available at: http://news.mongabay.com/2011/0420-protected_amazon.html.
Mongabay. 2011b. Majority of Brazilians Reject Changes in Amazon Forest Code. Available at: http://news.mongabay.com/2011/0611-amazon_code_poll.html.
Montgomery, David R. 2008. "Agriculture's No-till Revolution." *Journal of Soil and Water Conservation* 63:64–5.
Montgomery, Mark R. 2008. "The Urban Transformation of the Developing World." *Science* 319:761–4.
Moore, Sarah A. 2008. "The Politics of Garbage in Oaxaca, Mexico." *Society and Natural Resources* 21:597–610.
Morgan, S. Phillip. 2003. "Is Low Fertility a Twenty-first Century Demographic Crisis?" *Demography* 40:589–603.
Morton, D. C., R. DeFries, Y. Shimabukuro, L. Anderson, E. Arai, F. del Bon Espiritu-Santo, R. Frietas, and J. Morisette. 2006. "Cropland Expansion Changes Deforestation Dynamics in the Southern Brazilian Amazon." *Proceedings of the National Academy of Sciences* 103:14,637–41.
Moss, Richard, J. A. Edmonds, K. A. Hibbard, M. R. Manning, S. K. Rose, D. P. van Vuuren, T. R. Carter, S. Emori, M. Kainuma, T. Kram, G. A. Meehl, J. F. B. Mitchell, N. Nakicenovic, K. Riahi, S. J. Smith, R. J. Stouffer, A. M. Thomson, J. P. Weyan, and T. J. Wilbanks. 2010. "The Next Generation of Scenarios for Climate Change Research and Assessment." *Nature* 463:747–56. DOI:10.1038/nature08823.
Mouawad, Jad. 2009. 'Not So Green after All." *New York Times* April 7. Available at: www.nytimes.com/2009/04/08/business/energy-environment/08greenoil.html?
Mukherjee, S. D. 1997. "Is Handing over Forests to Local Communities a Solution to Deforestation?: Experience in Andra Pradesh-India." *Indian Forester* 123:460–71.
Murkoff, Heidi. 2010. *What to Expect: Eating Well When You're Expecting.* New York: Workman.
Mydans, Seth. 2008. "A Different Kind of Homework for Singapore Students: Get a Date." *New York Times* April 29. Available at: www.nytimes.com/2008/04/29/world/asia/29iht-29singapore.12416985.html.
Myers, Norman, R. A. Mittermeier, C. G. Mittermeier, G. A. B. da Fonseca, and J. Kent. 2000. "Biodiversity Hotspots for Conservation Priorities." *Nature* 403:853–8.
Myers, Ransom A. and B. Worm. 2003. "Rapid Worldwide Depletion of Predatory Fish Communities." *Nature* 423:280–3.

Nadeau, Robert L. 2006. *The Environmental Endgame: Mainstream Economics, Ecological Disaster, and Human Survival.* New Brunswick, NJ: Rutgers University Press.
Nader, Ralph. 1965. *Unsafe at Any Speed: The Designed-in Dangers of the American Automobile.* New York: Grossman Publishers.
Nagendra, Harini. 2007. "Drivers of Reforestation in Human-dominated Forests." *Proceedings of the National Academy of Sciences* 104:15218–15223.
National Aeronautics and Space Administration (NASA). 2011. Goddard Institute for Space Studies. GISS Surface Temperature Analysis (GISTEMP). Available at: http://data.giss.nasa.gov/gistemp/.
National Research Council. 2001. *Marine Protected Areas: Tools for Sustaining Ocean Ecosystems.* Washington, DC: National Academies Press.
Nepstad, Dan., S. Schwartzman, B. Bamberger, M. Santilli, D. Ray, P. Schlesinger, P. Lefebvre, A. Alencar, E. Prinz, G. Fiske, and A. Rolla. 2006a. "Inhibition of Amazon Deforestation and Fire by Parks and Indigenous Lands." *Conservation Biology* 20:65–73.
Nepstad, Daniel C., C. Stickler, and O. Almeida. 2006b. "Globalization of the Amazon Soy and Beef Industries: Opportunities for Conservation." *Conservation Biology* 20:1,595–1603.
Nepstad, Daniel, B. S. Soares-Filho, F. Merry, A. Lima, P. Moutinho, J. Carter, M. Bowman, A. Cattaneo, H. Rodrigues, S. Schwartzman, D. G. McGrath, C. M. Stickler, R. Lubowski, P. Piris-Cabezas, S. Rivero, A. Alencar, O. Almeida, and O. Stella. 2009. "The End of Deforestation in the Brazilian Amazon." *Science* 326:1,350–1.
Netting, R. Mac. 1981. *Balancing on an Alp: Ecological Change and Continuity in a Swiss Mountain Community.* Cambridge, UK: Cambridge University Press.
Netting, R. Mac. 1993. *Smallholders, Householders: The Ecology of Small Scale, Sustainable Agriculture.* Stanford, Calif.: Stanford University Press.
Neumann, Roderick P. 1998. *Imposing Wilderness: Struggles over Livelihood and Nature Preservation in Africa.* Berkeley, Calif.: University of California Press.
Neumann, Roderick P. 2002. "The Postwar Conservation Boom in British Colonial Africa." *Environmental History* 7:1,22–47.
Ng'weno, Bettina. 2001. "Reidentifying Ground Rules: Community Inheritance Disputes Among the Digo of Kenya." In *Communities and the Environment: Ethnicity, Gender, and the State in Community Based Conservation.* Edited by A. Agrawal and C. Gibson, 111–37. New Brunswick, NJ: Rutgers University Press.
Norgaard, Kari Marie. 2011. *Living in Denial: Climate Change, Emotions, and Everyday Life.* Cambridge, Mass.: MIT Press.
Norgaard, Richard B. 1994. *Development Betrayed: The End of Progress and a Coevolutionary Revisioning of the Future.* New York: Routledge.
Northwest Power and Conservation Council. 2011. Columbia River History Project. 2011. Available at: www.nwcouncil.org/history/ColumbiaRiver-Compact.asp.

Nowak, Martin A. 2006. "Five Rules for the Evolution of Cooperation." *Science* 314:1,559–63.
O'Connor, James. 1998. *Natural Causes: Essays in Ecological Marxism*. New York: Guilford.
Odum, Eugene P. 1969. "The Strategy of Ecosystem Development." *Science* 164:262–70.
Ogawa, Naohiro, R. Retherford, and R. Matsukura. 2009. "Japan's Declining Fertility and Policy Response." In *Ultra-low fertility in Pacific Asia: Trends, Causes, and Policy Issues*. Edited by P. Straughan, A. V. Chan, and G. Jones, 40–72. London: Taylor and Francis.
Olson, Mancur. 1982. *The Rise and Decline of Nations: Economic Growth, Stagflation, and Social Rigidities*. New Haven, Conn.: Yale University Press.
O'Neill, Brian C. 2010. "Climate Change and Population Growth." In *A Pivotal Moment: Population, Justice, and the Environmental Challenge*. Edited by L. Mazur, 81–94. Washington, DC: Island Press.
O'Neill, Brian C., M. Dalton, R. Fuchs, L. Jiang, S. Pachauri, and K. Zigova. 2010. "Global Demographic Trends and Future Carbon Emissions." *Proceedings of the National Academy of Sciences* 107:17,521–26. Available at: www.pnas.org/cgi/doi/10.1073/pnas.1004581107.
Onis, Ziya. 1991. "The Logic of the Developmental State." *Comparative Politics* 24:109–26.
Onishi, Norimitsu. 2005. "How Do Japanese Dump Trash?: Let Us Count the Myriad Ways." *New York Times* May 12.
Orlove, Ben, E. Wiegandt, and B. Luckman, editors. 2008. *Darkening Peaks: Glacier Retreat, Science, and Society*. Berkeley, Calif.: University of California Press.
O'Rourke, Dara. 2004. *Community-Driven Regulation: Balancing Development and the Environment in Vietnam*. Cambridge, Mass.: MIT Press.
Ostrom, Elinor. 1990. *Governing the Commons: The Evolution of Institutions for Collective Action*. New York: Cambridge University Press.
Ostrom, Elinor. 2005. *Understanding Institutional Diversity*. Princeton, NJ: Princeton University Press.
Ostrom, Elinor. 2009. "A General Framework for Analyzing Sustainability of Social-ecological Systems." *Science* 325:419–22.
Ostrom, Elinor. 2010. "Polycentric Systems for Coping with Collective Action and Global Environmental Change." *Global Environmental Change* 20:550–7.
Ostrom, Elinor, M. Janssen, and J. Anderies. 2007. "Going Beyond Panaceas." *Proceedings of the National Academy of Sciences* 104:15,176–8.
Ostrom, M. R. and R. Jussaume, Jr. 2007. "Assessing the Significance of Direct Farmer-Consumer Linkages as a Change Strategy in Washington State: Civic or Opportunistic?" In *Remaking the North American Food System: Strategies for Sustainability*. Edited by C. Clare Hinrichs and T. Lyson, 235–59. Lincoln and London: University of Nebraska Press.
Pacala, Stephen and R. Socolow. 2004. "Stabilization Wedges: Solving the Climate Problem for the Next 50 years with Current Technologies." *Science* 305:968–72.

Parrott, Nicholas, J. Olesen, and H. Hogh-Jensen. 2005. "Certified and Non-certified Organic Farming in the Developing World." In *The Global Development of Organic Agriculture*. Edited by N. Halberg, M. Knudsen, M. Alroe, and E. Kristensen, 153–80. London: CABI Publishers.

Pauly, Daniel, V. Christensen, S. Guenette, T. Pitcher, U. R. Sumaila, C. Walters, R. Watson, and D. Zeller. 2002. "Towards Sustainability in World Fisheries." *Nature* 418:689–95.

Pellow, David N. 2004. "The Politics of Illegal Dumping: An Environmental Justice Framework." *Qualitative Sociology* 27:511–25.

Pellow, David N. 2007. *Resisting Global Toxics: Transnational Movements for Environmental Justice*. Cambridge, Mass.: MIT Press.

Pellow, David N. and R. Brulle, editors. 2005. *Power, Justice, the Environment: A Critical Appraisal of the Environmental Justice Movement*. Boston, Mass.: MIT Press.

Pempel, T. J. 1999. "The Developmental Regime in a Changing World Economy." In *The Developmental State*. Edited by M. Woo-Cumings, 137–81. Ithaca, NY: Cornell University Press.

Perelli-Harris, Brienna. 2005. "The Path to Lowest Low Fertility in Ukraine." *Population Studies* 59:55–70.

Perelli-Harris, Brienna. 2006. "The Influence of Informal Work and Subjective Well-being on Child-bearing in Post-Soviet Russia." *Population and Development Review* 32:729–53.

Pereira, Alexius A. 2008. "Whither the Developmental State?: Explaining Singapore's Continued Developmentalism." *Third World Quarterly* 29(6):1,189–1,206.

Perkins, Richard. 2007. "Globalizing Corporate Environmentalism?: Convergence and Heterogeneity in Indian Industry." *Studies in Comparative International Development* 42:279–309.

Perkins, Richard and E. Neumayer. 2005. "The International Diffusion of New Technologies: Multitechnology Analysis of Latecomer Advantage and Global Economic Integration." *Annals of the Association of American Geographers* 95:789–808.

Perrow, Charles. 1999. *Normal Accidents: Living with High Risk Technologies*. 2nd edition. Princeton, NJ: Princeton University Press.

Perrow, Charles. 2007. *The Next Catastrophe: Reducing Our Vulnerabilities to Natural, Industrial, and Terrorist Disasters*. Princeton, NJ: Princeton University Press.

Perrow, Charles. 2008. "Complexity, Catastrophe, and Modularity." *Sociological Inquiry* 78:162–73.

Peters, B. Guy and B. W. Hogswood. 1985. "In Search of the Issue-Attention Cycle." *Journal of Politics* 47:238–53.

Peters, Glen P., G. Marland, C. Le Quéré, T. Boden, J. G. Canadell, and M. R. Raupach. 2012. "Rapid Growth in CO2 emissions after the 2008–2009 Global Financial Crisis." *Nature Climate Change* 2:2–4. DOI:10.1038/nclimate1332.

Petrolia, D. R. and T. Kim. 2011. "Preventing Land Loss in Coastal Louisiana: Estimates of WTP and WTA." *Journal of Environmental Management* 92:859–65.

Petroni, Suzanne. 2009. "Policy Review: Thoughts on Addressing Population and Climate Change in a Just and Ethical Manner." *Population and Environment* 30:275–89.

Philander, George. 1990. *El Nino, La Nina, and the Southern Oscillation*. San Diego, Calif.: Academic Press.

Pianka, Eric R. 1970. "On r- and K-selection." *American Naturalist* 104:592–7.

Pickett, Steward T. A., M. L. Cadenasso, and S. J. Meiners. 2009. "Ever Since Clements: From Succession to Vegetation Dynamics and Understanding to Intervention." *Applied Vegetation Science* 12:9–21.

Pickett, Steward T. A., J. Collins, and J. Armesto. 1987. "Models, Mechanisms, and Pathways of Plant Succession." *Botanical Review* 53:335–71.

Pickett, Steward T. A. and P. S. White. 1985. *The Ecology of Natural Disturbance and Patch Dynamics*. New York: Academic Press.

Pinedo-Vasquez, Miguel, D. Zarin, K. Coffey, C. Padoch, and F. Rabelo. 2001. "Post-boom Logging in Amazonia." *Human Ecology* 29:219–39.

Planet Ark. 2004. Recycling Olympics: An International Waste and Recycling Comparison. Sydney, Australia. Available at: http://recyclingnearyou.com.au/documents/TheRecyclingOlympics-2004.pdf.

Plasencia, Yomaira. 2011. Estudio sobre las Condiciones Laborales y Organizativas de los Trabajadores del Modelo Agroindustrial Bananero. Presentation at the V Encuentro de la Seccion de Estudios Ecuatorianos de LASA, May 29–31, Quito, Ecuador.

Poffenberger, Mark, B. McGean, and A. Khare. 1996. "Communities Sustaining India's Forests in the 21st Century." In *Village Voices, Forest Choices: Joint Forest Management in India*. Edited by M. Poffenberger and B. McGean, 17–55. Delhi: Oxford University Press.

Polidano, Charles. 2001. "Don't Discard State Autonomy: Revisiting the East Asian Experience of Development." *Political Studies* 49:513–27.

Pollan, Michael. 2001. "Behind the Organic-Industrial Complex." *New York Times Magazine* May 1. Available at: www.nytimes.com/2001/05/13/magazine/13ORGANIC.html?pagewanted=all.

Pollan, Michael. 2008. "Why Bother?: Looking for a Few Good Reasons to Go Green." *New York Times Magazine*. April 20. Available at: www.nytimes.com/2008/04/20/magazine/20wwln-lede-t.html?pagewanted=all.

Porter, Bryan E., F. C. Leeming, and W. D. Dryer. 1995. "Solid Waste Recovery: A Reward of Behavioral Programs to Increase Recycling." *Environment and Behavior* 27:122–52.

Porter-Bolland, Luciana, E. A. Ellis, M. R. Guariguata, I. Ruiz-Mallén, S. Negrete-Yankelevich, and V. Reyes-García. 2012. "Community Managed Forests and Forest Protected Areas: An Assessment of their Conservation Effectiveness across the Tropics." *Forest Ecology and Management* 268:6–17. DOI:10.1016/j.foreco.2011.05.034.

Pray, Carl, J. Huang, R. Hu, and S. Rozelle. 2002. "Five Years of Bt Cotton: Benefits Continue." *Plant Journal* 31:423–30.

Princen, Thomas. 2005. *The Logic of Sufficiency*. Cambridge, Mass.: MIT Press.

Pulver, Simone. 2007. "Making Sense of Corporate Environmentalism: An Environmental Contestation Approach to Analyzing the Causes and Consequences of the Climate Change Policy Split in the Oil Industry." *Organization and Environment* 20:44–83.

Pulver, Simone, N. Hultman, and L. Guimaraes. 2010. "Carbon Market Participation by Sugar Mills in Brazil." *Climate and Development*. 2:248–62.

Reardon, Sean F. and K. Bischoff. 2011. "Income Inequality and Income Segregation." *American Journal of Sociology* 116:1,092–153.

Reardon, T., C. P. Timmer, C. B. Barrett, and J. Berdegue. 2003. "The Rise of Supermarkets in Africa, Asia, and Latin America." *American Journal of Agricultural Economics* 85:1,140–6.

Redefining Progress. 2004. Ecological Footprints of Nations. Oakland, Calif. Available at: www.rprogress.org/publications/2004/footprintnations2004.pdf.

Reher, David S. 2007. "Towards Long-term Population Decline: A Discussion of Relevant Issues." *European Journal of Population* 23:189–207.

Reij, Chris and G. Tappan. 2008. Scale, Causes, and Impacts of Regreening in Niger. Presentation at the Social Life of Forests Workshop, University of Chicago, May. Available at: http://chicago.mirocommunity.org/video/3200/chris-reij-gray-tappan-scale-c.

Reij, Chris, G. Tappan, and Melinda Smale. 2009. Agroenvironmental Transformation in the Sahel: Another Kind of 'Green Revolution. IFPRI Discussion Paper 914. Washington, DC: International Food Policy Research Institute.

Reisner, Marc. 1986. *Cadillac Desert: The American West and Its Disappearing Water*. New York: Viking.

Repa, Edward. 2005a. Interstate Movement of Municipal Solid Wastes. NSWMA Bulletin 5-2. Washington, DC: National Solid Wastes Management Association.

Repa, Edward. 2005b. NSWMA's Tip Fee Survey. NSWMA Bulletin 5-3. Washington, DC: National Solid Wastes Management Association.

Repetto, Robert, editor. 2006. *Punctuated Equilibrium and the Dynamics of U.S. Environmental Policy*. New Haven, Conn.: Yale University Press.

Reuters. 2008. "Alcoa Sets Goal to Raise North American Aluminum Beverage Can Recycling Rate from...." January 22. Available at: www.reuters.com/article/pressRelease/idUS211970+22-Jan-2008+BW20080122.

Revkin, Andrew. 2007. "Are Words Worthless in the Climate Fight?" *New York Times*. December 3. Available at: http://dotearth.blogs.nytimes.com/2007/12/03/are-words-worthless-in-the-climate-fight/.

Reznick, David, M. J. Bryant, and F. Bashey. 2002. "R- and k-Selection Revisited: The Role of Population Regulation in Life-History Evolution." *Ecology* 83:1,509–20. DOI: 10.1890/0012–9658(2002)083[1509:RAKSRT]2.0.CO;2.

Rhoades, Robert, X. Z. Rios, and J. A. Ochoa. 2008. "Mama Cotacachi: History, Local, Perceptions, and Social Impacts of Climate Change and Glacier Retreat in the Ecuadorian Andes." In *Darkening Peaks: Glacier Retreat, Science, and Society*. Edited by B. Orlove, E. Wiegandt, and B. Luckman, 216–28. Berkeley, Calif.: University of California Press.

Richards, Peter D., R. J. Myers, S. M. Swinton, and R. T. Walker. 2012. "Exchange Rates, Soybean Supply Response, and Deforestation in South America." *Global Environmental Change* 22:454–62. Available at: http://dx.doi.org/10.1016/j.gloenvcha.2012.01.004.

Richerson, Peter J. 1977. "Ecology and Human Ecology: A Comparison of Theories in the Biological and the Social Sciences." *American Ethnologist* 4:1–26.
Richerson, Peter J. and R. Boyd. 2005. *Not by Genes Alone: How Culture Transformed Human Evolution.* Chicago, Ill.: University of Chicago Press.
Richtel, Marc. 2011. "Consumers Hold on to Products Longer." *New York Times* February 25. p. B1.
Riley, Mark. 2008. "From Salvage to Recycling – New Agendas or Same Old Rubbish?" *Area* 40:70–89.
Risgaard, Marie-Louise, P. Frederiksen, and P. Kaltoft. 2007. "Socio-Cultural Processes Behind the Differential Distribution of Organic Farming in Denmark: A Case Study." *Agriculture and Human Values* 24:445–59.
Ritzer, George. 2003. *The Macdonaldization of Society.* Revised edition. Thousand Oaks, Calif.: Pine Forge Press.
Roberts, C. M., J. A. Bohnsack, F. R. Gell, J. P. Hawkins, and R. Goodridge. 2001. "Effects of Marine Reserves on Adjacent Fisheries." *Science* 294:1, 920–3.
Roberts, T. John. 2007. "Debate on Voluntary Actions to Fight Climate Change." Envirosoc listserv. September 24.
Robinson, William I. 2004. *A Theory of Global Capitalism: Production, Class, and State in a Transnational World.* Baltimore, MD; Johns Hopkins University Press.
Robinson, William S. 1950. "Ecological Correlations and the Behavior of Individuals." *American Sociological Review* 15:351–7.
Rocheleau, Dianne, L. Ross, J. Morrobel, L. Malaret, R. Hernandez, and T. Kominiak. 2001. "Complex Communities and Emergent Ecologies in the Regional Agroforest of Zambrana-Chacuey, Dominican Republic." *Ecumene* 8:465–92.
Rock, M., J. Murphy, R. Rasich, P. van Seters, and S. Managi. 2009. "A Hard Slog, Not a Leapfrog: Globalization and Sustainability Transitions in Developing Asia." *Technological Forecasting and Social Change* 76:241–54.
Roett, Riordan. 1999. *Brazil: Politics in a Patrimonial Society.* Westport, Conn.: Greenwood Publishing.
Rogers, Will. 2004. "It's Easy Being Green." *New York Times.* November 20. Available at: www.nytimes.com/2004/11/20/opinion/20rogers.html.
Roitner-Schobesberger, Birgit, I. Darnhofer, S. Samsook, and C. Vogl. 2008. "Consumers and Organic Food." *Food Policy* 33:112–21.
Rome, Adam. 2001. *Bulldozer in the Countryside: Suburban Sprawl and the Rise of American Environmentalism.* Cambridge, UK: Cambridge University Press.
Rosa, Eugene A., R. York, and T. Dietz. 2004. "Tracking the Anthropogenic Drivers of Ecological Impacts." *AMBIO: A Journal of the Human Environment* 23:509–12.
Rosenbloom, Stephanie. 2009. "At Wal-Mart: Labeling to Reflect Green Intent." *New York Times* July 15. p. B1.
Rosenbluth, Frances M. 2007a. "The Political Economy of Low Fertility." In *The Political Economy of Japan's Low Fertility.* Edited by F. Rosenbluth, 3–36. Stanford, Calif.: Stanford University Press.

Rosenbluth, Frances M. 2007b. "Conclusion." In *The Political Economy of Japan's Low Fertility*. Edited by F. Rosenbluth, 201–15. Stanford, Calif.: Stanford University Press.

Rosenthal, Elizabeth. 2008. "Empty Seas: Europe's Appetite for Seafood Propels Illegal Trade." *New York Times*. January 15. Available at: www.nytimes.com/2008/01/15/world/europe/15fish.html?_r=1&oref=slogi.

Rosero-Bixby, Luis, T. Castro-Martín, and T. Martín-García. 2007. "Is Latin America Starting to Retreat from Early and Universal Child-bearing?" *Demographic Research* 20:169–93.

Rousmaniere, Peter. 2007. "Shipbreaking in the Developing World: Problems and Prospects." *International Journal of Occupational and Environmental Health* 13:359–68.

Rudel, Thomas K. 1989. *Situations and Strategies in American Land Use Planning*. Cambridge, UK: Cambridge University Press.

Rudel, Thomas K. 2007. "Changing Agents of Deforestation: From State Initiated to Enterprise Driven Processes, 1970–2000." *Land Use Policy* 24:35–41.

Rudel, Thomas K. 2009. "How Do People Transform Landscapes?: A Sociological Perspective on Suburban Sprawl and Tropical Deforestation." *American Journal of Sociology* 115:129–54.

Rudel, Thomas K and L. Hooper. 2005. "Is the Pace of Social Change Accelerating?: Latecomers, Common Languages, and Rapid Historical Declines in Fertility." *International Journal of Comparative Sociology* 46:275–96.

Rudel, Thomas K. with B. Horowitz. 1993. *Tropical Deforestation: Small Farmers and Land Clearing in the Ecuadorian Amazon*. New York: Columbia University Press.

Rudel, T. K., K. O'Neill, P. Gottlieb, M. McDermott, and C. Hatfield. 2011. "From Middle to Upper Class Sprawl?: Land Use Controls and Real Estate Development in Northern New Jersey." *Annals of the Association of American Geographers* 101:609–24. DOI: 10.1080/00045608.2011.560062.

Ruf, Francois. 2001."Tree Crops as Agents of Deforestation and Reforestation: The Case of Cocoa in Côte D'Ivoire and Sulawesi." In *Agricultural Technologies and Tropical Deforestation*. Edited by A. Angelsen and D. Kaimowitz, 304–15. Wallingford, UK: CABI Publishing.

Sahara and Sahel Observatory (SSO). 2008. *The Great Green Wall Initiative for the Sahara and the Sahel\ SSO*. Introductory Note Number 3. Tunis, Tunisia: CEN- SAD-SSO.

Sahota, Amarjit. 2010. "The Global Market for Food and Drink." In *The World of Organic Agriculture: Statistics and Emerging Trends, 2010*. Edited by H. Willer and L. Kilcher, 54–9. Bonn: FiBL and IFOAM.

Salamon, Sonya. 1995. *Prairie Patrimony: Family, Farming and Community in the Midwest*. Chapel Hill, NC: University of North Carolina Press.

Sanders, Richard. 2006. "A Market Road to Sustainable Agriculture? Ecological Agriculture, Green Food and Organic Agriculture in China." *Development and Change* 37:201–26.

Satake, Akiko, T. K. Rudel, and A. Onuma. 2008. "Scale Mismatches and Their Ecological and Economic Effects on Landscapes: A Spatially Explicit Model." *Global Environmental Change* 18:768–75.

Sayre, Nathan. 2008. "The Genesis, History, and Limits of Carrying Capacity." *Annals of the Association of American Geographers* 98:120–34.
Scheffer, Martin. 2009. *Critical Transitions in Nature and Society*. Princeton, NJ: Princeton University Press.
Schelhas, John and M. J. Pfeffer. 2008. *Saving Forests, Protecting People?: Environmental Conservation in Central America*. Lanham, Md.: Altamira Press.
Schnaiberg, Allan. 2007. Envirosoc Listserv. October 10. Available at: http://listserv.brown.edu/archives/cgi-bin/wa?.
Schneider, Laura C. 2006. "Invasive Species and Land Use: The Effect of Land Management Practices on Bracken Fern Invasion in the Region of Calakmul." *Journal of Latin American Geography* 5:91–107.
Scholte, J. A. 2005. *Globalization: A Critical Introduction*. 2nd edition. New York: Palgrave/MacMillan.
Schor, Juliet. 1998. *The Overspent American: Upscaling, Downshifting, and the New Consumer*. New York: Basic Books.
Schulman, Audrey. 2008. "How to be a Climate Hero." *Orion* May–June. Available at: www.orionmagazine.org/index.php/articles/article/2957.
Schultz, Duane P. and S. Schultz. 2008. *Theories of Personality*. 8th edition. Independence, KY: Wadsworth Publishing.
Schumpeter, Joseph A. 1934. *The Theory of Economic Development*. Cambridge, Mass.: Harvard University Press.
Schumpeter, Joseph A. 1942. *Capitalism, Socialism and Democracy*. New York: Harper.
Scialabba, Nadia. 2007. *Organic Agriculture and Food Security*. Rome: FAO.
Scialabba, Nadia and C. Hattam, editors. 2002. *Organic Agriculture, Environment, and Food Security*. Rome: FAO.
Scott, James C. 1998. *Seeing Like a State: How Certain Schemes to Improve the Human Condition Have Failed*. New Haven, Conn.: Yale University Press.
Scott, Lee. 2005. Twentieth Century Leadership. Wal-Mart, October 24. Available at: www.walmartstores.com/Files/21st%20Century%20Leadership.pdf.
Scott, Michael. 2009. "Cuyahoga River Fire Galvanized Clean Water and the Environment as a Public Issue." *Cleveland Plain Dealer*. April 12. Available at: www.cleveland.com/science/index.ssf/2009/04/cuyahoga_river_fire_galvanized.html.
Scruggs, L. and S. Benegal. 2012. "Declining Public Concern About Climate Change: Can We Blame the Great Recession?" *Global Environmental Change*. 22(2):505–515. DOI:10.1016/j.gloenvcha.2012.01.002.
Searchinger, T. R. Heimlich, R. A. Houghton, F. Dong, A. Elobeid, J. Fabiosa, S. Tokgoz, D. Hayes, and T. Yu. 2009. "Use of U.S. Croplands for Biofuels Increased Greenhouse Gases through Land Use Change." *Science* 326:1,238–40. DOI: 10,1126/Science. 1178797.
Sell, Jane and T. Love. 2009. "Common Fate, Crisis, and Cooperation in Social Dilemmas." In *Advances in Group Processes (Vol. 26): Altruism and Prosocial Behavior in Groups*. Edited by S. Thye and E. Lawler, 53–80. London: Emerald Publishing.
Sellen, Abigail and R. Harper. 2002. *The Myth of the Paperless Office*. Cambridge, Mass.: MIT Press.

Selznick, Philip. 1992. *The Moral Commonwealth: Social Theory and the Promise of Community*. Berkeley, Calif.: University of California Press.

Service, Robert F. 2007. "Delta Blues, California Style." *Science* 317:442–5.

Sewell, William, Jr. 2005. *The Logics of History: Social Theory and Social Transformation*. Chicago: University of Chicago Press.

Seyfang, Gill. 2006. "Ecological Citizenship and Sustainable Consumption: Examining Local Organic Food Networks." *Journal of Rural Studies* 22:383–95.

Simms, Andrew. 2001. *An Environmental War Economy: The Lessons of Ecological Debt and Global Warming*. London: New Economics Foundation.

Sirianni, Carmen and L. Friedland. 1995. "Social Capital and Civic Innovation." Paper presented at the American Sociological Association Annual Meetings, August 20, Washington, DC.

Smil, Vaclav. 1999. "Crop Residues: Agriculture's Largest Harvest." *Bioscience* 49:299–309.

Smith, Robert L. 1974. *Ecology and Field Biology*. 2nd edition. New York: Harper and Row.

Snow, D. A., E. Rochford, S. Worden, and R. Benford. 1986. "Frame Alignment Processes, Micromobilization, and Movement Participation." *American Sociological Review* 51:464–81.

Sober, Elliott. 1980. "Evolution, Population Thinking, and Essentialism." *Philosophy of Science* 47:350–83.

Sobotka, Tomas. 2004. "Is Lowest – Low Fertility in Europe Explained by the Postponement of Childbearing?" *Population and Development Review* 30:195–220.

Soil Association. 2009. *Soil Carbon and Climate Change*. Bristol, UK: Soil Association.

Soliday, Elizabeth. 2009. "Intensive Mothering, Intensive Visiting: How Mothers View Prenatal Care Schedules." *Journal of the Association for Research on Mothering* 11:49–58.

Solnit, Rebecca. 2009. *A Paradise Built in Hell: The Extraordinary Communities That Arise in Disasters*. New York: Viking.

Sonnenfeld, David. 2000. "Contradictions of Ecological Modernization: Pulp and Paper Manufacturing in South-east Asia." In *Ecological Modernization around the World*. Edited by A. P. J. Mol and D. Sonnenfeld, 235–56. London: Frank Cass.

Spencer, Herbert. 1876 (1967). *The Evolution of Society: Selections from Herbert Spencer's "Principles of Sociology."* Edited by Robert Carneiro. Chicago: University of Chicago Press.

Speth, J. G. 2008. *The Bridge at the Edge of the World: Capitalism, the Environment, and Crossing from Crisis to Sustainability*. New Haven, Conn.: Yale University Press.

Stark, Laura and H. P. Kohler. 2002. "The Debate over Low Fertility in the Popular Press, 1998–1999." *Population Research and Policy Review* 21:535–74.

Stark, Laura and H. P. Kohler. 2004. "The Popular Debate About Low Fertility: An Analysis of the German Press." *European Journal of Population* 20:293–321.

Stein, Karen. 2008. "Understanding Consumption and Environmental Change in China: A Cross-National Comparison of Consumer Patterns." *Human Ecology Review* 16:41–9.

Stein, Rob. 2010. "U.S. Birthrate Drops 2 Percent in 2008." *Washington Post* April 7. Available at: www.washingtonpost.com/wp-dyn/content/article/2010/04/06/AR2010040600758_2.html?sid=ST2010122105943.

Steinfeld, Hennings, P. Gerber, T. Wassenaar, V. Castel, M. Rosales, and C. de Haan. 2006. *Livestock's Long Shadow: Environmental Issues and Options*. Rome: FAO.

Stinchecombe, Arthur L. 1965. "Social Structure and Organizations." In *Handbook of Organizations*. Edited by James G. March, 142–93. Chicago, Ill.: Rand McNally.

Stobel-Richter, Yve, M. Beutel, C. Finck, and E. Brahler. 2005. "The 'Wish to Have a Child': Childlessness and Infertility in Germany." *Human Reproduction* 20:2,850–7.

Stone, Roger and C. D'Andrea. 2001. *Tropical Forests and the Human Spirit: Journeys to the Brink of Hope*. Berkeley, Calif.: University of California Press.

Strasser, Susan. 1999. *Waste and Want: A Social History of Trash*. New York and London: Metropolitan Books.

Straughan, Paulin, A. Chan, and G. Jones. 2009. "From Population Control to Fertility Promotion: A Case Study of Family Policies and Fertility Trends in Singapore." In *Ultra-low fertility in Pacific Asia: Trends, Causes, and Policy Issues*. Edited by P. Straughan, A. V. Chan, and G. Jones, 181–203. London: Taylor and Francis.

Streets, David G., K. Jiang, X. Hu, J. E. Sinton, X.-Q. Zhang, D. Xu, M. Z. Jacobson, and J. E. Hansen. 2001. "Recent Reductions in China's Greenhouse Gas Emissions." *Science* 294:1,835–7.

Sucato, Kirsty. 2008. "State Seeks to Regain Recycling Momentum." *New York Times*. March 16. Available at: www.nytimes.com/2008/03/16/nyregion/nyregionspecial2/16recyclingnj.html.

Swedberg, Richard. 2002. "The Economic Sociology of Capitalism: Weber and Schumpeter." *Journal of Classical Sociology* 2:227–55.

Swidler, Ann. 1986. "Culture in Action: Symbols and Strategies." *American Sociological Review* 51:273–86.

Szasz, Andrew. 1994. *Ecopopulism: Toxic Waste and the Movement for Environmental Justice*. Minneapolis: University of Minnesota Press.

Szasz, Andrew. 2007. *Shopping Our Way to Safety: How We Changed from Protecting the Environment to Protecting Ourselves*. Minneapolis: University of Minnesota Press.

Tacconi, Luca. 2003. Fires in Indonesia: Causes, Costs, and Consequences. CIFOR Occasional Paper No. 38. Bogor, Indonesia: Center for International Forestry Research.

Tainter, Joseph A. 1988. *The Collapse of Complex Societies*. Cambridge, UK: Cambridge University Press.

Tainter, Joseph. A. 2011. "Energy, Complexity, and Sustainability: A Historical Perspective." *Environmental Innovations and Societal Transitions* 1:89–96.

Taleb, Nassim. 2010. *The Black Swan: The Impact of the Highly Improbable: With a New Section on Robustness and Fragility*. 2nd edition. New York: Random House.
Tansley, Arthur G. 1935, "The Use and Abuse of Vegetational Concepts and Terms." *Ecology* 16:284–307.
Tarrow, Sidney. 2000. Beyond Globalization: Why Creating Transnational Social Movements Is So Hard and When It Is Most Likely to Happen. Global Solidarity Dialogue. Available at: www.antenna.nl/~waterman/tarrow.html.
Terborgh, John. 1992. *Biodiversity and the Tropical Rainforest*. New York: W. H. Freeman.
Thornton, Arland. 2005. *Reading History Sideways: The Fallacy and Enduring Impact of the Developmental Paradigm on Family Life*. Chicago: University of Chicago Press.
Tierney, Kathleen. 2011. Hazards, Risks, and Climate Change. Paper presented at the American Sociological Association meetings in Las Vegas, Nevada, August 20.
Tiffen, Mary, M. Mortimore, and F. Gichuki. 1994. *More People, Less Erosion: Environmental Recovery in Kenya*. New York: John Wiley.
Tilly, Charles. 1975. "Reflections on the History of European State-Making." In *The Formation of National States in Western Europe*. Edited by Charles Tilly, 3–83. Princeton, NJ: Princeton University Press.
Tomlinson, John. 1999. *Globalization and Culture*. Chicago: University of Chicago Press.
Trewavas, Anthony. 2001. "Urban Myths of Organic Farming." *Nature* 410:409–10.
Tripp, Robert and C. Longeley. 2006. *Self-sufficient Agriculture: Labour and Knowledge in Small Scale Farming*. London: Earthscan.
True, James L., B. D. Jones, and F. R. Baumgartner. 2006. "Punctuated Equilibrium Theory: Explaining Stability and Change in Policy Making." In *Theories of the Policy Process*. Edited by Paul Sabatier, 97–115. Boulder, Colo.: Westview Press.
Tu, E. J. C., X. Yuan, and X. Zhang. 2007. "Fertility Transition in Hong Kong and Taiwan." In *Transition and Challenge: China's Population at the Beginning of the 21st Century*. Edited by Z. Zhao and F. Guo, 71–86. London: Oxford University Press.
Tucker, C. M., J. C. Randolph, and E. J. Castellanos. 2007. "Institutions, Biophysical Factors, and History: An Integrative Analysis of Private and Common Property Forests in Guatemala and Honduras." *Human Ecology* 35:259–74.
Turner, Jonathan H. 1995. *Macrodynamics: Towards a Theory on the Organization of Human Populations*. ASA Rose Monograph Series. New Brunswick, NJ: Rutgers University Press.
United Kingdom. 2006. Stern Review on the Economics of Climate Change. London: Treasury Department.
United Kingdom, Foreign and Commonwealth Office. 2006. Heart of Borneo. Available at: www.fco.gov.uk/servlet/Front?pagename=OpenMarket/Xcelerate/ShowPag e&c=Page&cid=1177505205975.

United Nations. 1982. Convention on the Law of the Sea, 1982, Overview and Full Text. New York: Division for Ocean Affairs and the Law of the Sea. Available at: www.un.org/Depts/los/convention_agreements/convention_overview_convention.htm.

United Nations Environmental Program (UNEP) – World Conservation Monitoring Centre (WCMC). 2007. World Vision. Cambridge, UK. Available at: www.unep-wcmc.org/protected_Areas/docs/Besancon.pdf.

United Nations Environmental Program (UNEP) – World Meteorological Association. 2011. Integrated Assessment of Black Carbon and Tropospheric Ozone; Summary for Decision Makers. New York: UNEP. Available at: www.unep.org/dewa/Portals/67/pdf/Black_Carbon.pdf.

United Nations, Framework Convention on Climate Change (UNFCCC). Greenhouse Gas Inventory Data. Available at: http://unfccc.int/files/inc/graphics/image/gif/graph4_2007_ori.gif.

United Nations – Habitat (Human Settlements Programme). 2010. State of the World's Cities, 2008–2009. New York: Habitat. Available at: www.unhabitat.org/pmss/listItemDetails.aspx?publicationID=2562.

United Nations (UNPD), Population Division of the Department of Economic and Social Affairs. 2007. World Population Prospects: The 2006 Revision and World Urbanization Prospects: The 2005 Revision. Available at: http://esa.un.org/unpp.

United Nations (UNPD). Population Division of the Department of Economic and Social Affairs, United Nations. 2011. World Population Prospects: 2010 Revision. Available at: http://esa.un.org/unpp.

United States Department of Agriculture (USDA). 2000. Foot and Mouth Disease in Brazil. Impact Report. Available at: www.aphis.usda.gov/animal_health/emergingissues/impactworksheets/iw_2000_files/foreign/fmd_brazil0800e.htm.

United States Department of Agriculture (USDA). 2007. National Agricultural Statistics Service, Field Corn Statistics. Washington, DC: NASS. Available at: www.nass.usda.gov/QuickStats/index2.jsp.

U.S. Department of Agriculture (USDA). 2009. National Agricultural Statistics Service. 2007 Census of Agriculture – State Data, Selected Practices. Table 44. Available at: http://www.agcensus.usda.gov/Publications/2007/Full_Report/Volume_1,_Chapter_2_US_State_Level/st99_2_044_044.pdf.

United States Department of Agriculture (USDA). 2010. Economic Research Service, Briefing Room, Organic Agriculture. Washington, DC: ERS. Available at: www.ers.usda.gov/Briefing/Organic.

United States Department of Agriculture (USDA). 2011a. Facts and Figures About Farmers Markets. Washington, DC: Economic Research Service. Available at: www.ams.usda.gov/AMSv1.0/farmersmarkets.

United States Department of Agriculture (USDA). 2011b. Economic Research Service. Certified Organic Farmland Acreage, Livestock Numbers, and Farm Operations, 1992–2005. Available at: www.ers.usda.gov/Briefing/Organic.

United States Department of Agriculture (USDA). 2011c. USDA Agricultural Projections to 2020. Office of the Chief Economist. Washington DC. Available at: www.usda.gov/oce/reports/energy/index.htm.

United States Department of Energy. Energy Information Administration (USEIA). 2009. Emissions of Greenhouse Gases in the United States in 2008. Washington, DC. Available at: ftp://ftp.eia.doe.gov/pub/oiaf/1605/cdrom/pdf/ggrpt/057308.pdf.

United States Environmental Protection Agency (USEPA). 2007. Municipal Solid Waste Generation, Recycling, and Disposal: Facts and Figures. Washington, DC. Available at: www.epa.gov/garbage/facts.htm.

United States Environmental Protection Agency (USEPA). 2010. Climate Change and Extreme Events. Available at: www.epa.gov/climatechange/effects/extreme.html.

United States Environmental Protection Agency (USEPA). 2010. Municipal Solid Waste in the United States: Facts and Figures. Washington, DC: Office of Solid Waste.

Uphoff, Norman T. 1992. *Learning from Gal Oya: Possibilities for Participatory Development and Post-Newtonian Social Science*. Ithaca, NY and London: Cornell University Press.

Vale, Lawrence J. and T. J. Campanella. 2005. *The Resilient City: How Modern Cities Recover from Disasters*. New York: Oxford University Press.

van Beukering, Pieter and M. Bouman. 2001. "Empirical Evidence on Recycling and Trade of Paper and Lead in Developed and Developing Countries." *World Development* 29:1,717–37.

Van de Kaa, Dirk. 1987. "Europe's Second Demographic Transition." *Population Bulletin* 42:1–59.

van den Broeke, Michiel, J. Bamber, J. Ettema, E. Rignot, E. Schrama, W. Jan van de Berg, E. van Meijgaard, I. Velicogna, and B. Wouters. 2009. "Partitioning Recent Greenland Mass Loss." *Science* 326:984–6. DOI: 10.1126/science.1178176.

Vartiainen, Juhana. 1999. "The Economics of Successful State Intervention in Industrial Transformation." In *The Developmental State*. Edited by M. Woo-Cumings, 200–34. Ithaca, NY: Cornell University Press.

Vayda, Andrew P. 1969. *Environment and Cultural Behavior*. Garden City, NY: The Natural History Press.

Veblen, Thorsten. 1912. *The Theory of the Leisure Class: An Economic Study of Institutions*. New York: BW Huebsch.

Vedder, Amy, L. Naughton-Treves, A. Plumptre, L. Mabulama, E. Rutagarema, and W. Weber. 2001. "Epilogue: Conflict and Conservation in the African Rain Forest." In *African Rain Forest Ecology and Conservation*. Edited by W. Weber, L. White, A. Vedder, and L. Naughton-Treves, 557–62. New Haven, Conn.: Yale University Press.

Vithayathil, Trina. 2011. Below-replacement Fertility in India: Marriage, Early Child-bearing, and Female Sterilization. Paper presented at the American Sociological Association meetings, Las Vegas, Nevada, August 20.

Vitousek, Peter and W. A. Reiners. 1975. "Ecosystems, Succession and Nutrient Retention: A Hypothesis." *Bioscience* 25:376–81.

Wackernagel, Mathis and W. Rees. 1995. *Our Ecological Footprint: Reducing Human Impact on the Earth*. Gabriola Island, Canada and Philadelphia, Penn.: New Society Publishers.
Wai, Ong Kung. 2010. "Organic Asia, 2010." In *The World of Organic Agriculture: Statistics and Emerging Trends, 2010*. Edited by H. Willer and L. Kilcher, 122–7. Bonn: FiBL and IFOAM.
Wakker, Eric. 2006. The Kalimantan Border Oil Palm Mega-Project. Friends of the Earth – Netherlands. Amsterdam: Friends of the Earth. Available at: www.foe.co.uk/resource/reports/palm_oil_mega_project.pdf.
Wald, Matthew L. 2008. "Running in Circles over Carbon." *New York Times* June 8. Available at: www.nytimes.com/2008/06/08/weekinreview/08wald.html.
Walker, Brian and D. Salt. 2006. *Resilience Thinking: Sustaining Ecosystems and People in a Changing World*. Washington, DC: Island Press.
Wallerstein, Immanuel. 2004. *World Systems Analysis: An Introduction*. Durham, NC: Duke University Press.
Walters, Bradley and A. P. Vayda. 2009. "Event Ecology, Causal Historical Analysis, and Human-Environment Research." *Annals of the Association of American Geographers* 99:534–53.
Ward, David. 2011. Global Trends 2020 and Beyond: Automobile Use, Environment and Safety. Presentation at Our Future Mobility Now. Autoworld, June 22, Brussels, Belgium. Available at: www.acea.be/images/uploads/files/Presentation_Ward.pdf. July 8.
Warren, Keith D. 2007. *Agroecology in Action: Extending Alternative Agriculture Through Social Networks*. Cambridge, Mass.: MIT Press.
Washington State Department of Transportation (WSDOT). 2011. Volume of International Trade. Available at: www.wsdot.wa.gov/planning/wtp/datalibrary/freight/GrowingVolume.htm.
Weber, Max. 1922 (1978). *Economy and Society: An Outline of Interpretive Sociology*. 2 vols. Berkeley, Calif.: University of California Press.
Webster, P. J., G. Holland, J. Curry, and H. Chang. 2005. "Changes in Tropical Cyclone, Number, Duration, and Intensity in a Warming Environment." *Science* 309:1,844–6.
Weinberg, Adam, D. Pellow, and A. Schnaiberg. 2000. *Urban Recycling and the Search for Sustainable Community Development*. Princeton, NJ: Princeton University Press.
Wejnert, Barbara. 2003. "Integrating Models of Diffusion of Innovation: A Conceptual Framework." *Annual Review of Sociology* 28:297–326.
Westley, Frances, S. Carpenter, W. A. Brock, C. S. Holling, and L. Gunderson. 2002. "Why Systems of People and Nature Are Not Just Social and Ecological Systems." In *Panarchy: Understanding Transformations in Human and Natural Systems*. Edited by L. H. Gunderson and C. S. Holling, 103–20. Washington, DC: Island Press.
White, A. and A. Martin. 2002. *Who Owns the Forests?: Forest Tenure and Public Forests in Transition*. Washington, DC: Forest Trends and Center for International Environmental Law.

Wiarda, Howard J. 1996. *Corporatism and Comparative Politics: The Other Great "ism."* Armonk, NY: M. E. Sharpe.

Wier, Mette, J. O'Doherty, L. Andersen, and K. Millock. 2008. "The Character of Demand in Mature Organic Food Markets: Great Britain and Denmark Compared." *Food Policy* 33:406–21.

Wilkinson, Todd. 2003. "Organic Beef Gains amid Mad Cow Scare." *Christian Science Monitor*. December 29. Availalbe at: www.csmonitor.com/2003/1229/p03s01-usgn.html.

Willer, Helga and L. Kilcher, editors. 2010. *The World of Organic Agriculture: Statistics and Emerging Trends, 2010*. Bonn: FiBL and IFOAM.

Wilson, James, L. Yan, and C. Wilson. 2007. "The Precursors of Governance in the Maine Lobster Fishery." *Proceedings of the National Academy of Sciences* 104:15,212–17.

Winter, Michael. 2003. "Embeddedness, the New Food Economy, and Defensive Localism." *Journal of Rural Studies* 19:23–32.

Wiseman, Alan. 2007. *The World Without Us*. New York: St. Martin's Press.

Womack, John. 1969. *Zapata and the Mexican Revolution*. New York: Knopf.

Wong, Joseph. 2011. *Betting on Biotech: Innovation and the Limits of Asia's Developmental State*. Ithaca, NY: Cornell University Press.

Woo-Cumings, Meredith. 1999. "Introduction: Chalmers Johnson and the Politics of Nationalism and Development." In *The Developmental State*. Edited by M. Woo-Cumings, 1–17. Ithaca, NY: Cornell University Press.

World Commission on Environment and Development (WCED). 1987. *Our Common Future: Report of the World Commission on Environment and Development*. New York: Oxford University Press.

World Resources Institute (WRI). 2008. Earthtrends. Available at: http://earthtrends.wri.org.

World Resources Institute (WRI). 2009. Energy and Climate Policy Action in China. Available at: http://pdf.wri.org/factsheets/factsheet_china_energy_climate_policy.pdf.

World Wildlife Fund (WWF). 2006. Borneo: Treasure Island at Risk. London: WWF. Available at: www.wwf.org.uk/filelibrary/pdf/treasureisland_0605.pdf.

Worster, Donald. 1979. *Dust Bowl: The Southern Plains in the 1930s*. New York: Oxford University Press.

Worster, Donald. 1994. *Nature's Economy: A History of Ecological Ideas*. 2nd edition. Cambridge, UK: Cambridge University Press.

Wrobel, Sharon and D. Connelly. 2002. Revisiting the Issue-Attention Cycle: New Perspectives and Prospects. Paper presented at the annual meeting of the American Political Science Association, Boston, Massachusetts, August.

Wu, Jianguo and O. Loucks. 1995. "From Balance of Nature to Hierarchical Patch Dynamics: A Paradigm Shift in Ecology." *Quarterly Journal of Biology* 70:439–66.

Yamada, M. 2001. "Parasite Singles Feed on the Family System." *Japan Quarterly* 48:10–16.

Yashar, Deborah J. 2005. *Contesting Citizenship in Latin America: The Rise of Indigenous Movements and the Postliberal Challenge*. New York: Cambridge University Press.

Yip, Paul, C. Law, and K. Cheung. 2009. "Ultra Low Fertility in Hong Kong." In *Ultra-low Fertility in Pacific Asia: Trends, Causes, and Policy Issues*. Edited by P. Straughan, A. V. Chan, and G. Jones, 132–59. London: Taylor and Francis.

York, Richard. 2006. "Ecological Paradoxes: William Stanley Jevons and the Paperless Office." *Human Ecology Review* 13:141–46.

York, Richard and E. Rosa. 2003. "Key Challenges to Ecological Modernization Theory: Institutional Efficacy, Case Study Evidence, Units of Analysis, and the Pace of Eco-efficiency." *Organization and Environment* 16:273–88.

Yu, Eunice and J. Liu. 2007. "Environmental Impacts of Divorce." *Proceedings of the National Academy of Sciences* 104:20,629–34.

Zavestoski, Steve. 2007. Re.: Debate on Voluntary Actions to Fight Climate Change. Envirosoc listserv. September 25.

Zhang, Lei. 2003. "Ecologizing Industrialization in Chinese Small Towns." In *Greening Industrialization in Asian Transitional Economies: China and Vietnam*. Edited by A. J. P. Mol and J. van Buuren, 109–28. Lanham, MD: Lexington Books.

Zhang, Weiguo and X. Cao. 2009. "Family Planning During the Economic Reform Era." In *Transition and Challenge: China's Population at the Beginning of the 21st Century*. Edited by Z. Zhao and F. Guo, 18–33. New York: Oxford University Press.

Zhao, Zhongwei and F. Guo. 2009. Introduction. In *Transition and Challenge: China's Population at the Beginning of the 21st Century*. Edited by Z. Zhao and F. Guo, 1–17. New York: Oxford University Press.

Zimmerman, Erich. 1951. *World Resources and Industries*. Revised edition. New York: Harper.

Zimring, Carl A. 2005. *Cash for Your Trash: Scrap Recycling in America*. New Brunswick, NJ: Rutgers University Press.

Index

a drop in the bucket, local initiatives as, xiii, 1, 199
accountable autonomy, 189
Achuar, 52. See also indigenous peoples
agro-ecologies, 97, 115
agro-forests, 74
alternative agricultural practices, 9, 96–119
aluminum, 133
  consumption of, 133
Amerindians, 139. See also indigenous peoples
Argentina, 113
Arnalot, Jose, 52
Australia, 113

Bak, Per, 22. See also self-organized criticality (SOC)
Bangladesh, shipbreaking, 135
Beijing, air pollution, 157
Bennett, Hugh Hammond, 163
biofuels, 35, 44, 48
  corn-based ethanol, 45
  Energy Policy Act, 2005, 44
  European Directive, 2003, 44
  oil palm, 45
black carbon abatement as a defensive environmentalist strategy, 202
Black Swan, The, 23
body burdens, 112
Brazil, 45, 68, 75, 113, 166, 192
  Amazon, 46, 192
  Cerrado, 46, 49
  currency reform, 192
  government colonization programs, 192
  laws to preserve farm forests, 194
British Petroleum, 148
  Deep Water Horizon oil spill, 148
Brown, Lester, 3
business cycles, 154
  ecological modernization, effects on, 154
  greenhouse gas emissions, 154
Buttel, Fred, 1

CAFE (Corporate Average Fuel Economy) negotiations, 171
California, 104
  effects of California's regulations on subsequent debates about regulations elsewhere, 152
Calycophyllum spruceanum, 76
Canada, 113
capitalism, 8, 37–42, 82
  advertising, 40
  capitalism's impact on fertility, 82
  global expansion, 8
Carson, Rachel, 98. See also *Silent Spring*
cascades of events, 34, 35, 42–51
catalytic events. See focusing events
catastrophes, environmental. See focusing events
Catton, William R., 5
cement plants, 158
  China, 158
chain reactions, 44. See also cascades of events

245

children, costs of, 79. *See also* fertility declines
Chile, 116
China, 50, 73, 84, 86, 100, 134
   Chinese Ecological Agriculture (CEA) initiative, 118
   fertility rates, 84
   grain for green program, 73
   paper consumption, 133
   Yangtze River floods of 1998, 73
China Light and Power, 157
   biomass plants, 157
   coal-fired power plants, 157
CLAMP (concentrating locations at major plants), 138
Clarke, Lee, 42
classical theorists, 5
   modernization theorists, 6
   succession theorists, 6
   teleological thinking, 15
Clements, Frederic, 15. *See also* succession
climate change, 11, 14, 21, 27, 50
   adaptation, 11
   mitigation, 11
   "the sting is in the tail," 2
coal-fired capture-and-storage plants, 149
coevolution, 35
collapse of complex ancient societies, 23
Columbia River Commission, 20
commodity chains, 39
common fate, 19, 24, 164
   the egalitarian effects of wartime devastation, 187
   in egalitarian or stratified societies, 172
communities, 10. *See also* corporatism
   decentralization, 28
   modular changes, 4
   remodularization, 189
communities of practice, 145
community forests, 71
community-based natural resource management (CBNRM), 72
community-supported agriculture (CSA), 103
conservation, 58, 59
   conservation of open space, 65
   marine protected areas, 70
      Tortugas Ecological Preserve, 70
   parks and indigenous reserves, 65

   protected areas in the Brazilian Amazon, 194
   Virunga Park, Rwanda, 68
   "Heart of Borneo" biological reserve, 67
conservation (no-till) agriculture, 97, 105, 113
   carbon sequestration in agricultural soils, 99
   networks of innovators, 104
   no-till farmers, 98
   silvopastoral cattle ranching, 109
   silvopastoral landscapes, 99
   soil moisture, 107
Conservation Reserve program, 117
consumer cultures, 41, 101
   indigenous modernity, 41
   showcase modernity, 41
consumers, 111, 123, 137
   locavores, 116
conversion experiences, societal, 161
Copenhagen Climate summit, 168
corporations, transnational, 35, 40, 60, 138
corporatism, 189, 200
coupled natural and human systems, 5, 6, 19
   loosely coupled systems, 22, 168
   tightly coupled systems, 19, 22, 34, 35, 42, 162, 198
   "just-in-time" inventory systems, 43
crecive environmental problems, 172
   global warming as a crecive problem, 172
cultural change, 28
   schemata, role of, 28
   throwaway cultures, 123
Cuyahoga River fire, 166
   Clean Water Act of 1972, 166

Davis, Kingsley, 31, 200
Dean, Warren, 182
defensive environmentalist practices, 16, 52, 77, 97, 120, 141
   China, 156
   population declines in affluent societies, 94
   stratifying effects, 30
deforestation, rates of, 192
   Brazil, 192
deindustrialization, 154

Index

demographic momentum, 80
  negative demographic momentum, 81
  positive demographic momentum, 80
demographic transitions, 82
  demographic transition theory, 31
demonstration projects, 148
Dennett, Daniel, 2
density-dependent processes, 6, 78
detritus cycles, 16, 121
developmental states, 186, 202
  call forth their own grave diggers, 190
  in East Asia, 185
  as industrial latecomers, 186
Dietz, Thomas, 21
disaster capitalists, 172
disasters, 165. *See also* focusing events
Dole, 151
Dominican Republic, 74
Downs, Anthony, 29
Dunlap, Riley, 5
Durkheim, Emile, 6, 19

ecological footprints, 40
ecological modernization, 142, 149–159, 203
  in households, 156
  moments of ecological modernization, 149, 152
economic malthusian arguments, 37
Ecuador, 50, 109, 129
  Amazon, 67, 97, 139
  Cotacachi, 50
  Galapagos Islands, 54
  Mindo, 69
Eliasoph, Nina, 2
embedded autonomy, 188
embodied energy, 147
emotional burdens of global environmental change, 1
encompassing organizations, 19, 25, 170
  European Community, 25
  Intergovernmental Panel on Climate Change, 25
  nation-states as encompassing organizations, 183
  United Nations, 25
energy consumption, trends in, 142, 143. *See also* Jevons paradox
energy efficiency, 142
  Clean Development Mechanism, 151
  cap-and-trade carbon markets, 151
  economic expansion, 153
  Jevons paradox, 153
  energy efficiency of automobiles, 150
energy flows, 142
energy intensity, 143
environmental inequalities, 138. *See also* environmental injustices
environmental injustices, 120, 121. *See also* environmental inequalities
environmental justice movement, 139
  Citizens' Clearinghouse for Hazardous Waste, 174
environmental Kuznets curve, 38, 149
environmental movement, 101, 119, 126, 147, 160, 182. *See also* social movements
  apocalyptic, militarized terminology, 182
  environmental justice movement. *See* social movements
  Sierra Club, 202
environmental reforms, xiii, 2, 4, 6, 8, 19, 31, 165, 181, 201
  "big bang theory" of environmental reform, 168
  fatalism, 201
environmentalism, altruistic, 12, 66, 140, 184
environmentalism, defensive, 12, 18, 112, 120, 141
environmentalists, altruistic, xiv, 4, 9, 11, 19, 21, 29, 160, 164
environmentalists, defensive, xiv, 2, 8, 11, 17, 51, 62, 66, 77, 98, 137, 189
  social capital, effects on, 176
  stratifying effects, 17
extended producer responsibility, 130
  Bavarian Motor Works, 130
extreme weather events, 51
Exxon, 150
Exxon Valdez oil spill, 171

family-planning programs, 89, 90
  Sub-Saharan Africa, 89
farm forests, 73
  French colonial policy about tree tenure, 75
farmers' markets, 98, 102
  civic agriculture, 98

fertility declines, 31, 77–91. *See also*
    Ireland, Japan
  below-replacement fertility, 79, 203
  contraceptives, 93. *See also* population
    projections
  neo-liberal policies' impact on fertility,
    87
  pronatalist policies, 91
fertility rates, 84
  Argentina, 88
  Brazil, 88
  China, 84
  Colombia, 88
  depression during the 1930s, effects on,
    89
  Hong Kong, 85
  Italy, 88
  Japan, 84
  Kerala, India, 84
  Mexico, 88
  Russia, 84
  South Korea, 85
  Taiwan, 85
  Ukraine, 84
  United States, 82, 89
  volatility, 93
fertilizers, use of, 105
fires, 48
  peat fires, 48
Firey, Walter, 57
fishers, 70
  catch-share systems for fisheries, 71
  exclusive economic zones (EEZs), 69. *See*
    also resource partitioning
  roving bandits, 70
focusing events, 8, 19, 24, 29, 160–181.
    See also disasters
  catalysts, 175
  concentrations of wealth, effects on, 184
  extreme weather events, 23
  geographic reach, 162
  meteorological shocks, 23
  political effects from, 162
  political opportunities, 183. *See also*
    disasters
  press–pulse dynamics, 168
Food Security Act of 1985, 106
forest reforms, 171
  after a drought in the Sahel, 171
frontiers, 59

Gal Oya irrigation project, 185. *See also*
    Uphoff, Norman
game theory, 20
genetically modified crops, 114
Germany, 131
global forest compact, 191, 196. *See also*
    Redd+ (Reducing Emissions from
    Deforestation and Degradation)
globalization, 8, 34–50, 65, 102, 184
Gore, Al, 122
grain for green program (China), 158
Grand Banks cod fishery, collapse of, 161
greenhouse gas emissions, 39, 49, 50, 64,
    79, 94, 95, 98, 99, 117, 141, 145,
    152, 155, 157, 200
  China, 157
  household emissions, 155
  impact of low fertility rates, 94
Greenpeace, 152

Harriman, E. H., 66
Hawken, Paul, 3
Hirsch, Frederick, 40
Hofstadter, Richard, 5
Homer-Dixon, Thomas, 160
household sizes, declines in, 90
  natural resource use per capita, 91
human patch dynamics, 56. *See also*
    resource partitioning
Hurley, Andrew, 120
Hurricane Katrina, 162, 176
  New Orleans, 177

incinerators. *See* waste to energy projects
An Inconvenient Truth, 122
India, 71
indigenous peoples, 55, 68, 192
Indonesia, 46, 201
  Kalimantan, 67
  oil palm plantations, 67
industrial ecology, 121, 142
innovations, historical clusters of, 144
institutional sclerosis, 144. *See also* Olson,
    Mancur
intensive mothering, 77, 83, 111
interactive governance, 199
Intergovernmental Panel on Climate
    Change, 25
International Monetary Fund (IMF), 192
invasive species, 35

Index

inverted quarantine, 18. *See also* defensive environmentalist practices
Iowa, 106
Ireland, 31
issue attention cycles, 29, 166, 201
issue infrastructure, 167. *See also* issue attention cycles
Italy, 131
   recycling rates, 131

Japan, 31, 44, 86, 131, 188
   costs of children, 86
   garbage guardians, 131
   Juku schools, 85
Jevons paradox, 142
Johnson, Chalmers, 186. *See also* developmental states
joint forest management, 72

Kaimowitz, David, 197
Kentucky, 106, 108
Kenya, 74
Kingsolver, Barbara, 96
Klein, Naomi, 183

landfills, 136
   numbers of, 136
land-grant universities, 191
   energy-grant universities, 191
land-use controls, 61
land-use planners, 61
lash-ups, 24, 147
late developers, 187
leapfrog effects, 154
liability of newness, 146
Liu, Jianguo, 6, 7
livestock, 118
local-global environmental dynamic, 173. *See also* local-to-global links
local-to-global links, 4
   historical circumstances in which scaling up occurs, 4
loci of control, 203
   class position, 203

Mahogany (*Swietenia macrophylla*), 21
Malaysia, 46
Mars, Kettly, 160
McLaughlin, Paul, 5
McLuhan, Marshall, 141, 149

Mendes, Chico, 166
meta-narratives, 10–28
Miyata, Ken, 34
Mobro and Khian Sea garbage barges, 139
modernization theory, 14, 16
Monhegan Island, Maine, 56

natural capitalism. *See* ecological modernization
Natural Resources Defense Council, 148
neo-liberal regimes, 83
Nepal, 72
New England, 44
New Jersey, 55, 62
   Metuchen, 125
   recycling, 136
   Tewksbury, 62
New York City Department of Sanitation, 121
Niger, 75
Nigeria, 75
nongovernmental organizations (NGOs), 63
   environmental NGOs, 165
   information politics, 165
   international environmental NGOs, 68
      Conservation International, 68
      Nature Conservancy, 62
North America, 133
   paper consumption, 133
nuclear waste, 138

Odum, Eugene, xiii, 6, 15
   strategy of ecosystem development, 15
Olson, Mancur, 19. *See also* encompassing organizations
organic agriculture, 96, 100
   extent of, 105
   wild collection lands, 104
organic-industrial food complex, 117
Ostrom, Elinor, 3, 32, 57, 59

Panicum purapurascens, 109
paper, 133
   consumption, 133
Perrow, Charles, 22, 163
politics of global warming, 27, 28, 182–185, 197–203
Pollesta discolor, 114
polycentric, multiphasic responses, 31

population growth, 36–37
population projections, 92
  projections of fertility, 93
populations, aging, 90
  greenhouse gas emissions, 91
positional goods, 40, 123
prospect theory, 200
Pulver, Simone, 150
punctuated equilibria, 24, 169
  episodic patterns in, 171
  macropolitics is the politics of punctuation, 169
  in politics, 24
  press processes, 28
  pulse processes, 28

real-estate developers, 55, 145
recycling, 3, 9, 120–126
  China, 3, 4
  extended producer responsibility, 130
  globalization, 138
  greenhouse gas emissions, 133
  industrial producers, 137
  Japan, 3
  New Jersey, 4
  recycling rates, 129
    Japan, 129
    Sweden, 129
    Switzerland, 129
  subcultures of recycling, 126
  REDD+ (Reducing Emissions from Deforestation and Degradation), 117, 195
reproduction, r and K strategies, 78
resilience, 27
  Resilience Alliance, 26
resource partitioning, 9, 14, 52–73
  as a defensive environmentalist strategy, 60
  maritime partitioning, 55
    marine protected areas, 56
resource recovery, 134, 140. *See also* recycling
  aluminum, 132
    Tennessee, 133
Revkin, Andrew, 1, 2
Richerson, Peter, 5
Roberts, J. Timmons, 3
Rodale Institute, 115
Romer, A. S., 200
Romer's rule, 200

Royal Dutch Shell, 150
Rwanda, 68

Sahel, 75
  Great Green Wall project, the, 75
satellite imagery, to detect illegal deforestation, 194
  credit restrictions on farmers who deforest, 195
Scandinavia, 87
Schiff Nature Preserve, The, 63
Schnaiberg, Allan, 1
Schumpeter, Joseph A., 184
  creative destruction, processes of, 184
Scott, James, 33
Scott, Lee, 178. *See also* Wal-mart sustainability initiative
self-organized criticality (SOC), 22, 26. *See also* Bak, Per
Selznick, Philip, 10, 33
Senegal, 129
shipbreaking enterprises, 135
Shuar, 67. *See also* indigenous peoples
Silent Spring, 98, 119
silvopastoral cattle ranchers, 97
Singapore, 86
Slow Food International, 115
smallholders, 74, 100
  smallholders, Gal Oyo, Sri Lanka, 175
social capital, 58
Social Darwinist thinking, xiv, 4
social movements, 19, 29, 30, 114, 160. *See also* environmental movement
  anti-sprawl activists, 63
  food movement, 97
  political opportunities, 165
  political opportunities for reform, 30
Society for the Preservation of the Fauna of the Empire, 66
socio-ecological systems, 42. *See also* coupled natural and human systems
solid waste, 129
  tipping fees, 129
Solnit, Rebecca, 164
  "a paradise built in hell," 164
  "the Moral Equivalent of War," 164
South Korea, 188
Spencer, Herbert, 19
sprawl, 64
  middle-class sprawl, 64
  upper-class sprawl, 64

Index

Sri Lanka, 173
   Gal Oyo irrigation system, 174
Stang, Dorothy, 166
states, 60. *See also* sustainable development states
   as catalytic agents, 191
   hegemonic projects in, 183
   seeing like a state, 184
Sub-Saharan Africa, 133
   paper consumption, 133
suburbanization, 61
succession, 8, 11, 13
   human ecological succession, 8, 15, 51
   "hierarchical patch dynamics" paradigm, 16
Superfund legislation, 1984, 173
   Love Canal, 173
   Gibbs, Lois, 174
sustainable development states, 9, 181, 182–196, 201
   social equality in, 188
   strong states in weak societies, 188
Sweden, 87
Szasz, Andrew, 18. *See also* inverted quarantine
   Shopping Our Way to Safety, 111

Tainter, Joseph, 23
Taiwan, 134, 186
   "pay as you throw" system of waste management, 135
Taleb, Nassim, 23
Tanzania, 53
teleconnections, 2
think globally, but act locally, 2
three Rs (reducing, reusing, and recycling), 121, 127. *See also* recycling
   remanufacturing, 128
tipping fees, 136

treadmills of production, 38, 146
tropical rain forests, 48

United Nations, 192
United States, 65, 101, 113, 134, 177
   residential segregation, 65
   Soil Conservation Service, 1935 authorization, 163
Unsafe at Any Speed, 171
Uphoff, Norman, 173
urbanization, 90

Vayda, A. P., 7
vertical trade, 39
Vietnam, 73
virtual environmentalism, 199

Wal-Mart sustainability initiative, 177
   carbon index for products, 179
   EDLP, "everyday low prices," 177
   efficiency in energy use, 177
   elimination of waste, 177
   impact on suppliers, 179
   Katrina as a catalyzing event, 178
waste management, 122
   incinerators, 124
   landfills, 124
   solid waste, 124
waste removal, 123
   Chicago, nineteenth century, 123
   London, nineteenth century, 123
waste to energy projects, 136
Womack, John, vi, xiii, 200
World Bank, 192
world system, the, 38
Worldwide Opportunities on Organic Farms (WWOOF), 114

Zavestoski, Steve, 3
Zero Waste Alliance, 126

CPSIA information can be obtained
at www.ICGtesting.com
Printed in the USA
FSOW02n1440151214
3903FS